# It's Very Simple

# It's Very Simple

## THE TRUE STORY OF CIVIL RIGHTS

By
ALAN STANG

**WESTERN ISLANDS**

PUBLISHERS

BOSTON          LOS ANGELES

# Preface

On the evening of July 18, 1964, a riot was started on the streets of Harlem, in the city of New York. Within a few days rioting broke out in Brooklyn, in Rochester, in Jersey City and Philadelphia, and in still other cities across America. Many thousands of dollars worth of property was damaged and destroyed, and much was looted. A few men were killed.

On the afternoon of August 28, 1963, the Rev. Dr. Martin Luther King, Jr. addressed the many thousands who took part in the march on Washington to demand passage of the civil rights bill.

On July 12, 1964, Malcolm X, Black Nationalist-Muslim leader, arrived in Cairo to attend a meeting of the council of ministers of the Organization for African Unity. He said, according to the New York *Times,* that he wanted to acquaint the Africans "with the true plight of America's Negroes and to show them how our situation is as much a violation of the United Nations Human Rights Charter as the situation in South Africa or Angola." [1]

And on August 20, 1964, President Johnson signed the anti-poverty bill.

These are scenes from what has come to be called the Negro revolution. What do they mean? What is the relationship between them? What is the Negro revolution actually all about? These are the questions this book will answer. It will take you on a strange journey across many years and many countries—and return with the proof of what is really happening this year in your own.

This is *not* a book about segregation—or about integration. It says almost nothing about the moral issues at work in this very real problem—profound issues which require a book of

1. New York *Times* (July 14, 1964), p. 23.

their own. This book restricts itself to one *basic* question: What is the *real* purpose of the Negro revolution?

Many Americans think they know—that it has something to do with civil rights. Many others have no idea; they think the answer is very complex.

It isn't.

In fact:

*It's very simple.*

ALAN STANG
New York City

# Note

The story I have to tell, as I have indicated, has endless parallels in different times and different places. And, as I have also indicated, it is perhaps the most important purpose of this book to demonstrate that these parallels *do* exist, and why; to name both the symphony in which the "civil rights struggle" is one of the movements—and to name the composer of the music.

For this reason I have used the stylistic device of incorporating much of this material from other times and other places— the proof of these parallels—in italicized passages placed either before or after a specific development here and now in "civil rights."

\*   \*   \*

Several parts of this book are amplifications of material that originally appeared in magazine articles by this author. I appreciate the cooperation of the publisher of those articles in allowing that material to be used here.

—A.S.

# Table of Contents

"How will we bring the masses of a nation into the communist program? We have fashioned a number of organizations without which we could not wage war on capitalism: trade unions, cooperatives, work-shop committees, labor parties, women's associations, a labor press, educational leagues, youth societies.

"As often as not, these are non-party organizations and only a certain proportion of them are linked with the party. But under special conditions, every one of these organizations is necessary; for, lacking them, it is impossible to consolidate the class positions of the workers in the various spheres of the struggle.

"There is a veritable ant heap of independent organizations, commissions, and committees comprising millions of non-party members. Who decides upon the direction that all these organizations take? Where is the central unit of organization that wields sufficient authority to keep them within prescribed lines in order to achieve unity of command and to avoid confusion?

"The central unit is the Communist party!"[1]

JOSEPH STALIN

1. From the Stalin archives of the National War College in Washington, D. C., as quoted in *Coronet,* vol. 29, no. 3 (January 1951), p. 23.

It's Very Simple

The National Question

*The weaknesses of the capitalistic world which we can use are its insuperable antagonisms—antagonisms which dominate the whole international situation.*[1] Joseph Stalin

In 1913 Lenin assigned Stalin to prepare the Bolshevik position on the national and colonial questions, that is, on national minorities and the colonies of the major powers. Stalin came back with the idea that a group of this kind was actually a nation within a nation, and he wrote:

> The right of self-determination means that a nation can arrange its life according to its own will. It has the right to arrange its life on the basis of autonomy. It has the right to enter into federal relations with other nations. *It has the right to complete secession.* Nations are sovereign and all nations are equal.[2]

This did not mean, however, that a nation always *had* to secede:

> . . . A people has the right to secede, but it may or may not exercise that right, according to circumstances. Thus we are at liberty to agitate for or against secession, according to the interests of the proletariat, of the proletarian revolution. Hence, the question of secession must be determined in each particular case independently, in accordance with existing circumstances, and for this reason the question of the recognition of the right to secession must not be confused with the expediency of secession in any given circumstances. . . .[3]

The tactic of secession, then, is exactly that: a tactic, solely designed to further the interests of the "proletarian revolution." At certain times, Communists would endorse secession —that is, "self-determination"—at others they would oppose it, but only because it was at the moment inexpedient, inimical to the "interests of the proletariat"—as in Katanga—*not* because they opposed the principle.

1

Russia was the first country the Communists captured. And in 1917, just before the revolution, Lenin said he would apply the theory to the Russian minorities:

> As regards the national question, the proletarian must, first of all, insist on the promulgation and immediate realization of full freedom of separation from Russia for all nations and peoples who were oppressed by tsarism, who were forcibly included or forcibly retained within the boundaries of the state, i.e., annexed.[4]

Lenin wasn't giving anything away, of course. He wanted these people on his side, and knew he wasn't yet strong enough to oppress them himself.

Now, why is the principle of self-determination—that is, secession—so important?

Lenin gives the answer:

> The social revolution cannot come about except in the form of an epoch of proletarian civil war against the bourgeoisie in the advanced countries combined with a *whole series* of democratic and revolutionary movements, including movements for national liberation, in the undeveloped, backward and oppressed nations.[5]

But a question arises: Marx said it was one of the goals of socialism—that is, Communism—to produce one socialist world, by selling the idea of "internationalism," by destroying national barriers and inhibiting nationalism. In fact, Lenin tells us: "The aim of socialism is not only to abolish the present division of mankind into small states and end all national isolation; not only to bring the nations closer together, but to *merge* them. . . ." [6] (italics added)

How then can Lenin advocate a national revolution and the encouragement of nationalism? Isn't this a mistake? Some sort of contradiction?

Once again, Lenin himself gives the answer:

> . . . Just as mankind can achieve the abolition of classes only by passing through the dictatorship of the proletariat, so mankind can achieve the inevitable merging of nations only by passing through the transition period of complete liberation of all oppressed nations, i.e., their right to secede.[7]

National liberation then [writes Professor Wilson Record] was a transitory factor. It was a prelude to a working class movement within the nation, and its ultimate aim was socialism. Communists would support such movements, but at the same time *they would seek to obtain control over them and, where possible, turn them into workers' and peasants' revolutions.*[8]

. . . When these elements controlled the state apparatus, then the possibility of unifying that nation with the rest of the socialist world could be realized.[9] (italics added)

Why in fact was the national revolution alone—free from Communist control—out of the question? Why, for instance, couldn't a nation have a capitalist revolution, as, for instance, in 1776?

Stalin himself has the answer:

Only now has it become obvious to all that the national bourgeoisie is striving not for the liberation of "its own people" from national oppression but for the liberty of wringing profits from them, for the liberty of preserving its own privileges and capital. Only now has it become obvious that the liberation of the oppressed nationalities is inconceivable without breaking with imperialism, without *overthrowing the bourgeoisie of the oppressed nations, without power passing into the hands of the toiling masses of those nationalities.*[10]

In other words, writes Professor Record:

Working class elements might indeed favor the national liberation movement, but it would be the responsibility of the "most advanced elements" of that class to turn the conflict into a civil war against the native bourgeoisie, either during the course of the immediate struggle or at the first opportunity later. By the "most advanced elements" Stalin meant the various sections of the Communist International in the respective national states or the organizations which they either supported or controlled outright.[11]

Let's sum up: According to Lenin and Stalin it is the goal of socialism, i.e., Communism, to control the world: "The aim of socialism is . . . not only to bring the nations closer together, but to merge them." In order for the Communists to capture a "bourgeois" government, however, it is first necessary to disrupt that government. It is necessary to encourage "proletarian civil war against the bourgeoisie in the advanced countries combined with a *whole series*" of *"national liberation movements"* in the "oppressed nations." It is necessary, in short, to encourage civil war in the industrial nation, and secession in the primitive nation. "Mankind can achieve the inevitable merging of nations only by passing through the transition period of complete liberation of all oppressed nations, i.e., their right to secede." A "whole series" of such secessions will indicate that *everything is going according to plan.*

For the last step is to turn this revolutionary combination—civil war and secession—into a Communist revolution.

Victory will come when the Communists—*under the cloak of the national liberation movement*—take control of the government.[12]

## Notes

1. From the Stalin archives of the National War College in Washington, D.C., as quoted in *Coronet,* vol. 29, no. 3 (January 1951), p. 22.

2. Joseph Stalin, *Marxism and the National and Colonial Question* (London, Martin Lawrence Limited, 1936?), p. 19. Also, Joseph Stalin, *Marxism and the National Question* (New York, International Publishers, 1942), pp. 23-24. As quoted by William A. Nolan, *Communism Versus the Negro* (Chicago, Henry Regnery Company, 1951), p. 11.

3. Joseph Stalin, *Marxism and the National and Colonial Question,* p. 64. Speech delivered at the seventh all-Russian conference of the Russian Social Democratic Labor party (April 29, 1917).

4. V. I. Lenin, *The Tasks of the Proletariat in Our Revolution* (New York, International Publishers, 1932), p. 17. As quoted by Nolan, p. 42.

5. V. I. Lenin, "A Caricature of Marxism and 'Imperialist Economism,' " (August-October 1916), *Lenin on Proletarian Revolution and Proletarian Dictatorship* (Peking, Foreign Languages Press, 1960), p. 55.

6. V. I. Lenin, *The Right of Nations to Self-Determination* (New York, International Publishers, 1951), p. 76. Also, V. I. Lenin, "The Socialist Revolution and the Right of Self-Determination," *Collected Works,* vol. 14 (New York, International Publishers, 1942), p. 51. As quoted by Wilson Record, "The Development of the Communist Position on the Negro Question in the United States," *Phylon,* vol. 19, no. 3 (Fall 1958), p. 315.

7. Record, "The Development . . . ," p. 315.

8. *Ibid.*

9. *Ibid.,* p. 319.

10. As quoted by Emil Burns, ed., *A Handbook of Marxism* (New York, International Publishers, 1935), p. 817. Also, as quoted by Record, "The Development . . . ," p. 318.

11. Record, "The Development . . . ," p. 318.

12. See William T. Shinn, Jr., "The 'National Democratic State,'" *World Politics,* vol. 15, no. 3 (April 1963), pp. 377-389, for a discussion of the use of nationalism to produce a coalition state headed by a non-Communist as a transition to a complete Communist government.

## CHAPTER II

The War of National
Liberation

> Around the world there is a steady upsurge in demands for
> freedom, independence, and economic betterment—demands
> with which we sympathize and which we support. In no
> sense do these demands suggest a forthcoming victory for
> communism but rather a victory for freedom and democ-
> racy. . . .[1] Andrew H. Berding, U.S. State Department

The question arises: Are the Communists putting into effect
Lenin's and Stalin's theories on "the national and colonial
questions"? Or have these theories remained unrealized—nothing but the psychotic desires of a band of thugs? We know
what the Communists have wanted to do; now how can we be
sure that they are actually doing it?

Let us make a historical survey, examining several recent
national and colonial revolutions—and in each instance trying to answer two questions: What is supposed to have happened? What actually happened?

### CHINA

And let us begin with the case of China. You will recall that
for several years before the Communists captured that country,
many people warned that Mao Tse-tung and his fellow Communists were Communists—and that they were, and were
eagerly, everything a Communist is. You will recall further,
of course, that these people were either ignored, denounced,
pitied or urged to report for immediate psychiatric treatment.
Sure, Mao was a Communist—he said so himself—but he
wasn't a *bad* Communist like Joe Stalin—who wasn't a bad
Communist, either, until the end of the Second World War.

Mao was a good Communist. Granted, he made some mistakes in economics and probably had bad manners. But what he was doing was good for China and the world. He was fighting "corruption" and "colonialism." Indeed, he was struggling to "end colonialism" in China.

So, criticism of Mao and concern over his Communist beliefs and background were considered to be symptoms of political paranoia.

"We are confronted with this almost incredible fact," writes Dr. Fred Schwarz:

> The Chinese Communist leader, Mao Tse-tung, was writing such statements as this: "I am a Stalinist. Stalin is my leader. The Chinese Communist Party is a portion of the international proletarian party." "The Chinese revolution is a portion of the international proletarian revolution to destroy imperialism." While he was writing statements of this nature in English, available to anyone, the Information and Education section of the United States Army circularized the troops telling them that the Chinese Communists were not Communists at all. They were really "agrarian reformers." They had no connection with Soviet Russia; they were democrats as we were, and the Communist conquest in China posed no threat to American sovereignty and security.[2]

This statement has about it the odor of "wild charges," and Dr. Schwarz is of course a "right-wing extremist." So let us turn to the pages of the New York *Times:*

> One point which Mao Tse-tung and most other Communist leaders stress is that neither have they an alliance with the Soviets nor do they hope to impose on China the proletarian dictatorship set up in Moscow by the Bolsheviks in 1917. They admit a great friendship for Soviet Russia. They point out that Russia was their only friend abroad for many years. But they believe a different system is needed in China, a revolution based on land reform, a Government built on peasant foundations. Because China is industrially backward, they favor encouragement of investment in industry—but from Chinese, not foreign sources. They differ from the Bolsheviks, too, in proposing a coalition government of all democratic elements, and not one-party rule. . . .
>
> Most Americans who have visited Red China are accused of arriving at their judgments according to their previously held prejudices. None denies, however, that in Communist China they have found matters of law and order, public health, equitable dis-

tribution of food and wealth, and other operations of Government
carried out with greater earnestness and success than elsewhere in
China or in most of Asia. . . .

There is one thing that seems sure: the civil war is neither of
their making nor to their liking. . . .

Another certainty is that the idea they represent, the hope they
hold for the landless, overtaxed Chinese peasant, is not one that
can be destroyed by force. . . .

. . . there is no ground for the belief that Communism can be
eliminated from China in a military campaign. . . .[3]

So it's obvious, isn't it, that the planners in the State Department, and the thinkers in the New York *Times,* made a
mistake. Somebody, somewhere, was wrong.

For as we read, among many other places, in Joseph C.
Grew's *Invasion Alert!,* when Comrade Mao had been in power
only a few years—he had already murdered *twenty million* of
his fellow Chinese.

> The appalling figures on murders committed by the Peiping Com-
> munist government are neither propaganda, exaggerations nor
> guesses. Since the Communists drove Chiang Kai-shek and the Na-
> tionalists off the mainland in 1949, official accounts in Red news-
> papers have listed the executions of millions of Chinese. . . .
> . . . The real total of Chinese deaths administered by Peiping
> probably would total a great deal more than the estimates. Few
> Chinese marked for death by Peiping had a chance to escape their
> executioners. *The Communists masked their real intentions with a
> deceptively mild, restrained and orderly entry to power.*[4] (italics
> added)

And less than a year later, in June 1950, the Reds began
the Korean War—in which Chinese Communist troops killed
and imprisoned American husbands, brothers, fathers and
sons. In fact, at this moment in South Vietnam, American
servicemen are being killed and imprisoned by Communist
troops supplied and encouraged, and probably trained, by this
same Mao who was recommended by the New York *Times.*

No doubt you have already remembered that a sizable por-
tion of our foreign policy today is based on the fact that Mao
really isn't so nice, which is why we must take the side of the

Russians, who recently have "mellowed" and become agrarian reformers—according to the New York *Times*.

It becomes obvious that somehow, for some reason, you were fooled. But it isn't very funny, especially if your husband, brother, father or son got the joke. It is not the province of this book to ask who played this trick or how. All we want to establish here is that in the case of China at least, the trick was played.

## CUBA

The strange case of Fidel Castro has already become a legendary tale in the annals of reporting. You will recall that Castro was constructively engaged in destroying "oppression" and "imperialism" represented by Fulgencio Batista, whose corruption was probably equal to that found in the mayors' offices of certain large American cities. Castro said nothing about "Yankee imperialism." He said nothing about "national liberation." All he was doing was fighting for clean government—like George Washington.

There was even a rumor that Castro was some sort of agrarian reformer.

But it happened that even before Castro captured Cuba, the same people in the United States who had been correct about Mao—and many more—began to hint that Castro did not entirely agree with George Washington. They even charged that his motives smacked of something sinister.

The bearded beast soon struck back. According to the front page of the New York *Times* for April 18, 1959:

"Premier Fidel Castro of Cuba denied today charges of Communist influence in his regime. In a speech before the American Society of Newspaper Editors he asserted: 'I have said very clearly that we are not Communists.' " He further declared that "our revolution is a humanistic one"; what he was trying to do, said the *Times,* was "to develop industry and to end unemployment."

In an editorial a week later, the *Times* made it clear that as far as it was concerned Castro was in the clear: ". . . He made it quite clear that neither he nor anyone of importance in his Government so far as he knew was Communist or in agreement with communism. . . ." [5]

That should have done it. But it didn't. So one month later, on May 23, 1959, on the front page the *Times* recorded the following details:

> Extremists have no place in the Cuban revolution, Premier Fidel Castro said in a television interview early this morning.
> Asked whether the "extremists" he referred to were Communists, the Premier said:
> "Perhaps there is much coincidence in this."

And of course, if you're against "extremists," you're probably okay, aren't you?

Later on in the *same* story, and perhaps to reassure the initiate, there appeared the following sentence: "In the same broadcast the Premier dashed hopes of United States sugar interests to save their properties from seizure under the new land reform law."

That's *agrarian* reform, of course.

In an editorial in the same issue, the *Times* reported itself officially encouraged:

> It is encouraging to see Premier Fidel Castro of Cuba facing up to the Communists as he did in his television interview on Thursday night.
> . . . The aims of the Cuban Reds, with their links to Moscow and their totalitarian philosophy, were bound to be contrary, in the long run, to the aims of the 26th of July Movement, which fought for democracy, freedom, social justice and—rather unhappily—for an extreme nationalism. [6]

But still the attacks went on. Many people in the United States insisted that the evidence showed Castro to be a Communist, and, as you will recall, these people were denounced for their pains.

And then, on July 1, 1959, the *Times* reported that the chief of Cuba's air force had resigned, "charging there was Communist influence in the armed forces and Government. . . ." [7]

In its issue for July 15, 1959, the *Times* reported this man's testimony:

> The former head of the Cuban Air Force testified today [July 14] that Premier Fidel Castro was the chief Communist in Cuba and a member of the international Communist conspiracy. . . .
>
> Maj. Pedro Luis Diaz Lanz told the Senate Internal Security Subcommittee he was convinced that Dr. Castro was determined to impose an all-out Communist regime upon his country. . . .
>
> Major Diaz said he was convinced Dr. Castro was a Communist because of "many facts" including things the Premier had said to him about getting rid of the banks, taking land from "everybody" and giving Cuba "a system like Russia has." [8]

This was strong stuff. Major Diaz was not an American "right-wing extremist." He had been there and seen it. Something more would have to be said than the usual comment that Major Diaz should see a psychiatrist.

It was a day of much activity at the New York *Times*. Apparently a cable was sent—to Havana, of all places. For on the very next day, July 16, 1959, and of course on the front page, readers were treated to an amazing coincidence: a story datelined Havana, written by Herbert L. Matthews:

> This is not a Communist revolution in any sense of the word and there are no Communists in positions of control. This is the overwhelming consensus among Cubans in the best position to know and this writer subscribes to that opinion after searching inquiries and talks with Cubans in all walks of life and with many Americans.
>
> The accusations of the former head of the Cuban Air Force, Maj. Pedro Luis Diaz Lanz, before the United States Senate Internal Security Subcommittee yesterday are rejected by virtually all Cubans. It is stated here that before his resignation Major Diaz was removed . . . for incompetence, extravagance and nepotism. . . .
>
> There seem to be very few in Cuba—and one need have no hesitation in saying this—who believe Fidel Castro is a Communist, is under Communist influence or is a dupe of communism. The problem of communism, which aroused little interest in Cuba

until Americans picked it up, can be easily summarized. The point of view among the most experienced and knowledgeable Cubans is as follows:

There are no Reds in the Cabinet and none in high positions in the Government or army in the sense of being able to control either governmental or defense policies. The only power worth considering in Cuba is in the hands of Premier Castro, who is not only not Communist but decidedly anti-Communist, even though he does not consider it desirable in the present circumstances to attack or destroy the Reds—as he is in a position to do any time he wants. . . .

Even the agrarian reform, Cubans point out with irony, is not at all what the Communists were suggesting, for it is far more radical and drastic than the Reds consider wise as a first step to the collectivization they, but not the Cuban leaders, want. . . .

Premier Castro is avoiding elections in Cuba for two reasons. He feels that his social revolution now has dynamism and vast popular consent, and he does not want to interrupt the process. Moreover, most observers would agree that Cubans today do not want elections. The reason is that elections in the past have merely meant to them the coming of corrupt politicians seeking the spoils of power.

It was a mighty day of work. Premier Castro himself polished it off on page two of the issue of July 28, 1959:

Premier Fidel Castro likened himself today to the late President Roosevelt as a victim of attacks by "trusts and monopolies" against social reform.

"We are being attacked by the same interests that attacked Roosevelt," Dr. Castro declared. . . .

So great is Dr. Castro's preoccupation with unfavorable comment in the United States—he says the comment is "fabricated from lies"—that it apparently has colored his views on relations with the United States.

The *Times* reported the alarming news that Castro seemed to resent, "greatly resent," the open Senate hearings recently held for Major Diaz.

On the same page of the same newspaper—in fact in the same story—there appeared the following information:

Dr. Castro said at the news conference that United States owners of sugar land and cattle ranches, as well as other landowners in

Cuba, must accept the twenty-year bonds that the Cuban government had offered in compensation for expropriated land.

Dr. Castro . . . was emphatic in declaring that Cuba had no dollars to pay for the land, which is being expropriated under the new Agrarian Reform Law.

And of course, in an editorial on page twenty-six of the same issue, the *Times* warned that a little agrarian reform should not provoke anti-Castro reactions:

The basic problems, in the long run, are going to lie in the fact that Cuba is beginning a social revolution of a drastic nature. This has already hurt some American interests and shocked many Americans who, in our day, find it difficult to believe that revolutions are not necessarily communistic. . . .

On December 2, 1961, while such Americans, in growing numbers, were still being shocked—and ignored, ridiculed, vilified and abused—Castro announced that he was forming

a "united party of Cuba's Socialist revolution," a monolithic organization like the Soviet Communist party with restricted membership.

[He] acknowledged that he was a Marxist-Leninist and said that he was taking Cuba down the path to communism. He maintained that the world, too, "is on the road toward communism." . . .

"I am a Marxist-Leninist and will be one until the day I die," Dr. Castro declared in a nation-wide television speech that began about midnight. . . .

Castro added that by 1953, three years before his invasion of Cuba, his political thinking "was more or less like what it is now." [9]

Washington's collective jaw fell slack and there was trouble up at the *Times*.

Something, somewhere, had gone wrong—again.

Once again, someone, somewhere, had made—a "mistake."

Herbert L. Matthews? Since his days in Havana as a reporter, he has been promoted to the editorial board of the New York *Times*.

## Algeria

Let us turn to the case of Algeria. For here we observe the textbook application of the Communist theory of "self-determination." The story, you will recall, went as follows: Algeria contained nine million Moslem slaves, and one million French colonialists. The Moslems were innocent and defenseless, and were being brutalized by the vicious colonialists. This gave the Moslems psychological problems. They felt offended in the "national integrity." For it happened, you see, that they were a "nation."

Well of course you can't have nine million people with psychological problems, so it was necessary for this "historic nation" to "reassert its national pride," and to do this it was necessary to secede.

No nation had ever existed in the area known as Algeria, of course. And no citizen of any such nation had ever been born. Algeria was not a colony or a possession, but an integral part of France, more closely related to Paris than Hawaii is related to Washington.

But as you will remember, General de Gaulle decided to hold a referendum to see whether the Algerian nation desired to secede.

*Self-determination means "only the right of independence in a political sense, the right to free political secession from the oppressing nation. Concretely, this political, democratic demand implies complete freedom to carry on agitation in favor of secession and freedom to settle the question by means of a referendum of the nation that desires to secede."* [10] V. I. Lenin

And would you believe it—the Algerian nation *did* desire to secede.

It developed however that a small band of psychotic Americans began to make the amazing charge that Ahmed Ben Bella, "historic chief" of the revolution, was actually, and had always been, a Communist!

It was another piece of extremism, of course. The strongest

evidence they had was a photograph of Ben Bella taken by the Algerian police just before they locked him up for doing nothing more than killing an annoying woman during the course of an armed robbery designed to finance humanitarian political work.

*"From this it is likewise apparent that the party leaders also intended [in Indonesia in 1926] to enlist criminals in the illegal groups. That this was a means of propaganda recommended by the Communist International is confirmed not only by the passages quoted above from the statutes and conditions for admission into the Communist International, but also by what the press reported early in 1924 concerning revolutionary activities in Bengal following the attempted murder of the head of the Sakanritolla post office. It then came to light that political clubs had been formed there with the aim of committing murders and driving the Europeans out of the country; the clubs planned first to organize large-scale robberies in order to accumulate the necessary funds to carry out the plan. . . ."* [11]

In 1963, we read in *U.S. News & World Report:*

Cuba dispatched three shiploads of arms to Algeria during Algeria's border fight with Morocco. With them went Algerian military men who had been training in Cuba.

It is now believed that Fidel Castro is collaborating closely with Algeria's President Ben Bella in sponsoring and aiding African guerrillas. [12]

On Monday, March 30, 1964, the State Department handed a report on the world situation to the House Foreign Affairs Committee, in which was contained the charge that Algeria was a nation increasingly "marked by pro-Communist influence." [13]

The Algerians at once struck back: "Such a statement," said a foreign ministry spokesman, "serves no one but the Communists, who will surely make the most of it." [14]

It was in an editorial on April 23, [15] that the *Times* condescended to notice the situation. The *Times* saw a serious State Department blunder in its recent public warning against dangerous Communist influence in Algiers. The warning, in a report to the House Foreign Affairs Committee, provided grist for Communist propaganda mills and has noticeably cooled Algerian-American relations.

There are two mysteries about the report. The first is why the State Department should have permitted such remarks to be published, as they seemed almost designed to insure ill will.

The more important mystery is why such a misleading comment on the Algerian political situation should have appeared in any State Department report, public or private.

It is true that there are some pro-Communist French and Algerian intellectuals in the press, the radio and the student associations of Algeria. It is true that Premier Ben Bella has criticized "capitalists" and praised Fidel Castro. It is true that Algeria has obtained credits of $100 million from Moscow and $50 million from Peking.

But this apparently is not significant.

. . . similar remarks might be made about a score of other new nations the world around which equate their independence with neutralism and a native brand of socialism.

And this is not significant either.

Far more important facts are that Premier Ben Bella, though very much a dictator, is not a Communist. . . .

. . . the State Department's published analysis of the Algerian situation is wrong. Its policy, which has ignored that analysis, is right.

One week later, on May 1—May Day—at a dinner in Moscow, Ben Bella was awarded the title of Hero of the Soviet Union:

The Algerian leader is known to be an ardent admirer of Premier Fidel Castro. Significantly, Mr. Khrushchev in his speech hailed the close relations between Algeria and Cuba as well as the friendship between Algeria and the Soviet Union.[16]

Jaws fell slack again.

Because Ahmed Ben Bella, who is being kept in power by American aid, and who has been invited to the White House by the American president at the expense of the American taxpayer, is most certainly a Communist.

It was another mistake at the New York *Times*.

But Ben Bella kept his oar in. He just loves those Yankee dollars: "President Ahmed Ben Bella assured Algeria's Moslem traditionalists in a speech today that his 'Socialism' was not heading toward atheistic Communism."

Ben Bella declared: "We solemnly reply here that our Socialism stems from Islam. We repeat before world opinion that we are not Communist." [17]

## "TANZANIA"

At this point you may already be convinced. But with your permission, let's push on just a bit further. For it is necessary to make this point once and for all.

Let's push south into East Africa. You will recall that on January 12, 1964, the government of Zanzibar was captured by a Communist coup in which more than eighty were killed, five hundred injured, and many stores and homes were looted.[18]

The revolution in Zanzibar, says *U.S. News & World Report,* worked like this:

> Furthermore, Cuban-trained guerrillas often are reinforced by agents trained in Russia or Red China.
>
> In Zanzibar, for instance, 20 or so persons trained in Cuba reportedly formed the hard core of armed men who overthrew the pro-Western Government. They had been sent to Cuba, after January, 1962, by Sheik Abdul Rahman Mohammed Babu—a paid agent of Red China who now is Foreign Minister of Zanzibar's Marxist Government.
>
> Africans who have been or are being trained in Cuba are expected to play leading roles when all-out guerrilla warfare is launched against Portuguese rule in Angola and Mozambique. They may also be sent into white-ruled South Africa on trouble-making missions.[19]

Not long after, Julius Nyerere, the president of Tanganyika, decided to merge his country with the new Zanzibari Com-

munist state. The New York *Times* decided to sell the idea
that the merger was designed to prevent Communism:

> . . . President Nyerere was understood to have felt that armed
> African intervention might be the only means of preventing Zanzi-
> bar from becoming the "Cuba of Africa." He was deeply concerned
> about increasing penetration from the Soviet Union, Communist
> China and their allies.

Sheik Abdul Rahman Mohammed, who is described as "an
advocate of Peking's theory of violent revolution," is out as
minister for external affairs. ". . . His place in the United
Cabinet is occupied by a Tanganyikan, Ali Mogne Halona-
Tambwe." [20]

So Nyerere sounds really nasty, doesn't he—like a Tanganyikan version of Barry Goldwater.

And as we learn from Mr. C. L. Sulzberger on page thirty-
four of the same issue, this "non-Communist" Tanganyikan
shouldn't stop worrying: "A Chinese-tinged revolution that
seized Zanzibar has managed to retain power despite the
island's union with non-Communist Tanganyika. . . ."

This was the situation on October 19, 1964, when we turned
to page nine of our copy of the *Times:*

> Details have been disclosed here [in Dar Es Salaam, Tanganyika]
> of an offensive to free the East African territory of Mozambique
> from Portuguese rule.
>
> The details were reported this weekend by Oscar Kambona,
> Foreign Minister of the Republic of Tanganyika and Zanzibar,
> speaking as chairman of the African Liberation Committee.

A high official of the "Mozambique liberation movement"
said the offensive began September 24.

> The freedom fighters were trained mainly in *Algeria,* and some
> were trained in the United Arab Republic and elsewhere in Africa,
> the official said. He refused to confirm or deny that the national-
> ists were using arms of Soviet origin. (italics added)

According to Mr. Kambona—who is the foreign minister
of Tanganyika—the offensive is "a forceful assertion of the
right to self-determination. . . ."

"Mozambique's largest rebel group claims 9,000 members, including 500 guerrilla fighters training in *Tanganyika.*" (italics added)

In fact, as we have just seen, *U.S. News* has said that Africans who are "expected to play leading roles" in guerrilla warfare in Mozambique also "have been or are being trained in *Cuba.*" So, Communist troops trained in Communist Algeria and Communist Cuba are now conducting a Communist "revolution" in Mozambique from a base in *Tanganyika* with the blessings of the Tanganyikan government.

On November 5, 1964, the *Times* reported that President Nyerere had announced a cabinet revision: "Sheik Abdul Rahman Mohammed, the former Minister of State in the Directorate of Development and Planning, was appointed Minister of Cooperatives and Commerce. . . ." [21]

Abdul, according to the *Times,* is "an advocate of Peking's theory of violent revolution."

It looks as if the New York *Times* has made another mistake. Once again the Communists have captured a country under the cloak of "anti-colonialism"—this time Tanganyika —and the *Times* has told you nothing about it.

## GHANA

You will recall that not long ago, a furor broke out among Washington humanitarians when a Ghanaian exile had the temerity to charge that his country had become in effect a Communist state. Choosing at random from the New York *Times,* we find:

All university students, most new Ghanaian Ambassadors and many senior civil servants must undergo indoctrination at the Kwame Nkrumah Ideological Institute.

. . .

The bitterest anti-American campaign to date has started. The United States is no longer termed "neo-colonialist" but "Fascist-imperialist."

The institute, at Winneba, is charged with spreading the precepts of "Nkrumahism." More than half of its staff is from countries in the Communist bloc.[22]

In fact, we read in a pamphlet by Ghanaian exile K. A. Busia:

> . . . is it not also revealing that Nkrumah, who has been scream-ing so loudly about neo-colonialism, should be making Ghana more and more dependent on Soviet Russia? By means of a series of agreements and commercial transactions, and the employment of hordes of Russian experts maintained at fantastic cost, the economy of Ghana is being increasingly tied to the Soviet Union, and whilst the Soviet Union always gains, Ghana is always the loser in these cunning transactions. . . .[23]

## KENYA

Remember Jomo Kenyatta, now prime minister of Kenya, and the leader of the Mau Mau—a gang which murdered both blacks and whites in a campaign to encourage European colonialists to leave the country? Of course he did have one bad habit: He enjoyed killing people.

Now it turns out that he "retains in his Cabinet two ardent advocates of China. . . ." [24]

In fact, on December 12, 1964, in what the *Times* described as his "first official act," Kenyatta opened a

> Soviet-sponsored political training center . . . in memory of Pa-trice Lumumba. . . . The institute also intends to help African nationalist organizations in other countries to train what are termed militant "cadres." . . .
>
> Moscow's share of the costs was understood to amount to $84,000. . . .
>
> The Soviet Union was said to be prepared to provide two pro-fessors for the institute which is surrounded by a barbed-wire fence seven feet high.[25]

Moreover, we read in a recent British government publica-tion:

> To return to Jomo Kenyatta . . . he, with the help of Communist contacts, went to Russia in August, 1929, returning in October. . . . He next joined the Communist Party and in 1930 attended the Communist inspired International Negro Workers' Congress in Hamburg, proceeding to Berlin where he contacted leading Com-munists. . . .[26]

. . . He also had a full knowledge and understanding of the psychology of the Kikuyu and was able to blend the technique of revolution, undoubtedly learnt while he was in Russia, with an appeal to superstition and to the strong sense of tribal destiny which the Kikuyu possessed. In this way *Mau Mau* gradually but inexorably assumed the character of a tribal religion, albeit a religion based on evil, which bore remarkable resemblance to the witchcraft and black magic practised in Europe during the Middle Ages.[27]

## INDONESIA

Indonesia is the creature of the United States and her allies who helped the island empire to achieve independence from Dutch rule in 1949. The cry of "colonialism" had been raised, and the Department of State did everything it could to bring about the separation of the Dutch from the island possessions.[28]

Since then, your government has supplied Sukarno with military training,[29] arms,[30] and almost a billion dollars of your money in "foreign aid."

Is Sukarno a Communist?

Well, Bernard H. M. Vlekke describes him as a youth as follows:

Sukarno himself strongly leaned toward the Marxist concept of history and society. These views were rejected by many of the more mature nationalist leaders. It may be that Sukarno grew rather reckless in his exhortations to the people of Java to refuse cooperation with the Dutch "imperialist capitalists," he may have been embittered by the refusal of many other nationalist leaders to gather around him and to present a common front against the Dutch, in any case his speeches grew more and more incitatory and revolutionary. . . .[31]

As long ago as 1947, *Current Biography* said:

At this time Soekarno's [the Dutch spelling] political philosophy was Marxist, an ideology that was apparently too extreme for the mass of Indonesians. When Soekarno's agitators were arrested by the Dutch authorities, Soekarno organized "fighting squads." For this action he was subsequently tried by a native tribunal and imprisoned in a Dutch concentration camp on the island of Flores. . . .[32]

Hasan Muhummad Tiro, former head of research at the Indonesian embassy in Washington, said in 1955:

> Since the Sastroamidjojo regime [Sukarno's prime minister] took over the Government more than a year-and-a-half ago, no open criticism against the Communist party has been tolerated. Even the former Premier, Muhummad Natsir, Chairman of the Masjumi party, and Isa Anshary, prominent Moslem leader, were arraigned for interrogation by the Prosecutor General's office because of anti-Communist speeches they delivered on September 23, 1953. . . .
>
> Among those convicted and sentenced to jail in the Communist plot of 1946 were Iwa Kusumasumantri, a Moscow-trained Communist, and Mohammed Yamin. Soekarno not only pardoned these men, but appointed both of them to high office. Yamin is now Minister of Education, and Kusumasumantri is now Minister of Defense. It is beyond understanding how the Indonesian people can defend themselves against Soviet encroachment when their Defense Minister is a Communist party leader whose family, to this day, resides in Moscow.
>
> Little consolation can be drawn from the backgrounds of other members of Sastroamidjojo's cabinet. Gondokusumo, the Minister of Justice, participated in the Budapest Peace Conference and . . . ousted the anti-Communist Chinese leaders from Indonesia. Minister of Labor Abidin participated in the Peking Peace Conference. . . .[33]

Sukarno himself said after winning the Order of Lenin, "Thus, I am a Communist of the highest order."[34]

"I am Communist, religious and nationalist as well."[35]

"President Sukarno . . . said he prayed that Vietnam might soon be 'reunited in freedom' through the efforts of the Vietcong guerrillas."[36]

It is the Vietcong guerrillas of course who are now killing American servicemen.

Well, what do you think? Is this another mistake? Is that why your government has given this man almost a billion dollars of your money?

## Puerto Rico

Let's start getting closer to home. You will recall that there has recently been some trouble in Puerto Rico: "Nearly 1,000 high school and university students demonstrated outside the Capitol today," said the New York *Times,* "to protest alleged police brutality in repressing student disorders Wednesday night." [37]

What it is actually all about, writes Victor Riesel, is as follows:

. . . there have been riots, burnings of cars, clashes with police, stonings of buildings and damage to the University of Puerto Rico. . . .

This violence was forecast in this column last April. The street fighting broke out Oct. 28, when a band of "students" called for a demonstration against participation in the Nov. 3 election. The revolutionary hard core, numbering 60 trained men and women, soon merged into the melee as the demonstration grew and some 1,000 students fought the police.

[Riesel speaks of] the hard-core Puerto Rican revolutionists, some of whom were in Communist China earlier this year.

This peripatetic Puerto Rican group operated under the name "Puerto Rican University Students Federation for Independence."

Friends of the group which visited the Chinese—all expenses paid—also visited Cuba a few months later, and again all expenses were paid.

This is no hastily collected political potpourri. It is the youth infra-structure being set up by the Chinese Communists in the Western hemisphere, and those who don't view it seriously should remember those who first viewed Fidel Castro as simply an avant-garde refugee from a barber shop.[38]

## CANADA

Many Americans—and most Canadians—have wondered about the strange events now going on in Canada. A man has been killed, another seriously injured, and property destroyed, ostensibly as part of a campaign for the "national independence" of Quebec. Now of course, the idea that the good people of Quebec have developed the notion that they are some sort of nation, and that what they need is national independence, is about equivalent to a demand for secession from New York City by the people of Greenwich Village, and could be appreciated seriously only by the Messrs. Gilbert and Sullivan, if those talented gentlemen were happily still in operation. The New York *Times* apparently takes the view that the whole thing is a bit mystifying, but is probably the work of a band of unruly collegians who like nothing better than placing bombs in mailboxes.

What is it actually all about? Let us turn to a man who knows, the late Leslie Morris, former head of the Canadian Communist party:

> . . . there is a merging of a democratic *anti-capitalist,* anti-monopoly struggle with a *national revolution* in French Canada, spearheaded by a demand for *self-determination* up to and including *secession* from the present federal union with English-speaking Canada.[39] (italics added)

And how did all this happen to come about?

> . . . The impact of the national-liberation movements throughout the world, and particularly events in Cuba and the Negro liberation movement in the United States, have affected French Canadian public opinion.[40]

André Malraux also affected French Canadian public opinion:

> The French Minister of Cultural Affairs, Andre Malraux, stunned this French Canadian city [Montreal] today with an allusion to Quebec's nationalist movement. Raising his trembling voice, he proclaimed: "France needs you! We will build the next civilization together."
>
> . . .
>
> What surprised leaders of both the French-speaking and English-speaking communities of Montreal was the appeal to nationalist and separatist emotions contained in Mr. Malraux's speech, and the address by Mayor Drapeau, which was similar in tone.[41]

André Malraux is a member of the government of Charles de Gaulle, who as you will recall succeeded in separating a province of France—Algeria—from the rest of France, and giving it to the Communists.

And how do we know that the events in Canada as well are the work of the Communists?

The rise of the democratic and national French Canadian revolution in an imperialist state such as Canada constitutes an amazing verification of the truth of Marxism-Leninism that in the time of imperialism national movements *inevitably* take on an anti-imperialist character and are *a constituent part of the road to socialism.*[42] (italics added)

This, however, leaves one important matter unsettled. All that this proves is that the Communists *want* to capture the "French Canadian Revolution," yet inevitably the Communists *want* to capture all such revolutions. Where is the proof that in Canada they are succeeding?

Let us turn to the New York *Times:*

"The police arrested today eight men suspected of being members of the Quebec Liberation Front," said the *Times,* "the terrorist organization that has been blamed for a series of recent bombings in Quebec Province."

The *Times* then recorded the following sentence: "Most of the suspects were between 19 and 22 years of age, authorities said, *but one was a 33-year-old Belgian reported to have been trained for revolutionary work in Cuba.*" [43] (italics added)

Let us proceed carefully and examine for meaning what we have just read in the New York *Times:* A man who is not only a participant, but a leader—at least because of the age disparity—of the *conspiracy* to blow Canadians up with bombs, has been trained to do just that in Cuba. Cuba is, as we all know, a Communist state, operated by Fidel Castro—a self-proclaimed Communist.

Now, if Castro—a Communist—is doing any training, it would be moderate to conclude that he isn't training any capitalists. It would be reasonable to conclude that a Communist would be training more Communists. So let's draw the very reasonable conclusion that one of the leaders in the *conspiracy* to blow up Canadians—is actually a Communist.

Let's in fact draw the exceedingly probable conclusion that this Belgian Communist trained in Cuba has been *assigned* to kill people in Canada by an *international* association of Communists—that is, by an *international* conspiracy.

Now it happened that this information appeared on the front page of the New York *Times*. And the most moderate thing one can say about it is that it is information which should be loudly advertised to Americans in general and Canadians in particular. It should because it is essential to their survival that Americans and Canadians be made aware of it. It is therefore absolutely essential—and nothing more than barely adequate journalism—that this information should be investigated and developed by people trained for the job. However, to our knowledge nothing more has ever been said about it by the New York *Times*.

*    *    *

Let us draw some reasonable conclusions.

It is not the purpose of this chapter or this book to make an investigation or file an indictment of the New York *Times*. So let's say here only the most moderate thing we can say, which is that a trapeze artist, an employee or a doctor who made such a series of mistakes would long since be either dead, unemployed or locked up for criminal negligence.

All we should say, in short, is that there is something very peculiar going on up at the New York *Times*.

But what we want to underline now is only what we have *proved* so far:

1) We have proved—by quoting their own words—what the Communists mean to do.

2) We have proved—by using quotations from the pages of the New York *Times*—that they are doing what they mean to do, all over the world.

3) We have proved—through the use of reason applied to quotations from the *Times*—that over and over again *you have been fooled*.

### NOTES

1. Andrew H. Berding, "Strategy of Incitement," *Department of State Bulletin*, vol. 43, no. 1105 (August 29, 1960), p. 308.

2. Frederick C. Schwarz, "Blueprint for Conquest," *American Mercury*, vol. 77 (August 1953), p. 86.

3. Foster Hailey, New York *Times Magazine* (December 22, 1946), pp. 40-41.

4. Joseph C. Grew, *Invasion Alert!* (Baltimore, Maran Publishers, 1956), pp. 42-44.

5. New York *Times* (April 25, 1959), p. 20.

6. *Ibid.* (May 23, 1959), p. 24.

7. *Ibid.* (July 1, 1959), p. 1.

8. *Ibid.* (July 15, 1959), p. 1.

9. *Ibid.* (December 3, 1961), p. 1.

10. V. I. Lenin, *The Right of Nations to Self-Determination* (New York, International Publishers, 1951), pp. 76-77.

11. Harry J. Benda and Ruth T. McVey, editors, *The Communist Uprisings of 1926-1927 in Indonesia: Key Documents* (Ithaca, N.Y., Cornell University, 1960), p. 3.

12. *U.S. News & World Report*, vol. 56, no. 6 (February 10, 1964), p. 52.

13. New York *Times* (April 3, 1964), p. 6.

14. *Ibid.*

15. *Ibid.* (April 23, 1964), p. 38.

16. *Ibid.* (May 2, 1964), p. 1. Khrushchev was still grinning about the Lenin Peace Prize he had given Ben Bella the day before. See the New York *Times* (May 1, 1964), p. 10.

17. *Ibid.* (July 6, 1964), p. 4.

18. *U.S. News & World Report*, vol. 56, no. 4 (January 27, 1964), p. 6.

19. *Ibid.*, no. 6 (February 10, 1964), p. 52.

20. Robert Conley, New York *Times* (July 1, 1964), p. 2. Dispatch from Zanzibar.

21. New York *Times* (November 5, 1964), p. 4.

22. *Ibid.* (November 8, 1964), p. 37.

23. K. A. Busia, *Ghana Will Be Truly Free and Happy* (London, Ghana Students Association, n.d.), p. 9.

24. C. L. Sulzberger, New York *Times* (July 1, 1964), p. 34.

25. New York *Times* (December 13, 1964), pp. 1, 27.

26. F. D. Corfield, *Historical Survey of the Origins and Growth of Mau Mau* (London, Her Majesty's Stationery Office, 1960), p. 42.

27. *Ibid.*, p. 52.

28. Boston *Traveler* (December 26, 1957).

29. John Chamberlain, Boston *Record American* (May 4, 1964).

30. Manchester *Union Leader* (August 20, 1958). Also Boston *Traveler* (March 30, 1957).

31. Bernard H. M. Vlekke, *Nusantara, A History of Indonesia* (The Hague, W. van Hoeve, 1959), p. 374.

32. *Current Biography* (New York, H. W. Wilson Company, 1947), p. 590.

33. *U.S. News & World Report*, vol. 39 (July 1, 1955).

34. *Izvestia*. As quoted in *Human Events* (November 10, 1962).

35. New York *Times* (September 15, 1964), p. 11.

36. *Ibid.* (August 18, 1964), p. 7.

37. *Ibid.* (October 31, 1964), p. 33.

38. New York *Journal-American* (November 5, 1964), p. 15.

39. Leslie Morris, "National and Democratic Revolution in French Canada," *World Marxist Review*, vol. 7, no. 9 (September 1964), p. 15. Morris was the general secretary of the Communist party of Canada.

40. *Ibid.*, p. 16.

41. New York *Times* (October 11, 1963), p. 2.

42. Morris, pp. 20-21.

43. New York *Times* (June 3, 1963), p. 1.

## CHAPTER III

# The Communist Position on the Negro Question

> The program of the Communist Party demanded an end to the national inequalities suffered by the French Canadian people, but did not spell out the full program of national self-determination. It required the mass upsurge of the French Canadian people to produce the realization that in French Canada there existed not only grievances against national inequalities but potentially, and now actively, a mass demand for complete self-determination. This demand is now at the center of the Communist Party's position.[1]

As we have seen, the Communists really put themselves out to plan the future of every individual on the face of the earth. And so the question arises: What did they plan for us?

For more than a decade after the Russian revolution, the comrades floundered on the subject of the "Negro problem" in the United States. They discussed it, they studied it, but they were absolutely unable to make anything out of it. They were unable to form a revolutionary theory to guide the activities of their American members. And comrades were complaining that these ungrateful American Negroes simply didn't go for Communism.

At the Communist sixth world congress, in 1928, the problem was solved. For the American Negroes, the comrades had developed an amazing new theory. They called it "self-determination." [2]

It is important to record how and why the Communists decided to apply this theory to Negro Americans.

> After the Second Congress, the mystery deepens [writes Theodore Draper]. For the next eight years, there is no record in the Comintern or in the American party of any reference to the American Negroes as a "nation" or any implications of Negro "self-determination." On the contrary, all the documents and discussions

point in different directions. As we have seen, the Fourth Congress in 1922, during Lenin's lifetime, stressed the American Negroes' role in the liberation of Africa, not their own independent political existence. The Fifth Congress in 1924, soon after Lenin's death, arrived at a consensus that the right of self-determination did not apply to the United States. The American party's conventions in 1923, 1925, and 1927, all of them minutely scrutinized by Comintern commissions and representatives, did not give the slightest hint of an American Negro "national question." . . .[3]

But there was no mystery at all about the American comrades' opinion of this theory. Benjamin Gitlow, who was in the South campaigning as a Communist for the vice presidency of the United States in 1928 when the word came through about self-determination, reports his own hostility and shock.[4] William A. Nolan writes that

> . . . About twenty per cent of the articles which appeared in the official magazine of theory [*Communist*] during the first quarter of 1930 were devoted to the Negro question. But even in July, this high communist source had to concede that there existed only "great confusion" as to what self-determination could mean for the United States, and this was about two years after the Sixth World Congress had "clarified" the slogan. A former Negro communist told the author that the Negro comrades simply could not believe it, even those who for opportunist reasons gave it lip service. . . .[5]

The reason all this is so important to record is to show that the Communist notion that American Negroes might need, and want, "self-determination"—secession—just because they happened to be black, was so ludicrous, so alien to the facts, that even American comrades themselves, not noted for an excess of individualism, found it difficult to accept. It is important to show that the idea of "self-determination" was not an idea that would readily spring to mind after even a mildly rational examination of the facts.

Indeed, Earl Browder later explained as head of the American Communist party:

> The Bolshevik program on the Negro question was not simply a generalization of our own experience in America. It was an appli-

cation of Lenin's program on the national question which summarized the world experience of generations of revolutionary struggle and especially the experience of the revolutionary solution of the national question in the Soviet Union. *We could not have arrived at our program only upon the basis of our own American experience. It was the existence of the World Party of Communism which made possible for us the elaboration of a correct Leninist program on the Negro question.*[6] (italics added)

So, according to Earl Browder, it would not only have been difficult for a reasonable Negro looking at the facts to develop the idea of self-determination; it would have been impossible —without the use of Communist theory—simply because the idea of self-determination was one of the many discoveries of the "science" of Leninism. In fact, according to Earl Browder, only a Communist could develop the idea.

" 'Nearly all' non-Communist Negro leaders rejected the Communist theory . . ." Draper reports a Communist Negro leader to have written.[7]

The question naturally arises: If the idea of self-determination made so much trouble when applied to American Negroes, then why apply it at all?

There were probably two reasons: In the first place, it was Stalin's idea, his and Lenin's plan for the minorities in Russia, and in 1928 Stalin had recently come to power; and in 1915, Lenin had written as follows: ". . . There is a striking similarity between the economic position of the American Negro and that of the former serf of the central agricultural provinces of Russia." [8]

So the comrades applied it.

. . . The similarity between the program laid down for the Communist party of the United States and the earlier doctrines of Lenin and Stalin on the national and colonial questions is readily apparent; and the connection is a direct one, through the Sixth World Congress of the Communist International. Not only were the general ideas taken over; they were advocated in precisely the same terms, down to the slogans, and even to the sentences and phrases, employed by the Communist International.[9]

Now what did "self-determination for the Negroes in the Black Belt" actually mean? One of the earliest, if not the earliest, explanations, and certainly the most official, was offered by "John Pepper," who as Joseph Pogany had been a general in the Communist regime in post-World War I Hungary, and was at the time he wrote an official representative of the Comintern in the United States. "The 'black belt' of the south . . . *constitutes virtually a colony within the body of the United States of America*," Pepper tells us soon after the sixth world congress.[10] And therefore:

> The Negro Communists should emphasize in their propaganda *the establishment of a Negro Soviet Republic.*
> The Workers [Communist] Party of America puts forward correctly as its central slogan: *Abolition of the whole system of race discrimination. Full racial, social and political equality for the Negro people.* But it is necessary to supplement the struggle for the full racial, social and political equality of the Negroes with a struggle for their right of national self-determination. Self-determination means the right to establish their own state, to erect their own government, if they choose to do so. . . .[11]

As we have seen, however, this caused more problems than it solved, and so two years later, in October 1930, Moscow again sent word:

> The struggle of the communists for the *equal rights* of the Negroes applies to all Negroes, in the North as well as in the South. The struggle for this slogan embraces all or almost all of the important special interests of the Negroes in the North, but not in the South, where the main Communist slogan must be: *The Right of Self-Determination of the Negroes in the Black Belt.* . . .[12]

Remember this: The Communist policy toward the Negroes would consist of two slogans or strategies: first, a drive for equal rights for Negroes everywhere in America, and second, at the same time a drive for self-determination in the South.

Let us pursue this incredible idea.

In 1932, at the national nominating convention of the Communist party, comrade C. A. Hathaway made a speech called "Who Are the Friends of the Negro People?"

In the first place, our demand is that the land of the Southern white landlords, for years tilled by the Negro tenant farmers, be confiscated and turned over to the Negroes. This is the only way to insure economic and social equality for the tenant farmers.

Secondly, we propose to break up the present artificial state boundaries established for the convenience of the white master class, and to establish the state unity of the territory known as the "Black Belt," where the Negroes constitute the overwhelming majority of the population.

Thirdly, in this territory, we demand that the Negroes be given the complete right of self-determination; *the right to set up their own government* in this territory and the right to separate, if *they* wish, from the United States.[13]

The black belt in which the Negroes are to be self-determined was defined in 1935:

The actual extent of this new Negro Republic would in all probability be approximately the present area in which the Negroes constitute the majority of the population. In other words it would be approximately the present plantation area. It would be certain to include such cities as Richmond and Norfolk, Va., Columbia and Charleston, S.C., Atlanta, Augusta, Savannah and Macon, Georgia, Montgomery, Alabama, New Orleans and Shreveport, La., Little Rock, Arkansas, and Memphis, Tennessee. . . .[14]

In 1947, William Z. Foster, who then headed the party, again solved the problem:

It is a fact we must reckon with that, for the most part, the Negro people have not responded favorably to the slogan of self-determination for the Negro people in the Black Belt, a slogan first put forward by our Party in 1928. Because of this lack of response, which amounts in many cases to vigorous opposition, there are some comrades in our ranks who conclude incorrectly that the slogan of self-determination for the Negro people in the Black Belt is wrong.[15]

In other words, just because the "Negro people" vigorously oppose "self-determination" doesn't mean they aren't going to get it.

The point is, said Foster:

. . . the Negro people in the Black Belt are a nation . . . they possess the essential qualities of nationhood, as elaborated in the works of that great expert on the national question, Stalin. This lays a firm basis for the self-determination slogan. So I will not deal further with this basic matter of whether or not the Negroes in the Black Belt are a nation.

Secondly, we have made an important contribution in answering a question that has puzzled our comrades for the past twenty years, namely, why, if the Negro people are a nation, don't they put forth the slogan of self-determination. *Fundamentally, the reason is that they are essentially a young nation, a developing nation. A nation has to be at a certain stage of political growth before it advances the demand for self-determination. . . .*[16] (italics added)

The end of the war also saw a metamorphosis in language. The term "self-determination" was replaced by "national people's liberation." According to William Nolan:

There are several reasons for this new emphasis. In the first place, it escapes some of the embarrassment which had become associated with the slogan of self-determination. Secondly, it helps to bring the American communist movement into line with the "national people's liberation movements" behind the Iron Curtain, as well as in the Far East. And it also marks a more specific return to the leading terminology of the national and colonial theses of the Second and Sixth World Congresses of the Communist International.[17]

Indeed, it was necessary to hide what Communist policy was really about:

In the excess of his desire to make amends for his wartime deviations, Ben Davis printed his reapproval of the slogan of self-determination in the Black Belt in the Sunday edition of the *Daily Worker* for July 22, 1945. The effect on non communist Negroes was so instantaneous and so explosive that the slogan was thereafter withdrawn from the eyes of the rank and file. From that time on, the Negro masses would have to be content with circumlocutions, such as "free determination of their own destiny," and "fight against the semifeudal system of the South." [18]

Let's remember this. Such circumlocutions are *nothing but* circumlocutions. What they *really* mean is self-determination.

Nevertheless, as late as 1951 we find Gus Hall, the present head of the party, writing openly as follows:

. . . what is the Negro nation we speak about? There are some who say that all the 15 million Negro people in the U.S.A. comprise the oppressed nation. This, of course, is not so. We are speaking about the subjugated Negro nation . . . in the Black Belt area of the South. . . .

When one states this, the question immediately arises, what about the millions of Negro people who live in the North and other parts of the country? The Negro people outside of the area of the Negro nation constitute a national minority.

In this connection there are a number of questions that need further elucidation. First, what are the possible dangers and wrong conclusions that can be drawn from the formulation that the 15 million Negroes comprise a nation?

. . .

It leaves room for confusion as to the tasks, outlook, program of the *Negro nation in the South* and its struggle for self-determination, and the *struggle for full equality of the Negro people* in the rest of the country. As a rule, this confusion results in a watering down of the program and tasks of the national liberation struggle, an ignoring of the particular and distinctive features, of the unequal levels and forms of struggle, demanded by the requirements of the "equal rights" goals of the national minority and the "liberation" goals of the Black Belt nation.[19]

And in 1953, Hugh Bradley was saying the following in a report delivered at the national conference of the Communist party:

In addition, the entire Negro people are confronted with the problem of national oppression, arising from the heart of the Deep South where the Negro people constitute a distinct nation, held in subjugation, and denied all major rights as a nation.

. . .

While helping to unite the Negro people in support of a minimum national program for complete equal rights the Communist Party must advance a class program in behalf of the Negro workers in industry, a program designed to relieve the burden of the Negro farming masses, as well as to raise and popularize the demand of self-determination for the Negro nation in the South.[20]

In fact, writes former Royal Canadian Mounted Police undercover agent Pat Walsh, "the executive of the USA Communist Party discreetly distributed *in June 1964* thousands of copies of a 1935 pamphlet entitled The Negroes In A Soviet America." (italics added)[21]

Let us proceed carefully and ask ourselves what we have proved. Well, we have proved that the Communists have decided to apply here in America the same strategy we have proved they are applying everywhere in the world. We have proved that they *openly* decided to apply it here more than thirty-five years ago. And we have demonstrated that since this strategy was the work of Lenin and Stalin, they could do nothing else but apply it, *being Communists.*

But a question arises. As we have seen, the Communists prescribed two strategies for American Negroes: equal rights and self-determination. Equal rights would seem to refer to "integration," whatever that is, but self-determination would seem to refer to "segregation," whatever that is.

Isn't this some sort of contradiction? Doesn't one strategy tend to negate the other?

It is of supreme importance that we understand the answer to this question.

At the plenary meeting of the national committee of the Communist party in 1946, William Z. Foster complained:

> One of the major difficulties we have had to contend with has been a tendency of our opponents to pose one of these currents to the other, thus making it appear that the demand for self-determination slogans is in contradiction to the propositions that Negroes fight for the fullest rights as Americans. Comrade Strong knocked this nonsense on the head when he pointed out so forcefully that *it is impossible for the Negro people to achieve their full economic, political, and social equality as Americans unless they organize as a nation, unless they forward the slogan of self-determination for the Black Belt of the South.*[22] (italics added)

In other words, equal rights and self-determination not only aren't antagonistic, they aren't even complementary; *they are one and the same thing.* If it is impossible for the Negro people to get equal rights without self-determination, then it follows, does it not, that the struggle for equal rights *is* the struggle for self-determination.

At the same meeting, General Secretary Eugene Dennis spoke of

> the main slogan of action which our Party champions nationally in behalf of the Negro people, namely, the right of full political, economic and social equality for the Negro people. . . . if this basic democratic slogan and Marxist principle is to mean what it says, then its application in the Black Belt . . . *requires the exercise of the right to self-determination.*[23] (italics added)

"Before a people can have equal rights with other peoples of the world, it must have the right itself to determine its relations with other nations," James S. Allen tells us in 1932. "We can in no sense speak of the Negro people having achieved full equal rights until it has won the right of self-determination." [24]

". . . is there a close connection, an interrelation between the subjugated nation in the South and the Negro people generally?" asks Gus Hall in 1951.

> How could anyone deny this? Of course there is. There is in fact a very close kinship. Each influences the other. . . . Thus, the struggles for full equality of the Negro national minority and the struggle for national liberation of the oppressed nation are very closely interlinked.[25]

Self-determination, in short, is in no way opposed to equal rights. It is simply the name of the *last* victory in the struggle for those rights. Self-determination means *full* equal rights, and all the equal rights won before it are only *partial.*

> The slogan for the right of self-determination and the other fundamental slogans of the Negro question in the Black Belt do not exclude but rather pre-suppose an energetic development of the struggle for concrete *partial demands* linked up with the daily needs and afflictions of wide masses of working Negroes. . . .[26]

And the point of it all, of course, is to bring socialism-communism to the United States:

> The point I wish to make is that the development of the American Negroes in the Black Belt into a full-fledged nation in the classical sense is a basic requirement for the progressive [that is,

socialist-communist] development of the United States. . . . It means as a result of this struggle the unfolding of the most fundamental and the most profound struggles for democracy in the United States, anti-imperialist struggles leading to socialism.[27]

Here is a large part of the Communist plan for the destruction and communization of the United States. But again a question arises: Like a bunch of psychotics in a hospital, the Communists can *say* whatever they like.

Where's the proof that they're doing it?

## NOTES

1. Leslie Morris, "National and Democratic Revolution in French Canada," *World Marxist Review*, vol. 7, no. 9 (September 1964), p. 20.

2. "Theses on the Revolutionary Movement in the Colonies and Semi-Colonies, Sixth World Congress," *International Press Correspondence*, vol. 8, pp. 1659-1676.

3. Theodore Draper, *American Communism and Soviet Russia* (New York, The Viking Press, 1960), pp. 339-340.

4. Benjamin Gitlow, *I Confess* (New York, E. P. Dutton and Co. Inc., 1940), pp. 480-481.

5. William A. Nolan, *Communism Versus the Negro* (Chicago, Henry Regnery Company, 1951), p. 48.

6. This position of Browder is contained on page 5 of a pamphlet by the Communist party of the U.S.A., "The Communist Position on the Negro Question" (New York, Workers Library Publishers, 1934). Because there is another pamphlet with the same title, we will refer to this first pamphlet as "The Communist Position (1934)." See footnote 16 of this chapter.

7. Draper, p. 354.

8. V. I. Lenin, *Capitalism and Agriculture in the United States of America* (translation in manuscript, New York Public Library), p. 8.

9. Wilson Record, *The Negro and the Communist Party* (Chapel Hill, The University of North Carolina Press, 1951), p. 60.

10. John Pepper, "American Negro Problems," *Communist*, vol. 7, no. 10 (October 1928). This and other Pepper quotes on p. 628 ff.

11. *Ibid.* Also quoted by Nolan, p. 47.

12. "The Communist Position (1934)," p. 42. Also quoted by Nolan, pp. 39-40.

13. "The Communist Position (1934)," p. 28.

14. James S. Allen and James W. Ford, *The Negroes in a Soviet America* (New York, Workers Library Publishers, June 1935), p. 39. Also quoted by Nolan, p. 45.

15. William Z. Foster, "On Self-Determination for the Negro People,"

*Political Affairs,* vol. 25, no. 26 (June 1946), pp. 549-554. Also quoted by Nolan, p. 58.

16. This position of Foster is contained on page 14 of a pamphlet by the Communist party of the U.S.A., National Committee, "The Communist Position on the Negro Question" (New York, New Century Publishers, 1947). We will refer to this pamphlet as "The Communist Position (1947)." See footnote 6 of this chapter. Contained also in William Z. Foster, "On the Question of Negro Self-Determination," *Political Affairs,* vol. 26 (January 1947), p. 54. Also quoted by Nolan, p. 59.

17. Nolan, p. 60.

18. *Ibid.,* p. 61.

19. Gus Hall, *Marxism and Negro Liberation* (New York, New Century Publishers, 1951), pp. 17-19.

20. Hugh Bradley, *Next Steps in the Struggle for Negro Freedom* (New York, New Century Publishers, 1953), pp. 24-25.

21. *TAB,* vol. 9, no. 15 (Toronto, August 29, 1964).

22. As quoted in "The Communist Position (1947)," pp. 14-16.

23. *Ibid.,* pp. 24-25.

24. James S. Allen, "Negro Liberation," International Pamphlets, no. 29 (New York, International Publishers, 1932), p. 21.

25. Hall, pp. 17-19.

26. Resolutions of the Communist International on the Negro Question in the United States in "The Communist Position (1934)," p. 53.

27. Alexander Bittelman, as quoted in "The Communist Position (1947)," p. 43. Bittelman was a member of the national committee of the Communist party.

## CHAPTER IV

# The Black Muslims

> For many years this policy [self-determination] was exclusively associated with the Communists and, more than any other theoretical and practical program, distinguished them from other American radical movements.[1]

Some time in the summer of 1930, when the comrades in Moscow were busy clarifying the policy of "self-determination for the Negroes in the Black Belt," a peddler appeared in the Negro community of Detroit. "He was welcomed into the homes of the culture-hungry Negroes, who were eager to purchase his silks and artifacts," writes Professor C. Eric Lincoln, "which he claimed were like those the Negro people wore in their homeland across the sea."

> "He came first to our houses selling raincoats, and then afterwards, silks. In this way he could get into the people's houses, for every woman was eager to see the nice things the peddler had for sale. He told us that the silks he carried were the same kind that our people used in their home country, and that he was from there. So we asked him to tell us about our own country." [2]

So he did. He began holding meetings from house to house throughout the community.

> At first, the "prophet," as he came to be known, confined his teachings to a recitation of his experiences in foreign lands, admonitions against certain foods and suggestions for improving his listeners' physical health. He was kind, friendly, unassuming and patient.

> But after a while, his teachings changed.

> Eventually the stranger's teachings took the form of increasingly bitter denouncements against the white race; and as his prestige grew he "began to attack the teachings of the Bible in such a way as to shock his hearers and bring them to an emotional crisis." People experienced sudden conversions and became his followers.[3]

Thus was born the movement whose followers are called Black Muslims.

Who in fact was this itinerant peddler and prophet? His name was usually Mr. Farrad Mohammad or Mr. F. Mohammad Ali, except when it was Professor Ford, Mr. Wali Farrad or W. D. Fard. Legends about him abounded, says Lincoln, one having him a Palestinian Arab "who had participated in various racial agitations in India, South Africa and London before moving on to Detroit." [4] Another says he was educated at a London university in preparation for a diplomatic career in the service of the kingdom of Hejaz, but that he sacrificed his personal future "to bring 'freedom, justice, and equality' to the 'black men in the wilderness of North America, surrounded and robbed completely by the Cave Man.'" [5]

It was really all very simple, Fard later explained to the Detroit police: It seems he was "The Supreme Ruler of the Universe."

It now appears, however, that the truth is even more amazing. For according to reporter Ed Montgomery:

> [Fard] is not a Negro. He is a white man masquerading as a Negro! His true name is Wallace Dodd.
>
> He was born in New Zealand on Feb. 26, 1891.
>
> [His police record] includes a conviction for bootlegging and a San Quentin prison term for the sale of narcotics.
>
> To the FBI he is number 56062—and a man of many aliases. The California Bureau of Identification and Investigation lists him as Wallace Ford, number 1797924. At San Quentin, as Ford, he was number 42314. With the Michigan state police he is Wallace Farad, number 98076.
>
> Although the names and numbers vary, the fingerprints are always the same.

It seems that at 26, Dodd took as his common-law wife a 25 year old Los Angeles waitress, and on September 1, 1920, she bore him a son, Wallace Dodd Ford.

On the son's birth certificate, Dodd listed himself as "White."

. . .

Dodd was arrested by Detroit police on May 25, 1933. The official report states that Dodd admitted his teachings "were strictly a racket" and that he was "getting all the money out of it he could." [6]

So here is a white man teaching Negroes to hate white men, which to say the least is very peculiar.

Fard-Dodd established a "religion," named Elijah Muhammad to succeed him, and then disappeared as suddenly as he had come. Mr. Muhammad, also known as Gulam Bogans, Elijah Poole, Muhammad Rassouli, Elijah Muck Muhd, "and various other aliases," [7] now says that Fard returned to Mecca and keeps in touch—spiritually; Mr. Montgomery says that police records show he returned to New Zealand.

Now, what were the essential teachings of this very mysterious man? The prophet taught that white men were "blue-eyed devils," and "incapable of telling the truth." He spoke of "the glorious history of Black Afro-Asia."

> [Fard explained] that his followers were not Americans and that they owed no allegiance to the American flag. It was stupid, he argued, to pledge allegiance to a flag that offered no protection against "the depravities·of the white devils [who] by their tricknology . . . keep our peoples illiterate to use as tools and slaves." . . .[8]

Mr. Muhammad, the present prophet, has developed these simple principles into an even simpler political program, which reads as follows:

> . . . we believe our contributions to this land and the suffering forced upon us by white America, justifies our demand for complete separation in a state or territory of our own.
>
> If the white people are truthful about their professed friendship toward the so-called Negro, they can prove it by dividing up America with their slaves.[9]

It seems, you see, that American Negroes are "a nation within a nation," an "occupied people." [10]

Muhammad usually asks for "two or three states," but at the Muslim convention of 1960 he asked for "four or five." [11] The late Malcolm X thought "nine or ten states would be enough." [12]

In *The Negroes in a Soviet America,* the Communist plan for the "Negro Soviet Republic," we read the following:

*"The same will occur throughout the plantation area—from southeastern Virginia, down through the Carolinas and central Georgia, across Alabama, Mississippi and Louisiana, reaching even into Arkansas and parts of Tennessee and Texas. . . ."* [13]

And what would be the result of such an amputation?

. . . Let us say that the Muslims were to achieve the possession of the six or seven states that they claim are owed to Negroes by the United States as "back payment" for slave labor [writes James Baldwin]. Clearly, the United States would never surrender this territory, on any terms whatever, unless it found it impossible, for whatever reason, to hold it—unless, that is, the United States were to be reduced as a world power, exactly the way, and at the same degree of speed, that England has been forced to relinquish her Empire. . . . If the states were Southern states—and the Muslims seem to favor this—then the borders of a hostile Latin America would be raised, in effect, to, say, Maryland. Of the American borders on the sea, one would face toward a powerless Europe and the other toward an untrustworthy and non-white East, and on the North, after Canada, there would be only Alaska, which is a Russian border. The effect of this would be that the white people of the United States and Canada would find themselves marooned on a hostile continent, with the rest of the white world probably unwilling and certainly unable to come to their aid. All this is not, to my mind, the most imminent of possibilities, but if I were a Muslim, this is the possibility that I would find myself holding in the center of my mind, and driving toward. And if I were a Muslim, I would not hesitate to utilize—or, indeed, to exacerbate—the social and spiritual discontent that reigns here. . . .[14]

So the question arises:

Are Muhammad's teachings in fact seditious? No one can say [says Professor Lincoln], for his goals—and the ultimate methods he would use to reach them—are never baldly stated. . . .

. . . He speaks knowingly of an impending "Battle of Armageddon" and has promised that Negroes "will soon gain control of

New York City—and that 'white rule' in the United States will be overthrown by 1970." [15]

Now, what sort of people are these Black Muslims?

Well, some are in jail. At Clinton state prison in Utica, New York, for instance, officials refused to let four Negro inmates practice their new faith. ". . . Prison officials did not dispute that discipline improves markedly among those converted to Islam, but they protested that the Muslims have 'ulterior motives,' aimed at 'forcing supremacy over whites, although they do not express it.' " [16]

*"But the revolution will not stop with the seizure of the land. . . . With the power of the plantation owners destroyed, a new kind of government will be set up by the farmers and the workers in this territory. . . . The Negroes will play the leading role both in the land revolution and in the new revolutionary governments.*

*". . . It can be proclaimed as a new country . . . where the majority—the Negro people—rule with the cooperation of the white masses in the territory."* [17] The Negroes in a Soviet America

It must not be supposed, however, that all Muslims spend time in jail. Most of them apparently are workmen and thoroughly solid citizens: "Recruitment for the Movement is still predominantly from among low-income groups at the lower end of the educational scale. . . . a majority of the membership of any given temple is composed of domestic and factory workers, common laborers and the like. . . ." [18]

*". . . The aim of the Communist Party must be to fight for the hegemony of the working-class elements in the national liberation movement. The basic task of the communists is to form working-class organizations for the Negro proletariat and agricultural workers, and farmers' organizations for the Negro farmers and to turn these organizations into energetic integral forces of the whole class struggle. . . ."* [19]

In fact: ". . . Where Negroes of middle- and upper-class status have developed—or moved into—residential areas consistent with their new prosperity, Muslims have not followed, for the Movement continues to emphasize its affiliations with the working class. . . ." [20]

And this brings us to the Muslim ideal:

". . . *It is permissible to form a united front (for example in the form of a Negro Race Congress) of the working-class elements with the petit-bourgeois elements. . . .*" [21] John Pepper, 1928

> The Muslim ideal is "a United Front of Black Men," who will "take the offensive and carry the fight for justice and freedom to the enemy." Through such a united front, "the American Negroes will discover themselves, elevate their distinguished men and women . . . give outlets to their talented youth, and assume the contours of a nation." [22]

"*The Negro liberation movement, in my opinion will not be confined to the scope of any one organization, but will take the form of a united Negro people's front, embracing all organized sections of the Negro people, around a common program of liberation. While the leadership of such a movement must represent all sections of the Negro population, the Negro workers must constitute the main driving force. The Negro workers must strive to build and strengthen the alliance between the organized labor movement and the Negro people.*" [23] Ray Hansborough, secretary, National Negro Commission, Communist Party, USA, 1947

> Such then [writes Professor Lincoln] is the Muslim vision of a United Front of Black Men—a phalanx of American Negroes no longer torn by dissension but standing shoulder to shoulder, ready for battle. The leader and the enemy are known, *but everything else is shrouded in mystery: the methods of combat, the terms of surrender and the new way of life to be established after the victory.*[24] (italics added)
> . . . It is doubtful whether any except the top leadership know exactly what the Movement's political aspirations are, or why. . . .[25]

It is necessary as always to be absolutely punctilious. And the question arises of whether or not everything we have already learned could be nothing more than coincidence. So in order to give the Muslims a chance to speak for themselves, let us turn to the Muslim newspaper, *Muhammad Speaks.*

On page nine of the issue for October 11, 1963, we learn that "this is a time," here in America, "of mass murder of innocent children; of day-to-day police brutality; of mass arrests and torture and frame-up trials—all of it openly directed against those who fight to throw off the yoke of slavery. . . ."

On page eleven, Charles P. Howard, Sr., "UN and Foreign Correspondent," presents a laudatory story of Cuba's "educational" activities: "Cuba today has the highest literacy rate of any country in Latin America. Thus Cuba is well on the way to becoming a nation of people free of discrimination and hatreds based on ignorance."

On the next page, Mr. Howard speaks of the "immense significance of the Cuban revolution, with its deep implications for the peoples of African descent the world over. . . ."

*"At the same time the Negro question in the United States of America must be treated in its relations to the huge Negro masses of farmers and workers oppressed and exploited by white imperialism in Africa and South America."* [26] John Pepper, 1928

On page twenty-three of this same issue of *Muhammad Speaks* for October 11, 1963, a photograph shows Ben Bella, president of what used to be Moslem Algeria, giving an award to Dr. W. E. B. DuBois—a Communist—in DuBois' adopted country, Ghana—a Communist state. The caption reads in part: ". . . President Ben Bella is the young revolutionary who led Algeria's successful seven-year struggle for freedom from French rule, and looked up to Dr. DuBois as a champion in the cause of liberty for all Africa."

The late Dr. DuBois was of course a Negro, and at one time was an American.

The Muslim dream [Professor Lincoln explains] is to have a solid Black Muslim community in the United States, recognized and supported by Moslems throughout the world as an integral part of Islam. . . .

. . .

Like Christianity and Judaism, Islam is more than a religion: it has served also as a political force, drawing together coalitions of states for various purposes at various times. Today it is dynamically important in shaping political alignments among Moslem nations from Morocco to Indonesia—that is to say, across the entire span of the African-Asian land mass. If these states could establish a large and influential Moslem bloc in the United States, their coalition would circle the earth.[27]

*"To the extent that the idea of the Negro question as but a 'race question' is being replaced by the concept that the root of the Negro question is the oppression and subjugation of a nation in the Black Belt, and therefore a national question, to that extent do we see the influence of Marxism. . . .*

*". . .*

*". . . The growing extent to which the Negro people see their own struggle in relationship to, and in unity with, the world-wide colonial struggle is further evidence of this influence."* [28] Gus Hall

In the *Muhammad Speaks* issue for January 31, 1964, on page two, Mr. Howard strikes again, this time from Tanganyika, "where the young and charming Julius Nyerere presides as President." Tanganyika, as you will recall, according to *U.S. News & World Report* and the New York *Times,* is also where the young and charming Julius Nyerere has established a base from which "freedom fighters," trained mainly in Communist Algeria and probably in Communist Cuba, and probably using Russian arms, are conducting a campaign to capture and communize Mozambique.

Jomo Kenyatta, Mr. Howard goes on, is an "African freedom fighter." "It was in Kenya . . . that the African surge for freedom began. And it was Kenyatta who lit the torch for that freedom drive." It was also Kenyatta who conducted the murder and dismemberment of both black and white Africans. And it is Kenyatta who, as we have seen, has been a member of the Communist party since 1929.

President Nkrumah of Ghana "continues to move forward in the way he feels is best for his country . . . ," Mr. Howard tells us. And the way he feels is best, according to K. A. Busia, is "increasingly" to tie the economy of Ghana to the Soviet Union.

What Mr. Howard is doing, then, is trying to convince his readers, who may not know the truth, that Nyerere, Nkrumah and Kenyatta, three black Communist leaders, should be some sort of idols to American Negroes.

> . . . although the Black Muslims call their Movement a religion [Professor Lincoln explains] religious values are of secondary importance. They are not part of the Movement's basic appeal, except to the extent that they foster and strengthen the sense of group solidarity.
>
> The Muslims make no secret of the fact that they count themselves a part of the growing alliance of non-white peoples, which they expect eventually to inundate the white race. . . .[29]

*In 1963, Communist leader Benjamin Davis spoke of "the increasing consciousness of American Negroes of a community of interests between the Africans fighting against white supremacy and colonialism and the Negro in the United States fighting white supremacy and the Jim Crow system. This sense of solidarity will grow."* [30]

On page seven of the January 31, 1964, issue of *Muhammad Speaks,* Herbert Muhammad, son of Elijah, hails Nasser's revolution,

> which set about building a new kind of society, totally different from the old Western Christian systems.
>
> . . .
>
> . . . Egypt's courageous struggle for the ownership and control of the Suez—its own possession—makes it easier to understand the current struggle of the peoples of Panama now for some realistic control of their own canal.

On page eleven Mr. Howard strikes yet again, this time from Algiers:

> History may yet say that the greatest benefactors of the Algerian revolution have been the orphans.
>
> . . .
>
> Today the tender concern exhibited by the revolutionary government, led by Algeria's President Ahmed Ben Bella, for these destitute children is bringing startling results.
>
> Thousands of children who saw their mothers and fathers gunned down in cold blood by Nazi-like French settlers bent on destroying what they could not hold, look upon Ahmed Ben Bella literally as both "father and mother."

That thousands of children saw their parents gunned down, is true. But that their parents were gunned down by "Nazi-like French settlers" is a lie—a vicious lie—as Mr. Howard is probably aware.

Their parents were gunned down by the very man who now claims to be their benefactor—the Communist bank bandit Ahmed Ben Bella. It's all in the record.[31]

Mr. Howard tells us instead on page twelve: "Now, color plays no part in how high an ambitious young person may rise." On the faces of the youth "I see a joy and eagerness; a confidence which rarely reaches the youth of many other more prosperous countries."

Incredible.

A story on page fourteen of this same issue of *Muhammad Speaks* for January 31, 1964, reports the Communist revolution in Zanzibar: ". . . the new government indicates a keen interest in a federation with Kenya, Uganda and Tanganyika." Prime Minister Abdullah Kassim Hanga is reported to have said "we support all African liberation movements." Sheik Abdul Rahman Mohammed—who is, remember, "an advocate of Peking's theory of violent revolution," according to the New York *Times*—is identified only as the leader of the Umma party and minister of external affairs and defense in the new government. Not a word is said about Communism.

The issue for February 28, 1964, of *Muhammad Speaks* contains a three-page article beginning on page twelve on the wonders of Ghana and President Nkrumah, who is "leading his country toward African socialism. . . ."

The issue for March 27, 1964, on page seventeen awards a favorable review ("one fails to read this book at his own peril") to a book called *The Yahoos* by one Mike Newberry. Mention is made of "the diabolical design and intent of the racist, fascist, right wing reactionary forces in America. . . ."

The masthead of the *Worker,* official Communist party newspaper, lists as a member of the editorial staff a Mike Newberry. This man and the author of *The Yahoos* are one and the same!

But of course this is not mentioned in *Muhammad Speaks.*

In fact, something else isn't mentioned in *Muhammad Speaks* and it's the most important thing to be learned from the whole publication: As we have seen, the Muslims teach that white men are "blue-eyed devils," and "incapable of telling the truth"; they are hopelessly depraved and love nothing better than to commit "tricknology," whatever that is. In fact, whatever goes wrong, some white man did it.

Yet, as we have seen, *Muhammad Speaks* has praise—fulsome praise—not only for Nkrumah, who is black, and for Kenyatta, who is black, but for Sheik Abdul Rahman Mohammed, who is probably white, and for Ahmed Ben Bella and Fidel Castro, who are definitely white.

Why? If what they have in common isn't race—then what is it?

It's very simple: It's Communism.

In 1963 Jack Lotto reported on the closed convention of the Socialist Workers party:

> Attending the sessions of this Marxist-Leninist party as delegates and guests were members of the Muslims. The Muslim members participated in the SWP discussions on resolutions on Negro activities, which called for closer SWP orientation toward the Muslim movement. . . .[32]

The Socialist Workers party is of course a Communist party.

## NOTES

1. Theodore Draper, *American Communism and Soviet Russia* (New York, The Viking Press, 1960), p. 315.

2. C. Eric Lincoln, *The Black Muslims in America* (Boston, Beacon Press, 1961), p. 10.

3. *Ibid.*, pp. 10-11.

4. *Ibid.*, p. 12.

5. *Ibid.* Also, E. D. Beynon, "The Voodoo Cult Among Negro Migrants in Detroit," *The American Journal of Sociology*, vol. 43 (July 1937-May 1938), p. 896.

6. New York *Mirror* (July 30, 1963).

7. Lincoln, p. 180.

8. *Ibid.*, p. 12-16.

9. Elijah Muhammad, "The Muslim Program," *Muhammad Speaks*, vol. 3, no. 2 (October 11, 1963), p. 24. Also, the last page of any issue of *Muhammad Speaks*.

10. Lincoln, p. 85.

11. *Ibid.*, p. 95. Also, Chicago *Daily Defender* (March 5, 1960).

12. Lincoln, p. 95 (interview, WMEX, Boston, April 2, 1960).

13. James S. Allen and James W. Ford, *The Negroes in a Soviet America* (New York, Workers Library Publishers, June 1935), pp. 26-27.

14. James Baldwin, *The Fire Next Time* (New York, The Dial Press, 1963), pp. 88-89.

15. Lincoln, pp. 86-87.

16. *Ibid.*, p. 211. From the New York *Amsterdam News* (November 7, 1959).

17. Allen and Ford, pp. 26-27.

18. Lincoln, p. 24.

19. John Pepper, "American Negro Problems," *Communist*, vol. 7, no. 10 (October 1928), p. 636.

20. Lincoln, p. 25.

21. Pepper, p. 636.

22. Lincoln, p. 85. From the Los Angeles *Herald-Express* (February 6, 1958).

23. As quoted in "The Communist Position (1947)," pp. 46-47. See footnote 16, chapter 3.

24. Lincoln, p. 87.

25. *Ibid.*, p. 94.

26. Pepper, p. 628. Also quoted by Wilson Record, "The Development of the Communist Position on the Negro Question in the United States," *Phylon*, vol. 19, no. 3 (Fall 1958), p. 257.

27. Lincoln, pp. 218-219, 223.

28. Gus Hall, *Marxism and Negro Liberation* (New York, New Century Publishers, 1951), pp. 16-17.

29. Lincoln, p. 27.

30. Benjamin J. Davis, *Against Tokenism and Gradualism* (New York, New Century Publishers, April 1963), p. 12.

31. See "The Green Book," *Aspects Véritables de la Rébellion Algérienne* (Ministère de l'Algérie, Cabinet du Ministre, n.d.); and *Documents on the Crimes and Outrages Committed by the Terrorists in Algeria* (Algiers, Société d'Editions et de Régie Publicitaire, n.d.) for a description and photographs of the crimes committed by the forces of Ben Bella against Christian *and Moslem* Algerians. These books are not recommended for women and children.

32. Los Angeles *Herald-Examiner* (August 31, 1963).

## CHAPTER V

The Blood Brothers

> So far, this has taken the form of massive peaceful political
> agitation, but already there is in existence among young peo-
> ple the conviction that only violence will bring about the
> satisfaction of French Canadian national rights. Already young
> people are in prison as a result of activity flowing from this
> conviction.[1]

On October 21, 1963, Jules Bulgach, a seventy-one-year-old
white fruit peddler, was stabbed to death on a Harlem street
by a gang of boys.[2] And rational men were aware at once that
the act had something or other to do with "right-wing extremism."

You've heard of the "atmosphere of hate." What doubtless
happened was that the atmosphere of hate worked its way
into the physiology of these unfortunate lads, where it probably activated the evil present in us all, with the inevitable
result that they just had to go out and stab somebody.

On March 23, 1964, David L. Watts, twenty-nine, a white
man who had come from Idaho seven years before to live as
a missionary in Harlem, was murdered. He was stabbed repeatedly in the chest and stomach. No one knew why.[3]

On April 11, Eileen Johnson, twenty-eight, a white department of welfare social worker, was stabbed to death on a
Harlem street as she walked with a Negro co-worker. As usual,
no one knew why.[4]

On April 29 just before 5:00 p.m., Mrs. Magit Sugar, fifty,
a Hungarian refugee, was stabbed to death by one of a gang
of boys in her second-hand clothing store on West 125th
Street. When she told one of the boys that she had no suit
in his size, another drew a knife and stabbed her in the heart.[5]

You can't blame him, of course; no suit in his size, indeed!
—and of course, there's the atmosphere of hate.

Soon afterward, however, the criminals were caught, and, on May 6, the *Times* revealed in a front page story, continued to page thirty, that they were among "about 400" youths who are members of an anti-white Harlem gang.

"Members of the youth gang refer to themselves as 'Blood Brothers.' They have infiltrated many community centers in Harlem by obtaining positions on committees."

The purpose of the gang is said to be "to oppose the police if trouble should develop in Harlem. . . . Some members of the gang are used as drug pushers and numbers runners. Others are taught to steal."

> The Blood Brothers appear to be distinguished from other youth gangs [we read in the *Times* of May 29, page thirteen] chiefly by their intensive training in karate and judo fighting techniques. According to members, they are organized into divisions, each division consisting of a junior and senior league. Communication among divisions is maintained by a system of runners.
>
> . . . A gang leader told this reporter that there were now 200 trained Blood Brothers, and that each trainee was obligated to train at least 10 juniors."

In fact, according to one of what the *Times* describes as "youngsters," there is already in existence "an offshoot of the Brotherhood known as the Black Mollyzuls," a league of young gentlemen who "believe in violence and killing white."

"The Blood Brothers is two organizations," we learn. "One believes in killing and murdering and one believes in helping and fighting back—if they be hit first, of course."

What do you make of it?

Well of course, if you have ever conducted a war of national liberation you'll already know.

You see, you can't simply appear in a country with your two hundred goons and say, "Look, I'm a criminal degenerate who enjoys killing and I'm going to capture your country." You'd be laughed off the lot.

In fact, the whole point to the war of national liberation is to create the impression that it isn't what it actually is in fact—a play for power by two hundred goons—but that it is a "mass movement" of a "heroic people," "united as one," etcetera and so on, and that it has something to do with self-determination.

Now, how would you do that?

Well of course, if the country you were after is the United States, the first thing you'd do is kill some white men. That would probably provoke some white men to retaliate against Negroes, which would probably provoke some Negroes to retaliate.

But that's still no good. Because all you'd still have, wouldn't you, is a couple of *incidents*. You wouldn't have a "mass of people marching as one."

Your problem is that since most black men—like most white men and most red men, and most other men—are decent people, they won't have anything to do with you once you tell them what the war of national liberation is actually about. Your problem is simply that because the overwhelming majority of people everywhere—of any race, region or religion—are decent, they derive no pleasure from committing murders.

So your first step is to recruit some Negro goons to kill some white men.

And your next step—once they have gone too far to get out —is to have your Negro goons kill some *Negroes*.

Because the most important part of the war of national liberation isn't to fight the "exploiters" doing the "suppressing." That is important, yes. But the most important part is to terrorize the people you are supposed to be liberating—and so force them to join you.

*"Most Simbas are former Congolese Army Soldiers who deserted or were captured and then persuaded to join, some under the threat of death."* [6]

And for this you need a band of goons.

George Washington didn't need a band of goons because he wasn't a criminal degenerate. What he was fighting was a real war of national liberation, so he didn't have to force anybody to join him.

But the Communists do.

So *their* war of national liberation always begins with the killing of some "colonialists": Belgians in the Congo, English-speaking Canadians in Quebec, Frenchmen in Algeria—and white men in New York.

*"In connection with the propaganda carried on in this direction it was apparent particularly in the months of February and March of last year [1925 in Indonesia] that the Communists were planning to create disturbances by means of strikes, arson and murders carried out by organized bands of criminals."* [7]

It always continues—when enough reliable killers are outside the law—with the killing, not only of hundreds of colonialists, but also of thousands of "toilers": Congolese in the Congo, French in Quebec, Moslems in Algeria—*and Negroes in New York.*

*"In the countryside, the Viet Cong, who had been careful to avoid harming the peasantry, have begun mining roads and paths used by farmers. In recent weeks, jam-packed intercity buses have been blown off roads and tiny three-wheeled motor-scooter buses have virtually vanished in land-mine explosions. The unreal, carnival mood along Tu Do is a long step removed from the horror endured by the ordinary people of Vietnam."* [8]

And it always ends with a State Department announcement that the victorious rebels seem to be Communists after all.

It is happening in every country that the Communists are trying to capture. It is happening in Quebec. It is happening in Caracas. It is happening in Angola, the Congo, Malaysia and Vietnam.

What happened in Algeria, as you will recall, was that the FLN rebels told the people that the revolt was really about the Korean. They said that it was a revolt of the Moslems, the true believers, against the infidels—who happened to be French.

Then of course the FLN cut the throats of any Moslems who disagreed.

*"With the murder of the* adat *head in Kamang there came to light the existence of a Communist conspiracy in which native heads were involved and which aimed at overthrowing the authorities by means of actual rebellion and by murdering opponents of the rebellion."* [9]

Let us turn to the trouble in New York.

*8/28/59: Mr. Cherif Benhabyles is assassinated in Vichy by the FLN.*

5/10/64: Druggist Archie Galanter is found shot to death on the floor of a phone booth in his Brooklyn store. According to the New York *Times,* "The police of the 66th precinct reported that there was $291 in cash boxes. They also said that the pharmacist's narcotics stock was intact. . . ." [10]

*7/31/60: On a beach near Tipaza, FLN terrorists machine-gun bathers. The eleven dead include two women.*

6/13/64: The body of Mrs. Sallye Mae Hart, forty-eight, of 1964 East 24th Street, Brooklyn, is found in an empty parking lot at 2920 West 21st Street, two blocks west of the Steeplechase amusement area in Coney Island. "The police said that she had been struck on the skull several hours earlier by a heavy object, probably a rock." [11]

*3/1/61: In Oran, Algeria, two women are burnt alive in their car.*

7/5/64: Regina Marshall, sixteen, is stabbed to death as she enters the hall of her Brooklyn apartment house. According to the New York *Times,* "The police reported that the girl's clothing had not been disarranged and that nothing had been taken from her handbag." [12]

There's no point in taking narcotics or stealing cash if you are a rebel, for two reasons: First, your motive is simply to kill for the pleasure and reward of killing, and second, it shows your contempt for the victim.

But of course, if you're very clever and can show your contempt by taking the cash—then you take it.

*"Twenty-six persons were killed yesterday when Communist guerrillas blew up a bus near Tavoy, 300 miles southwest of Rangoon.*

*"After the explosion the guerrillas stripped the victims of all valuables and cut off the ears of dead women to remove their earrings."* [13]

You will recall that Professor Lincoln describes the "entire" Black Muslim movement as "a kind of reserve fighting corps—a potential phalanx of Black Men ready to wage open war against the entire white community in case of white provocation." [14]

And so the question naturally arises: Have the Black Muslims anything to do with the gang called the Blood Brothers? Well, Mr. Muhammad says on May 7, 1964, according to the New York *Times,* that he has no knowledge of the Blood Brothers and that his followers are devoted to peace. All they want is to be given land they can call their own so they can set up their own nation.[15]

*11/3/54: The Voice of the Arabs, 7:00 p.m.: "The heart of every Algerian is filled with hatred toward the French who have deprived them of their liberty and flouted their honour.*

*"Every Algerian is resolved to sacrifice his blood and his life to raise the flag of his country over the bodies of the French."*

According to page twenty-seven of the *Times* for May 7, Black Muslims and black nationalists refer to white Harlem businessmen as "colonialists."

*9/6/56: Radio Damascus: "O colonialists and imperialists!*
*"Go back to your country before you are carried there, covered with wounds stained with blood or on stretchers."*

And on May 1, the New York *Post* on page three says the police have been told that factions of the Black Muslim movement—"dissident" factions, whatever they are—are urging teenagers to "hit" white people and to "drive them out of Harlem."

In fact a detective says of the suspects in the murder of Mrs. Sugar, "that it was the knowledge of the youths' link with the Muslims that had led to their speedy arrests."

The detective said that "while the three youths had denied being members of the Black Muslims, a police informant has definitely identified them as belonging to the Muslim group." [16]

And on May 6, the *Times* revealed that according to an informant, "rebel" Black Muslims are "indoctrinating" the Blood Brothers. The story goes that these Black Muslims "left the parent Black Muslim group when Malcolm X did, but that they later left Malcolm because they considered him too mild in his denunciation of whites.

"Most of the rebel Muslims, the researcher said, belonged to the fruit of Islam, the security arm of the Black Muslim organization, whose members are trained in karate and judo fighting techniques."

As part of their tactic of respectability [writes Professor Lincoln] the Muslim leaders present the FOI as an ordinary physical training program, like those of "the YMCA, CYO, Masons or Boy Scouts." . . . Unlike most Boy Scout troops, however, they also receive training in judo, military drill and the use of knives and blackjacks. There is no evidence that the FOI sections still receive small-arms training—as Beynon reported in 1937—or that the FOI high command is gathering an armory for emergency use. Such activities are not unlikely, however, for the FOI looks forward to playing an heroic role in the impending "Battle of Armageddon."

[It is] probably the most powerful single organization within the Movement. It now has a "section" in every temple, and its local officers report not to the minister but to the Supreme Captain of the FOI, Raymond Sharrieff. . . . This virtually autonomous body is an elite group, carefully chosen, rigorously trained. . . . It is entrusted with top security assignments and remains on constant alert. Most ominous of all, it shrouds its activities in nearly absolute secrecy—a tactic that has aroused the deepest suspicions of observers as experienced and sophisticated as the FBI.

. . . The FOI no longer dedicates itself solely to guarding the Black Nation against "trouble with the unbelievers, especially with the police." *It now acts also as a police force and judiciary —or, more exactly, a constabulary and court-martial—to root out and punish any hint of heterodoxy or any slackening of obedience among the Muslims themselves.* . . . (italics added)

Lincoln describes an FOI trial:

The defendant is not allowed to offer any defense; the charges against him are read, and the verdict is thereupon pronounced. . . . This verdict is final; there is no appeal.[17]

. . . Some police authorities suggest that Sharrieff . . . through a hand-picked corps of lieutenants, effectively silences any defectors from the Movement who may wish to cooperate with the police in exposing its secrets. . . .[18]

In fact, in a Muslim training manual we read as follows:

. . . A Committee of three must be formed by the minister or captain to report of any undesirable conditions going on by moslems in their homes. All traitors, who betray their sisters or brothers be murdered without mercy.[19]

And that's not all. The FOI could easily begin to regulate the lives not only of black men who belong, but of black men who don't—of all black men. Indeed, "the FOI might easily degenerate into a strong-arm elite keeping a restive people in line. . . ."[20]

. . . The distinguishing feature of both the Black Muslims and the F.L.Q. [Quebec Liberation Front] is that each aspires to bully its way into power over an important minority [writes C. L. Sulzberger].
. . . The F.L.Q. has . . . begun a program of limited terrorism. Its primitive bombs have already caused casualties, and it has prepared what purport to be lists of intended assassinations of personages opposing secession of French Canada.[21]

*Muhammad speaks of Negro professionals who won't cooperate because of "advantages." They go to the police and*

*FBI and accuse Muhammad of "trying to overthrow the gov-*
*ernment or even with causing trouble.*

"*. . .*

"*. . . This is the enemy; but Elijah Muhammad is laid as a*
*stumbling stone. That stone that has been rejected by the*
*builders. And whosoever falls on that stone will be broken to*
*pieces and whosoever the stone falls upon will be ground into*
*powder.*" [22]

"*. . .* Some police authorities suggest," writes Lincoln,
"that Sharrieff . . . collects tithes from delinquent members. . . ." [23]

"*Once a month, right after the roll call at the workers'*
*meeting [we read of the complete Communist control over*
*some parts of Colombia] comes the payment of contributions*
*to the Communist war chest. One peso is the minimum ex-*
*pected of all; more is paid, up to 20 pesos, according to the*
*individual's means and income. Once a year a special tax is*
*levied to meet the quota assigned by the party to each region*
*of Colombia. . . .*" [24]

In fact, Lincoln tells us, members are urged to hold steady
jobs, and gambling, smoking, drinking, installment buying
and luxuries are barred, the main purpose of which is to leave
money for the movement, to which members must give a fixed
percentage of their incomes each year. In 1952, aside from contributions for various funds, the percentage was set at one
third of all earnings.[25]

You will recall that some Muslims have practiced their new
faith while in prison:

Many Muslims have come into the movement from various levels
of extralegal activity. Some are ex-convicts—or even convicts, for
at least three temples are behind prison walls. Some have come
into the Movement as dope addicts and alcoholics, or from ca-
reers as pimps and prostitutes, pool sharks and gamblers. But all
who remain in the Movement are rehabilitated and put to
work. . . .[26]

*". . . in which connection the PKI [Indonesian Communist Party] proposed to search the kampungs for criminals (pendjahat) who would then assume the leadership over fellow-criminals."* [27]

Indeed, we read in *Saga* magazine: ". . . 'This may come as a shock to your white readers,' Malcolm X says, 'but today we've got Muslim ministers working inside every prison in the country.' What he says is true. . . ." [28]

In fact, Malcolm himself was "converted" in 1947, by one of his brothers, while a guest of the Commonwealth of Massachusetts in the maximum-security prison at Concord, where he had been detained by Massachusetts authorities after a conviction for armed robbery. [29]

And this, as you will recall, was exactly why the Algerian police happened to lock up Ahmed Ben Bella, at about the time that the Communist FLN uprising was getting underway.

As for the white man, that's no problem:

. . . All Moslems will murder the devil because they know he is a snake and also if he be allowed to live, he would sting someone else. Each Moslem is required to bring four devils and by bringing and presenting four at one time his reward is a button to wear on the lapel of his coat, also a free transportation to the Holy City Mecca to see brother Mohammad. [30]

Compare this with one of the oaths of the Mau Mau, the band of criminals, founded and led by Jomo Kenyatta, that terrorized black and white Africans alike in Kenya in the mid-1950's. Some of the purposes of the organization, we read, are:

(a) To burn European crops, and to kill European-owned cattle.
  (b) To steal firearms.
  (c) If ordered to kill, to kill, no matter who is to be the victim, even one's father or brother.
  (d) When killing, to cut off heads, extract the eyeballs and drink the liquid from them.
  (e) Particularly to kill Europeans. [31]

And you will recall that according to Dodd-Fard, the "blue-eyed devil" is "the white man."

*"Furthermore there is the so-called Reichscheka as a sec-
tion of this military organization at the disposal of the party
—which 'Cheka' was straightforwardly labelled an 'organization for murder' in connection with what came to light at the
Leipzig trials in February, 1925."* [32]

In the so-called war of national liberation, among the first
things needed are a test and a reward for the new recruits.

*12/1/59: Mr. Krim Belcacem, vice-president and minister of
war in the provisional government of the Algerian republic,
writes in "Views and Opinions," published by the "Review of
International Affairs" in Belgrade, of the young volunteers in
the FLN: "Another test of their aptitude and preparedness is
assassination: a new recruit, before qualifying to serve with
the Army* must *murder* at least *a colonialist or a known
traitor."*

5/10/64: The gang members, says the New York *Times* on
page sixty-one, "are seeking to win recognition from Malcolm
X and other rebel Black Muslim leaders and the right to use
the letter 'X' instead of their surnames.

"The police said that the gang members become eligible to
use the letter 'X' when they seriously maim or kill a white
person."

The next thing needed is discipline.

*"(a) If I am sent to bring in the head of an enemy or Euro-
pean, and I fail to do so, may this [Mau Mau] oath kill me.*

*"(b) If I fail to steal anything from a European, may this
oath kill me.*

*"(c) If I know of any enemy to our organization, and fail to
report it to my leader, may this oath kill me.*

*"(d) If I am ever sent by my leader to do something big for
the House of Kikuyu, and I refuse, may this oath kill me.*

*"(e) If I refuse to help in driving the Europeans from this
country, may this oath kill me.*

*"(f) If I worship any leader but Jomo Kenyatta, may this
oath kill me."* [33]

7/10/64: The New York *News* on page three reports the arrest of two men believed to be Malcolm X's followers, and the capture of a small notebook. The notebook contains a list of penalties:

> Anyone who betrays the organization penalty death.
> No. Two. Notice must be given 12 hours except for an emergency meeting.
> No. Three, lateness. First time five lashes. Second time 10 lashes. Third time serious beating.
> No. Four, absence. First time beating. Third time death.

But the most important thing needed is something to complain about.

*6/20/59: In documents seized on FLN leaders captured recently, we find the following orders: "In all circumstances, the Algerian Patriot (when tried by Court) will never hesitate to accuse the police of torture and brutalities; this greatly influences the judges, particularly with the application of the new code."*

5/29/64: A Blood Brothers leader tells us, according to the *Times,* page thirteen, that "the main reason the gang started was to protect ourselves in a group against police brutality."

Police brutality is a terrible problem. It is a well-known fact that the reason most men join the police is to give vent to their sadistic natures. Everybody knows that.

In fact, as everybody knows, police brutality is an absolutely imperative part of the war of national liberation. Everyone knows that wherever a war of national liberation breaks out, there suddenly develops police brutality.

7/20/64: New York *News,* page three: "I walked through the streets for four hours and saw the most nauseating demonstration of police malfeasance. It was an orgy of blood, violence and sadism, which was uncalled for," says James Farmer of CORE.

"I say with much sadness that I have not seen anything like this before, even in Alabama or Mississippi."

The solution, according to Mr. Farmer and others, is a

"civilian police review board," which would begin by deciding which police action was brutal and which wasn't—and would eventually wind up deciding what could be done to protect the people of the City of New York and elsewhere, and what couldn't.

Police Commissioner Michael J. Murphy charged yesterday that his department was being subjected to a "planned pattern of attack" in connection with civil rights disorders.

He said the attack, if successful, would destroy the department's effectiveness and "leave the city open to confusion."

Mr. Murphy declined to identify any organization or individuals directing the attack, but he hinted that details might be given in the future.

. . .

Mr. Murphy reported that "during—and before—the opening of the World's Fair, prearranged protests of brutality were heard even before there had been any encounters between the police and demonstrators." [34]

Who's behind it, do you think?

## NOTES

1. Leslie Morris, "National and Democratic Revolution in French Canada," *World Marxist Review,* vol. 7, no. 9 (September 1964), p. 17.

2. New York *Times* (May 29, 1964), p. 13.

3. *Ibid.*

4. *Ibid.*

5. *Ibid.* (May 1, 1964), p. 31.

6. *Ibid.* (December 4, 1964), p. 14.

7. Harry J. Benda and Ruth T. McVey, editors, *The Communist Uprisings of 1926-1927 in Indonesia: Key Documents* (Ithaca, N.Y., Cornell University, 1960), p. 10.

8. *Newsweek,* vol. 63 (June 8, 1964), p. 27.

9. Benda and McVey, p. 11.

10. New York *Times* (May 11, 1964), p. 25.

11. *Ibid.* (June 14, 1964), p. 71.

12. *Ibid.* (July 6, 1964), p. 18.

13. *Ibid.* (December 4, 1964), p. 6.

14. C. Eric Lincoln, *The Black Muslims in America* (Boston, Beacon Press, 1961), p. 109.

15. New York *Times* (May 8, 1964), p. 67.

16. *Ibid.* (May 1, 1964), p. 31.

17. Lincoln, pp. 199-201.

18. *Ibid.*, p. 193.

19. As quoted in *Activities of "The Nation of Islam" or the Muslim Cult of Islam, in Louisiana,* report of the Joint Legislative Committee on Un-American Activities, State of Louisiana (January 9, 1963), p. 29.

20. Lincoln, p. 203.

21. New York *Times* (May 29, 1963), p. 32.

22. *Muhammad Speaks,* vol. 3, no. 10 (January 31, 1964), p. 8.

23. Lincoln, p. 193.

24. Eugene K. Culhane, *America,* vol. 102, no. 23 (March 12, 1960), p. 702.

25. Lincoln, p. 17.

26. *Ibid.*, p. 24.

27. Benda and McVey, p. 3.

28. Joseph T. Friscia, *Saga* (July 1962), pp. 72-73.

29. Lincoln, p. 191.

30. Louisiana report, p. 27. See footnote 19 above.

31. F. D. Corfield, *Historical Survey of the Origins and Growth of Mau Mau* (London, Her Majesty's Stationery Office, 1960), p. 167.

32. Benda and McVey, p. 3.

33. Corfield, p. 166.

34. New York *Times* (April 29, 1964), p. 28.

CHAPTER VI  The Making of the
Revolution

*As Lenin has said, a terrible clash between Soviet Russia
and the capitalist States must inevitably occur. . . .*

*The ruling classes must be in the throes of a major govern-
ment crisis, so that the government is so enfeebled the revolutionists can speedily overthrow it.*[1] Joseph Stalin

Soon after the assassination of President Kennedy, Malcolm X
made it known in a speech that he was not displeased with the
event. The remark caused Elijah Muhammad to chastise his
lieutenant, and this in turn caused a "split."

The nature of the split has never been revealed, but it does
make Mr. Muhammad a moderate, so that he plays Khrushchev to Malcolm's Mao.

Malcolm then formed a party, a Black Nationalist party,
and opened his doors not only to Muslims but to people of all
religions, or of no religion, as long as they were black.

Then Malcolm took a trip to Mecca. There he had an experience; some called it holy. Malcolm described it in a letter
to a New York friend, and the letter was obtained by and appeared on the front page of the New York *Times* of May 8,
1964:

I have never before witnessed such sincere hospitality and the
practice of true brotherhood as I have seen and experienced
during this pilgrimage here in Arabia.

In fact, what I have seen and experienced on this pilgrimage
has forced me to "rearrange" much of my own thought-pattern,
and to toss aside some of my previous conclusions.

Malcolm did not say whether he had seen and experienced
any money. But he did say that the white Muslims on the

67

pilgrimage turned out to be okay—unlike the vicious, white Americans:

> Their sincere submission to the Oneness of God, and their true acceptance of all nonwhites as equals makes the so-called "whites" also acceptable as equals into the brotherhood of Islam with the "nonwhites." Color ceases to be a determining factor of a man's worth or value once he becomes a Muslim. I hope I am making this part very clear, because it is now very clear to me.

What could be clearer?

> If white Americans would accept the religion of Islam, if they would accept the Oneness of God (Allah), then they could also sincerely accept the Oneness of Man, and they would cease to measure others always in terms of their "differences in color."

So that the reason white Americans exploit Negroes isn't just that they're white. It isn't because, as Malcolm used to crack, they are "blue-eyed devils and white dogs." It's simply that they aren't Muslims. It's simply that they're Americans.

*"It has been pointed out in this general connection (and I think this throws much light on the question) that some of the nations of India are advancing their self-determination slogan under the guise of religion. It is also true that in certain circumstances national slogans are put out by other peoples in primitive or in distorted forms, for example, as racial slogans. One of the characteristics of the American Negro people has been that they, too, have put out what are basically national slogans very largely in a racial sense. Hence we have to look more closely than we have in the past at these racial slogans and at the conceptions the Negro people have with regard to race and racial oppression. Behind these prevalent concepts of race are actually developing national concepts. I think the discussion has proved that it is no decisive sign that a people does not constitute a nation if it does not advance clear-cut slogans for self-determination."* [2] Communist leader William Z. Foster

What Malcolm brought back from Mecca, then, was a message, printed on the front page of the *Times,* for Nasser and Ben Bella—and American Negroes—to see, and which clearly defines the true nature of the conflict:

> . . . as America's insane obsession with racism leads her up the suicidal path, nearer and nearer to the precipice that leads to the bottomless pits below, I do believe that whites of the younger generation, in the colleges and universities, through their own young, less hampered intellect, will see the "handwriting on the wall" and turn for spiritual salvation to the religion of Islam *and force the older generation of American whites to turn with them.* (italics added)

Which would make quite an impression in Algiers.

*5/19/57: The Voice of the Arabs: "The Algerian fighters of the holy war know perfectly well which is the way to follow that which was marked out and imposed on them, by God, by the Koran, by the Prophet and by their Fathers. 'It is meet for us to give victory to the believers.' "*

Indeed, as early as the summer of 1959, Malcolm visited the United Arab Republic[3]—a few months before Mr. Muhammad himself—where five years earlier, in Cairo, the decision was made and the money spent to launch the Communist coup in Algeria.

Malcolm has pledged that Negro Americans "would be completely in sympathy with the Arab cause." [4]

"He believes," says reporter William Worthy, himself a frequent visitor to Communist China and a perennial defender of Fidel Castro, "that any Negro freedom movement not international in scope and perspective is foredoomed to failure. . . ." Indeed:

> At his March 12 press conference announcing his split with Elijah Muhammad he declined, in an exchange with a British reporter, to rule out acceptance of possible Communist support.
> . . .
> "Outside the UN," he told an interviewer recently, "we have friends—700,000,000 Chinese who are ready to die for human rights." Malcolm has observed that the most thunderous applause from Negro audiences comes when he reminds them that, with China now openly in support, "we are not alone." [5]

[Worthy speaks of] the reaction of Malcolm X to the racial goodwill policy of Mao. Reporting to his supporters this past spring after a tour of Africa, he said, "I had tea at the home of the Chinese ambassador in Accra. He very politely reminded me that Mao Tse-tung was the first head of state to declare the open support of his government and its 800,000,000 [sic, Worthy] people behind the Afro-American struggle." [6]

And that isn't all: ". . . Fidel Castro, during his dramatic sojourn in Harlem in the autumn of 1960, invited Malcolm X to a secret conference which lasted some two hours. . . ."[7]

In the same article, Worthy describes what he calls the "spreading Negro underground":

In May of this year a conference of seventy-five Negro students in Nashville (convened by some of the undergraduates of Fisk University) called for unity with the African, Asian and Latin-American revolution and for efforts to obtain "financial help from friendly forces." Another resolution was for the "development of a permanent underground secretariat to carry out plans."

"Plans" include the "elimination of capitalism in this country and the world and support for revolutionary black international-ism."

Worthy describes an outfit called RAM (Revolutionary Action Movement), which on July 4, 1964, sent the following message to the "National Liberation Front" of South Vietnam:

Congratulating our Vietcong brothers for their inspiring victories against American imperialism in South Vietnam and declaring our independence from the policies of the American government abroad and at home. . . . we will not join in the American counterrevolution that is attempting, at home and abroad, to crush the mounting revolutionary struggles.

RAM calls for the use of "the three basic principal powers" held by Negroes:

"1. The power to stop the machinery of government.

"2. The power to hurt the economy.

"3. The power of unleashing violence." [8]

And how would this be done?

Worthy quotes an "underground leader" who calls himself "Mr. Lumumba":

> Black youth with the right orientation can stop this entire country. Small bands can damage the eight major dams that supply most of the electricity. Electricity means mass communications.
>
> Gasoline can be poured into sewer systems in major urban areas and then ignited. This would burn out communications lines in an entire city.
>
> What would emerge from this chaos? Most likely, guerrilla warfare. I don't think the entire white community will fight. The Minutemen, Klansmen, the American Nazi party and other organized groups in the racist-fascist coalition will fight. But the entire black community will be fighting.
>
> We call the whites "cream puffs." We feel that when TV stops, when the telephone no longer rings, their world will almost come to an end. Like during a major air raid, they will stay in the house. They'll sit and wait for television to come back on.[9]

Worthy quotes Charles Johnson of Detroit, a member of Uhuru—Bantu for freedom—who wrote to his draft board: "There ain't no way in the hell that I'm going out like a fool and fight my nonwhite brothers in China, Africa and Latin America for White Devils. . . ."[10]

"It is probable that substantial monies will soon begin to flow to the nationalist underground. . . ." says Worthy, and that "sympathetic governments and revolutionary forces abroad" will support the "freedom" movement because of "the extent of the police apparatus in this country." He says the government is infiltrating the nationalists but that "no amount of police infiltration can stop a revolutionary thrust *so closely paralleling colonial wars abroad.*"[11] (italics added)

Mr. Worthy also reports the plans of one Robert F. Williams, a Communist and former chapter president of the NAACP, with whom North Carolina authorities are eager to discuss a kidnapping. Mr. Williams publishes a monthly newsletter in Havana which he calls the *Crusader,* the February 1964 issue of which predicts as follows:

> When massive violence comes, the U.S.A. will become a bedlam of confusion and chaos. . . . The factory . . . telephone . . .

and radio workers will be afraid to report to their jobs. All transportation will grind to a complete standstill. . . . Essential pipelines will be severed and blown up and all manner of sabotage will occur. . . . A clash will occur inside the Armed Forces. At U.S. military bases around the world local revolutionaries will side with Afro G.I.'s. . . .[12]

In the May-June issue, Mr. Williams discusses various means of killing policemen and other "domestic enemies," and explains that "flame throwers can be manufactured at home."[13]

*"The Crusader* loves the Muslims because they love oppressed black people and are teaching 'Negroes' to love themselves, and Malcolm X is the greatest leader on the American scene today. . . ." [14]

Mr. Williams also conducts a broadcast which he calls "Radio Free Dixie," originating in Havana—and heard from Florida to the city of Washington—on which he regularly recommends a new form of Negro protest: the "kill-in." [15]

"Non-violence is what is dead," Mr. Williams explained on July 13, 1964.

> . . . our people must be willing to die and to kill for freedom. Our lives have been miserable and tormented since the first slave ships brought us to America. They will continue to remain so until we prove ourselves willing and ready to meet the violence and terror of oppression with the violence and terror of liberation.[16]

Columnist Victor Riesel describes four new, terrible groups,

> The Provisional Organizing Committee for a Marxist-Leninist Communist Party (POC), the Progressive Labor Movement (PLM), Hammer and Steel and the Workers World party. They apparently are never short of funds.
>
> In all, they run over 100 "clubs" in 10 major cities and in a number of communities in New England, North Carolina, Georgia, and on the West Coast. According to their boasts, these neo-radical operatives have some kind of organization in New York, Boston, Philadelphia, Chicago, Cleveland, Buffalo, Williamsport, Pa., San Francisco, Los Angeles and Seattle.
>
> Some have ties with the violent fringe of the Black Muslims. Some organize youth groups for Cuba and for the "independence"

of Puerto Rico. Some call for outfitting squads with rifles. Others infiltrate unions and attempt to stir violent action on picket lines.
. . .

Most active in the championing of Communist China's policies of guerrilla warfare and violent revolution, has been the group known as Hammer and Steel. It operates out of Boston and boasts of covering all New England. It also calls for emulation of the Cuban revolution in the United States and actually demands an armed Negro revolt.[17]

Why? one wonders. What's behind it all?

Mr. Worthy has the answer.

He speaks of an amazing new political theory:

. . . a growing acceptance of a concept that the U.S. is really composed of two nations, one the colonizer, the other the colonized, that Negroes are engaged in what Joseph Alsop has called a colonial war at home, that 20,000,000 black Americans are part of an international colored majority, and that victory here will come only when the world revolution against colonialism and neocolonialism finally triumphs. . . .[18]

## NOTES

1. From the Stalin archives of the National War College in Washington, D.C., as quoted in *Coronet*, vol. 29, no. 3 (January 1951), p. 25.

2. As quoted in "The Communist Position (1947)," p. 14 ff. See footnote 16, chapter 3.

3. Pittsburgh *Courier* (August 15, 1959).

4. C. Eric Lincoln, *The Black Muslims in America* (Boston, Beacon Press, 1961), p. 224.

5. William Worthy, "The Red Chinese American Negro," *Esquire*, vol. 62, no. 4 (October 1964), p. 174.

6. *Ibid.*, p. 173.

7. Lincoln, p. 18.

8. Worthy, pp. 174-176.

9. *Ibid.*, pp. 177-178.

10. *Ibid.*, p. 175.

11. *Ibid.*, p. 179.

12. *Ibid.*, p. 176.

13. New York *Times* (July 28, 1964), p. 13.

14. *Crusader*, vol. 4, no. 8 (May 1963), p. 7. This issue of *Crusader* is reproduced in full in *Activities of the Southern Conference Educational Fund, Inc. in Louisiana*, part 2, report of the Joint Legislative Committee on Un-American Activities, State of Louisiana (April 13, 1964), pp. 31-38.

15. New York *Times* (July 28, 1964), p. 13.

16. As quoted by Senator James O. Eastland (D., Miss.), speech, *Congressional Record* (July 22, 1964), p. 16040.

17. Los Angeles *Times,* part 2 (September 9, 1964), p. 5.

18. Worthy, p. 176.

## CHAPTER VII

The Revolution

> [The Communist party] *strives only to exploit what are often legitimate Negro complaints and grievances for the advancement of Communist objectives.*
>
> *Controversial or potentially controversial racial issues are deliberately and avidly seized upon by Communists for the fullest possible exploitation. Racial incidents are magnified and dramatized by Communists in an effort to generate racial tensions. As a result, such campaigns are actually utilized as a stepping-stone to extend Communist influence among the Negroes.*[1] J. Edgar Hoover

Late in May 1964, students of the Blood Brothers who opened the New York *Times* were intrigued to learn that the Brothers were

> looking forward to a planned "hit," or attack, against Harlem police, probably some time in July, to protest the enforcement of the "no-knock" and "stop-and-frisk" laws, which become effective July 1.
>     . . .
> The exact date of the "hit," according to one gang leader, will be decided within 48 hours of the attack in order to lessen chances of betrayal.[2]

On the morning of July 16, a police lieutenant shot and killed a fifteen-year-old Negro boy named James Powell. All he had to say for himself was that young Powell had repeatedly attacked him with a knife.

On the night of July 18—little more than forty-eight hours later—a riot "somehow broke out" during a march on a police station, and only a few hours after that, large sections of New York City were fast approaching open warfare.

*"The instructions [to Communist terrorists in Vietnam] stress the desirability of violence and serious injuries—even*

*deaths—to produce martyrs and a focus for further resentment.*

*"All these elements were noted during last week's disorders, including a death—that of a 15-year-old boy killed in circumstances that are not clear. His funeral provided the occasion for a demonstration Sunday during which paratroopers seized at least 10 youths with knives hidden under their shirts."* [3]

Some time later, it developed that young Mr. Powell had not been what is called a model boy:

> FBI report on summer riots in NYC, Philadelphia, Rochester, reveals for first time that 15-year-old James Powell, whose killing by New York policeman Gilligan touched off the three-day NY riots, had long history of street fighting, bullying younger children; had once been treated for a stab wound, had been arrested earlier in the year for robbery. [4]

But that didn't mean anything. There had to be a "hit," you see, to protest the phenomenon called police brutality.

*"The second phase, according to one document, is 'to get people out into the streets [of Saigon].' Quarrels are to be provoked, youth groups are to be armed with clubs and knives, allegedly to protect themselves in a manufactured tension."* [5]

So the "freedom fighters" went to work:

Posters appeared in the streets bearing the legend: "Wanted for Murder—Gilligan the Cop."

> *Almost from the inception of the Harlem riots,* an army of some 200 young toughs, mostly Negroes, but with a scattering of whites, descended on two streets in the W. 80s, between Broadway and Columbus Ave., in about 50 cars, *most of them from out of town,* and camped there for the duration of the turbulent week. . . .[6] (italics added)

*"Black youth with the right orientation can stop this entire country. Small bands can damage the eight major dams that supply most of the electricity. . . ."* [7] "Mr. Lumumba"

Despite the obvious resentment of the residents, the burly young men set up what amounted to command posts from which they moved on to the racial battlegrounds in Harlem and Bedford-Stuyvesant. They returned to the cars to change clothes, get some sleep and food, consume quantities of booze and, sometimes, nurse their wounds.

*"In the first phase of fear and insecurity, the Communists [in Saigon] are trying to establish what they call 'safe zones' in sections of the city. These are areas in which arms could be stored and agents, even military personnel, could gather secretly in the guise of youths or workers, ready for a full-scale revolt against the Government."* [8]

. . . Police who infiltrated the meetings said the conspirators were heard making plans for participation in the Rochester troubles. . . .

Police believe the campers were part of a hard core of troublemakers who have been traveling around to racially tense areas, taking advantage of, if not provoking, the rioting.

*". . . The only serious organizational principle the active workers of our movement can accept is: Strict secrecy, strict selection of members, and the training of professional revolutionists. . . ."* [9] V. I. Lenin

[They] were spotted in the forefront of the Harlem rioting, participating in the blood-letting, brick-tossing and the throwing of Molotov cocktails.

*Communist cadres [in Saigon] have also been told to have grenades ready to throw into crowds. One boy seized Sunday had a grenade hidden in his clothing."* [10]

Malcolm X, however, was in the clear. In fact, six days earlier, on July 12, he arrived in Cairo to attend a meeting of the council of ministers of the Organization for African Unity.

So he's in the clear.

*"There ought to be a Mau Mau in the U.S."* [11] Malcolm X

In the streets, steel-helmeted policemen by the hundreds fought nightstick battles with Negro gangs. Other Negroes, high on the roofs of tenements, bombarded the police with bricks and bottles. Police cars were attacked by Negroes armed with "Molotov cocktails"—homemade fire bombs.[12]

*May, 1929: "What happened these past May days in Berlin was not accidental disorder resulting from the disregard by the working classes of the order issued by the police not to organize street manifestations, but was really a deliberate attack on the police by a Communist band armed with rifles. . . ."* [13] (emphasis added)

According to a front page story in the New York *Journal-American* of July 21, many incidents broke out in different places at the same time; several men seen rioting in Harlem at midnight were seen rioting at two a.m. in Brooklyn; and organizers were everywhere equipped with walkie-talkies. Yes, walkie-talkies.

*June, 1960: "The whole thing, it is now clear, was manipulated by Communists [in Tokyo] as part of an organized, world-wide campaign. . . . The signals are called in Moscow.*
*". . .*
*"There were evidences of careful planning behind the seemingly hysterical mob. Rioting flared, subsided, flared again as though on signal. . . ."* [14]

It is in those areas [Harlem and Brooklyn] that Negroes are being organized for guerrilla warfare.[15]

*"The new concept of revolution defies military science and tactics. The new concept is lightning campaigns conducted in highly sensitive urban communities, with the paralysis reaching the small communities and spreading to the farm areas."* [16]
Robert Williams

A Negro civil-rights leader says that thousands of Negroes in Harlem are armed and that "sooner or later they will use their guns against the cops."

*"The new concept is to huddle as close to the enemy as possible so as to neutralize his modern and fierce weapons. The new concept . . . dislocates the organs of harmony and order*

*and reduces central power to the level of a helpless, sprawling
octopus. During the hours of day sporadic rioting takes place
and massive sniping. Night brings all out warfare, organized
fighting, and unlimited terror against the oppressor and his
forces. . . ." *[17]

> Screams of the injured, bursts of flame from "bottle bombs," the
> sharp crack of pistol shots, shrieking sirens of police cars and am-
> bulances, the crashing of bricks through store windows made it a
> bedlam.[18]

And if you didn't know how to make a "bottle bomb," you
could of course refer to a handbill circulated by the "Harlem
Freedom Fighters": "Any empty bottle filled with gasoline,
use rag as a wick. Light rag, toss bottle and see them run." [19]

On July 19, Jesse Gray got mad. Mr. Gray is usually described by the New York *Times* as a "rent-strike" leader. He
was also described under oath before the House Committee
on Un-American Activities in February 1963 as an organizer
for the Communist party.[20] *Counterattack* of July 3, 1964, reports that he also found time to manage the campaign of
Communist official Benjamin Davis in his 1958 try for the
New York state senate.

*Counterattack* reports also the testimony on February 3,
1960, of Albert Gaillard, before the House Committee on Un-
American Activities:

> Gaillard quoted both Gray and Davis as saying that the con-
> spiracy badly needed to organize and stimulate a Negro youth
> movement in Harlem.
>
> Gaillard swore that Davis assigned Gray, whom he identified as
> a regional organizer for the Communist Party in Harlem, to work
> with him.
>
> Gaillard said that later he called at Gray's home, 1809 Seventh
> Avenue, to receive the Party briefing.
>
> He swore that Gray told him that "You cannot bring the idea
> of Communism over to the Negro Youth of this community."
>
> And that "You have it on a social basis and then you can trick
> them into this youth movement."

And so on July 19, 1964, the day after the trick worked,
Jesse Gray appeared at a "protest" rally, where he made the

following statement, according to the New York *Times:*
"There is only one thing that can correct the situation, and
that's guerrilla warfare." He called for "100 skilled black
revolutionaries who are ready to die." Mr. Gray said that he
was seeking platoon captains, who could each recruit one
hundred men loyal to themselves.[21]

" . . . *Another way in which the above statement has been
confirmed is through knowledge acquired concerning the
preparations made by the Communist Party in Germany in
the fields of politics and military strategy, viz. that the German Communist Party's organization of armed force is
planned along the lines of* hundred-men groups (*in factories,
etc.*) *which can be united into regiments and battalions and
. . . trained in the use of fire-arms and street-fighting. . . ."* [22]
(emphasis added)

"This city can be changed by 50,000 well organized Negroes," says Mr. Gray. "They can determine what will happen
in New York City."

"*Today the Ku Klux Klan has taken off its sheets and
donned a uniform—a police uniform. Guerrilla tactics are
the only way of letting the underdog equalize a situation.*" [23]
Malcolm X

Among those in the audience were William L. Patterson
and Robert G. Thompson, top state Communist party officials.[24]

That fact was nowhere to be found in the New York *Times.*
At the time, as you will recall, Malcolm X was still in Cairo.

On the morning of July 22 in a front page story of the
*Times,* Acting Mayor Paul Screvane was reported to have
charged that "known Communists" had something to do with
causing the trouble.

And on the same day, Americans read as follows on pages
three and thirteen in the *News:*

A five-month investigation by dozens of top detectives, working in
close cooperation with FBI, has disclosed widespread Communist
infiltration—so much so that they command 1,000 young fanatics

dedicated to violence. Their instructions are: "Deploy! Incite!" One high source described them as "beatniks, crumbums, addicts and thieves," some of whom are paid in narcotics as well as cash. . . .

. . .

In the W. 125th St. area up to 50 paid Communist agitators are known to be working, the rallying point being a store near 125th and Seventh Ave. Here, each Friday at 4 p.m. the professional agitators have reported to receive their pay envelopes. *The store also is known to be frequented by UN attaches from the United Arab Republic and various leftist African nations.* (italics added)

Those of you who remember your geography will forgive me for emphasizing that the capital of the United Arab Republic is Cairo.

Cairo of course is where the decision was made and the money spent to launch the Communist coup in Algeria—under the cloak of Islam.

Cairo—of all places—was where Malcolm X was at the moment.

On the same night that all this was revealed, Dr. Martin Luther King, Jr. said in Jackson, Mississippi, according to the New York *World-Telegram* of July 23, page two, that he is "sick and tired of people saying this movement has been infiltrated by Communists and Communist sympathizers.

"There are as many Communists in this freedom movement as there are Eskimos in Florida."

On July 24, the *Journal-American,* on pages one and four, published an interview with an Eskimo by the name of William Epton, chairman of both the Progressive Labor Movement (PLM)—which describes the 135th Street police station as "the Auschwitz of Harlem"—and of the Harlem Defense Council—whose leaflets urged Harlemites to organize "with the purpose of defending each and every block in Harlem from the cops"—both of which share offices at 336 Lenox Avenue.

"It's no crime to be a Communist," Mr. Epton states. "They can't put us in jail because of our political beliefs. As a matter of fact, I would like to see the police try it."

Mr. Epton readily admits that he is a Communist and that his organization is a Communist organization, the *Journal* reports.

"We arrived at what we consider to be a correct Marxist-Leninist position. Our position happens to be almost the same as that of the Chinese."

Mr. Epton says that PLM has four offices in New York and others throughout the country. He estimates national membership at "more than 1000." Mr. Epton, who is a Negro, says that seventy-five percent of his membership is white. He says that his members "are very generous. They contribute all of the money."

At two p.m. on July 26, station WPAT reported that police files show PLM's money comes "from Red China through Cuba."

*"Williams [Robert F. Williams: the Communist and former NAACP official who now broadcasts from Havana] did not arrive unheralded in Peking from Cuba last autumn. Chairman Mao had paid him tribute in a rare public statement. Six weeks before Williams came, the Party Leader was receiving a group of African visitors and opened his audience with them by declaring that Robert Williams, writing from Havana, had asked him to speak 'in support of the American Negroes' struggle against racial discrimination. On behalf of the Chinese people I wish to . . . express our resolute support.'"* [25]

*"People of all countries always encourage and support each other in the struggle against imperialism and old and new colonialism and for national liberation. . . . we consider it our unshirkable international duty to support all just, revolutionary struggles of the peoples throughout the world."* [26] Kuo Mo-jo, chairman of the China Peace Committee, at a rally in Peking

The New York *Times* of July 28 reports on page fifteen, the New York state supreme court testimony of Detective John Rivera, who says he heard Mr. Epton make the follow-

ing announcement at a meeting on July 18: "We're going to
have to kill cops and judges."

Two Negro patrolmen, Clifton King and Clarence Crabb,
told of attending another meeting on the next day at Mr.
Epton's headquarters, where Mr. Crabb says Epton made the
following remarks: "If there was any opposition, it should
not be dealt with on the avenue but the police should be
sucked into the side streets where they should be bombarded
with missiles." Patrolman King added that Mr. Epton said
"people were wasting their time throwing empty bottles but
if they filled them with some kind of liquid it could create
more disturbance."

So it was interesting indeed to read the following paragraphs in the same story:

> Mr. Gray, who has been leading Harlem rent strikes, protested
> at the start of the hearing that he had no lawyer present. During
> the session, Abraham Unger, a lawyer, came up to represent him
> and contended the only link between the Epton and Gray groups
> was a Harlem Defense Council circular listing a rally by Mr.
> Gray's group.
>
> Thereupon, Corporation Counsel Larkin presented Detective
> Fritz O. Behr, who testified he had heard Mr. Gray tell a reporter
> during a demonstration outside the United Nations last Monday
> that he was "connected with the Harlem Defense Council" and
> that "the Progressive Labor Movement made up this leaflet for
> his use."

> *"Another building in Brasil [a town in Colombia] a smaller
> one, is the two story Casa Communista, where a mimeograph
> machine grinds out cheap propaganda sheets urging support
> of the 'Democratic Front of National Liberation'—the euphe-
> mism that now replaces the former, more explicit 'Commu-
> nist party.' . . ."* [27]

That Friday night, July 24, rioting broke out in Rochester,
New York. As residents of that city will probably recall,

> a shouting, cursing group of about 20 persons descended on a
> nearby police car, pelting it with vegetables, rocks and cans of
> paint.
>
>   . . .

The gang then overturned the police car, smashed its windows and smeared it with paint. . . .[28]

*June, 1952: "Around the world last week the Communists exploded in uprisings, upsets and general uproar. . . . from the similar patterns of their uprisings everywhere, it seemed clear that they were all centrally directed as part of a master program. . . ."* [29]

As the officers tried to clear the walks and pavement by pushing demonstrators into doorways and side streets, they were pelted with eggs, beer cans, bottles and broken window glass.[30]

*"During the original rioting Saturday night [in New York] one policeman reported, he and other cops—white and Negro —were insulted by youngsters 'who didn't even speak New York English. They had obviously been brought up from the South.'"* [31]

*"They [the White Shirters] were seen at the Jesse Gray '100 men willing to die' rally, and in Bedford-Stuyvesant. At least one of them was spotted in Rochester."* [32]

Burglar alarms were ringing all over Joseph Avenue now. We couldn't see a store window that wasn't broken.

Negroes were walking around with clothes, television sets, boxes of merchandise.[33]

*". . . the party is not hostile towards those who steal from the enemy because this would bring the government into difficulties and would prevent the money which had been obtained by bleeding the little man dry from being put by or taken to Europe. . . . A third of the goods obtained by crime would be for the offenders and two-thirds for the PKI [Indonesian Communist Party]."* [34]

7/26/64: New York *Journal-American,* front page story:

All of Rochester's gun shops were ordered closed.

Most motion picture houses in the downtown area were told to close their doors.

As sultry darkness settled, the third largest municipality in the state was like a city under siege.

. . . Public transportation was halted throughout the city mainly to keep citizens off the streets, or to protect passengers from attacks.

*10/13/55: The 40th Moroccan Goum Regiment finds some papers in the Djebel Krouma belonging to Belkacemi Mohamed ben Messaoud, the terrorist chief of the region south of the Aurés. A document headed "Moghrebin Army of Liberation—Directives for September/October 1955—Zone of Tebessa," reads in broken French as follows:*

*"Anything of use to the enemy must be destroyed: schools, churches, stations, post offices, camps, telephone installations, etc. . . .*

*"Attacks on coaches, trains, taxis, bicycles. Insecurity on all the roads. These actions are to be unceasingly continued. . . .*

*"Kill all the caids, khodjas, presidents, councillors, etc. . . . Kill the wives of the Moroccans.*

*"Do all that you can against the colons, goums, traitors, gardens, houses, farms. Lock them in, burn them up."*

Rioting bands of Negroes fired shotguns and pistols into the air. Police fought back with tear gas barrages.[35]

Of the riots in Rochester we read as follows:

Federal investigators are increasingly leaning to the view that communist planning, instigation and leadership played a major role in this savage rioting.

On the basis of what these authorities have uncovered so far, they are strongly inclined to the conclusion that this world-headlined racial outbreak has unmistakable manifestation of a basic and widely exploited communist revolutionary tactic—"ethnological warfare."

Under this doctrine, the Communists deliberately incite dissension and conflict between nationalities—in the jarring Rochester instance, Negroes against Jews.

Highlighting the evidence underlying this explosive finding are the following:

Most of the small neighborhood stores robbed and wrecked are owned by Jews.

These shops apparently were carefully pinpointed and marked

out in advance. For example: Jewish-owned stores located between non-Jewish establishments were attacked while the others were not. This was a distinct "pattern" in all affected sections, whether Negro or white.[36]

The riots in Philadelphia, which broke out soon after, were explained as follows:

> The Negro riots that ravaged North Philadelphia were caused by a small band of Communist-influenced agitators who used lies and command-like precision to trigger an "explosion" that still has the city reeling.
>
> Seizing on a minor incident, these agitators quickly put into operation a well-organized plan that touched off the violence along Columbia Ave., much like demolition experts would touch off a series of charges.

According to a top police official, "as few as 20 men" put the plan into effect.

> These men had been stationed along Columbia Ave. for the last few weeks, one or two in every block, waiting for a chance—an incident involving the police—to go to work.
>
> . . .
>
> Then the terrorists weaved through the rapidly forming crowds spreading lies: "Police have killed a woman." "The cops have shot a boy." "Police have beaten a pregnant woman." [37]

Meanwhile Malcolm X, as you will recall, was in the clear—in Cairo.

What he was doing there, among other things, says Leonard Lyons, was "negotiating for munitions." [38]

In fact, says Victor Riesel, while in Africa Malcolm

> spent a considerable amount of his time in the presence of international Communist propagandists. . . .
>
> Not only did he endorse the rioting back home, but he publicly called for retaliation against the white community. He said the time had come to meet "violence with violence; an eye for an eye and a tooth for a tooth."
>
> [He made speeches] so anti-U.S., so incendiary, that they could be printed only on asbestos.
>
> It is also being noticed that the Chinese Communists' broadcasts have been featuring him and his splinter sect.[39]

In fact, on December 20, 1964, he said—*again*—that like the people of Kenya, " 'we need a Mau Mau' to win freedom and equality for Negroes in the United States." [40]

Soon after the 1964 New York riots were over, the Negro leaders and their groups formed the Unity Council of Harlem Organizations, which is composed of "such diverse organizations as the Black Muslim, the recognized civil rights groups, three African nationalist associations, and various church and civic groups." [41]

*April, 1963: ". . . The first step, it seems, would be the convening of a national convention of the Negro people, representative of all points of view without exception, which would address itself to the task of uniting the national Negro community around a common, effective method of achieving freedom now . . ."* [42] Communist official Benjamin J. Davis

## NOTES

1. Testimony of J. Edgar Hoover before a House subcommittee, January 29, 1964, as quoted by David Lawrence, *U.S. News & World Report*, vol. 56, no. 18 (May 4, 1964), p. 108.

2. New York *Times* (May 29, 1964), p. 13.

3. *Ibid*. (December 2, 1964), p. 9.

4. *National Review* (October 13, 1964), p. 3.

5. New York *Times* (December 2, 1964), p. 9.

6. New York *News* (August 2, 1964), p. 5.

7. William Worthy, "The Red Chinese American Negro," *Esquire*, vol. 62, no. 4 (October 1964), p. 177.

8. New York *Times* (December 2, 1964), p. 9.

9. V. I. Lenin, *What Is to Be Done?* (New York, International Publishers, 1929), p. 131.

10. New York *Times* (December 2, 1964), p. 9.

11. As quoted by syndicated columnist Dorothy Kilgallen (April 22, 1964).

12. *U.S. News & World Report*, vol. 57, no. 5 (August 3, 1964), p. 22.

13. *Literary Digest*, vol. 101, no. 8 (May 25, 1929), p. 14.

14. *U.S. News & World Report*, vol. 48, no. 25 (June 20, 1960), p. 61. This was the riot that greeted Presidential Press Secretary James C. Hagerty, who was supposed to be followed by President Eisenhower.

15. *U.S. News & World Report* (August 3, 1964), p. 24.

16. As quoted by Worthy, p. 176.

17. *Ibid*.

18. *U.S. News & World Report* (August 3, 1964), p. 22.

19. *Ibid.*, p. 24.

20. Senator James O. Eastland (D., Miss.), speech, *Congressional Record* (July 22, 1964), p. 16037.

21. New York *Times* (July 20, 1964), p. 16.

22. Harry J. Benda and Ruth T. McVey, editors, *The Communist Uprisings of 1926-1927 in Indonesia: Key Documents* (Ithaca, N.Y., Cornell University, 1960), p. 3.

23. New York *Journal-American* (July 1, 1964), pp. 1, 8.

24. New York *News* (July 20, 1964), p. 18.

25. Worthy, p. 132.

26. *Ibid.*

27. Eugene K. Culhane, *America,* vol. 102, no. 23 (March 12, 1960), p. 702.

28. Rochester *Times-Union* (July 25, 1964), p. 2A.

29. *Life,* vol. 32, no. 23 (June 9, 1952), p. 30.

30. Rochester *Times-Union* (July 25, 1964), p. 1.

31. New York *News* (July 22, 1964), p. 13.

32. *Ibid.* (August 2, 1964), p. 5.

33. Rochester *Times-Union* (July 25, 1964), p. 3A.

34. Benda and McVey, p. 3.

35. Rochester *Democrat and Chronicle* (July 26, 1964), p. 1.

36. "Allen-Scott Report," Chicago *American* (August 4, 1964).

37. Philadelphia *News* (September 1, 1964), p. 3.

38. Boston *Herald* (July 31, 1964), p. 29.

39. Hollywood *Citizen-News* (September 8, 1964).

40. New York *Times* (December 21, 1964), p. 20.

41. *Ibid.* (November 8, 1964), p. 47.

42. Benjamin J. Davis, *Against Tokenism and Gradualism* (New York, New Century Publishers, April 1963), preface.

CHAPTER VIII **The United Nations**

> Now that national-liberation revolutions throughout the world
> join with the socialist revolution in a massive struggle for
> democracy and national independence directed against U.S.
> imperialism, the French Canadian national struggle will re-
> ceive great impetus from outside of Canada. . . .[1] Leslie
> Morris, Communist party of Canada

Suppose that you're a Communist and you want to capture
the United States. You've already succeeded in setting every
sort of person against every other sort of person: Jews against
Christians, Negroes against whites, Mississippians against New
Yorkers, women against men—all of course according to plan;
and you're doing very well in what Lenin called "the battle
of the streets." Even your war of national liberation is beginning to take shape.

But the United States isn't Czechoslovakia. It isn't Albania.
At this point in those countries you could almost forget this
annoying nonsense about "humanity" and turn to the last
step: that of killing people. The United States, however, is
the fountainhead of capitalism, and therefore the last bastion
of fascism. And, also unlike Albania, it's a huge country con-
taining millions of fascists and armed nazis, all vicious. Even
the women are vicious.

So it's obvious that you can't just crawl out of the American's plumbing with your two hundred goons and announce
that you're here to capture his country. You are fully aware
that if he didn't believe you he'd simply laugh himself sick,
and if he did he would rise up against you with the rest of
the Americans, black and white, man and woman, Mississip-
pian and New Yorker, butcher, baker, candlestick maker and
industrialist—and that when it was all over there wouldn't be
enough left of you to put under a microscope.

So—if you were a Communist—what would you do?

Well of course, you would call in the United Nations—if you were a Communist.

Why?

"One resolution after another protesting new colonialist trends which America's rulers support and the racist practices they endorse, emerges from the Human Rights Commission of the General Assembly of the United Nations," says Communist official William L. Patterson. "Notice must be taken of this historic fact, for *herein lies an international bond of the liberation movements of progressive mankind.*" [2] (italics added)

And, says William Worthy, "Negro nationalists" are noticing it: ". . . Negro nationalists have already begun to 'by-pass the American government and to look upon the Afro-Asian bloc in the UN as their representatives,' as a Negro writer asserted in *Correspondence* magazine last year." [3]

The point is—if you are a Communist—that you would orchestrate your strategies; you would combine the "liberation movements of progressive mankind," all bound by the "international bond" that is the United Nations—with the civil rights and national liberation movements in the United States.

But the question at once arises: Didn't the UN *oppose* "self-determination" when the province of Katanga tried to apply it? Because of course, when Katanga seceded from the Congo, the United Nations got nasty. In fact, the United Nations got brutal, as the bombed-out hospitals there will attest.

The answer of course is that since President Tshombe of Katanga is an outspoken enemy of Communism, then what he was doing couldn't possibly be a war of national liberation—simply because, as Communists insist, anyone who opposes Communism is a fascist. As you will recall, both Lenin and Stalin emphasized that the tactic of the "war of national liberation" is exactly that: a tactic, to be used only when tactically profitable:

. . . A people has the right to secede, but it may or may not exercise that right, according to circumstances. Thus we are at liberty to agitate for or against secession, according to the interests of the proletariat, of the proletarian revolution. Hence, the question of secession must be determined in each particular case independently, in accordance with existing circumstances. . . .[4]

If, in short, a Communist faction secedes from a non-Communist country, that is a war of national liberation. But if a non-Communist province secedes from a Communist country, that's morally wrong, that's fascist exploitation of the laboring masses.

And of course, you'd apply this strategy—as we have seen —to the United States:

The right of self-determination does not necessarily imply separation. It means the right to separate, if the citizens of the proposed new republic so choose, and it means the right to remain a federated part of the United States, if that suits the interests of the Negro people better, which depends on the circumstances. For instance, under conditions of capitalism in the United States today, when they are ground under by the heel of Yankee imperialism, the Negroes would achieve immeasurably greater freedom by separation. Should there, on the other hand, be a truly workers' and farmers' government in the United States today, the real interests of the Negro masses would be served best by federation with such a government, as is shown by the position enjoyed by the numerous formerly subject nationalities in the Soviet Union.[5]

So the point is—if you are a Communist—that you would apply the international power of the world's "liberation movements" through the UN—as in the case of Algeria—to the national liberation movement within the United States, with the aim of breaking up the huge territory of the United States, so that, as James Baldwin has mentioned, *it would become more manageable.*

How can we be sure that this is true?

Well, the Communists say so.

The National Negro Congress was a Communist operation.[6] ". . . The crowning achievement of the communists was their getting A. Philip Randolph to serve as first chairman of the NNC," writes William A. Nolan.[7]

In May 1947, the National Negro Congress published "a petition to the United Nations on behalf of 13 million oppressed Negro citizens of the United States of America." [8]

Dr. Max Yergan, then a Communist,[9] is listed in the pamphlet as president. Revels Cayton, also a Communist,[10] is listed as executive secretary.

The "Proof in Support of the Petition" is presented under a heading called "The Oppression of the American Negro: The Facts," by Dr. Herbert Aptheker. Dr. Herbert Aptheker is identified as: "Ph.D. Columbia U., Member American Historical Society." [11] He is not identified as a Communist, though he has been a leading one for years.

The pamphlet begins with the following paragraphs, in an attempt to establish that the UN has jurisdiction to act within the United States:

> 4. Reference: Article 55, Sec. 1(c), Charter of the United Nations.
> "With a view to the creation of conditions of stability and well-being which are necessary for peaceful and friendly relations among nations based on respect for the principle of *equal rights and self-determination of peoples,* the United Nations shall promote: Universal respect for, and observance of, human rights and fundamental freedoms for all without distinction as to race, sex, language or religion." [12] (italics added)

The petition asks that the UN do as follows:

> 2. Make such recommendations and *take such other actions as it may deem proper* with respect to the facts herein stated, to the end that "higher standards" in the field of human rights may be achieved in the United States of America and "discrimination and other abuses" on the grounds of race and color, may be "checked and eliminated."
> 3. *Take such other and further steps as may seem just and proper* to the end that the oppression of the American Negro be brought to an end.[13] (italics added)

Now remember, we are not arguing here about whether or not "the oppression of the American Negro" should be brought to an end; all men of good will are against oppression—real oppression. We are simply trying to show how the NNC is trying to internationalize this tragic *American* problem by bringing in the UN.

And since the UN has jurisdiction only over international disputes, it is implicit, is it not, that the dispute is between the Negro "nation" and the United States.

> There are many . . . signs, of course, of the developing national consciousness of the American Negro people [said William Z. Foster]. They are building up many movements that are definitely of a national liberation character. They are also closely identifying themselves with the national liberation struggles of colonial peoples all over the world. They feel a kinship with these movements. Very significant in this general respect was the demand made by the National Negro Congress to the United Nations to take up the grievances of the Negro people in this country. . . . *Such an act was essentially that of a nation appealing over the head of the American government to the peoples of the world for justice, much as almost any other colonial or oppressed nation might do.*[14] (italics added)

In December 1947, the NNC was merged with the Civil Rights Congress, which was also a Communist operation.[15]

In 1951, the Civil Rights Congress issued its own petition: *We Charge Genocide, The Historic Petition to the United Nations for Relief from a Crime of the United States Government Against the Negro People.*[16]

The editor of the petition is identified as William L. Patterson, who is not only still a top Communist official, but is the same William L. Patterson who was seen enjoying the rally at which Jesse Gray called for "100 skilled black revolutionaries who are ready to die."

The staff for the petition includes Richard O. Boyer, Howard Fast, Dr. Oakley Johnson, Leon Josephson and Elizabeth Lawson, all Communists. The petitioners include Isadore Begun, Richard O. Boyer, Benjamin J. Davis, Jr., Howard Fast, James Ford, Abner Green, Harry Haywood, Arnold Johnson, Claudia Jones, Albert Kahn, Elizabeth Lawson, William L. Patterson, Pettis Perry, John Pittman and Paul Robeson, all Communists.

Nowhere in the petition does it say that the Civil Rights Congress was a Communist operation.

But in the introduction by Communist William L. Patterson, who is there identified as national executive secretary of the CRC, we read as follows:

> It is sometimes incorrectly thought that genocide means the complete and definitive destruction of a race or people. The Genocide Convention, however, adopted by the General Assembly of the United Nations on December 9, 1948, defines genocide as any killings on the basis of race, or, in its specific words, as "killing members of the group." Any intent to destroy, *in whole or in part,* a national, racial, ethnic or religious group is genocide, according to the Convention. Thus, the Convention states, "causing serious bodily or mental harm to members of the group" is genocide as well as "killing members of the group."

You will recall that the U.S. Supreme Court said in *Brown v. Board of Education* on May 17, 1954, that segregated schools produce in the Negro child "a feeling of inferiority as to his status." This would imply not only that those Americans who want segregated schools are guilty of genocide, but that the genocide convention can somehow intervene to forbid segregation.

> We maintain, therefore, that the oppressed Negro citizens of the United States, segregated, discriminated against and long the target of violence, suffer from genocide as the result of the consistent, conscious, unified, policies of every branch of government.
> . . .
> . . . We further submit that this Convention on Genocide is, *by virtue of our avowed acceptance of the Covenant of the United Nations, an inseparable part of the law of the United States of America.* (italics added)

And Mr. Patterson is correct.

> According to international law, and according to our own law, the Genocide Convention, as well as the provisions of the United Nations Charter, supersedes, negates and displaces all discriminatory racist law on the books of the United States and the several states."

Such as the Constitution of the United States.

. . . The General Assembly of the United Nations, by reason of the United Nations Charter and the Genocide Convention, itself is invested with power to receive this indictment and act on it.

The proof of this fact is its action upon the similar complaint of the Government of India against South Africa.

The United Nations, in short, *already has the right* to send an army of "neutral" troops—from Ghana, Indonesia, India and Burma—to the American South, just as it did to the Congo.

The NAACP also got into the act:

This question then, which is without doubt primarily an internal and national question [wrote W. E. B. DuBois, who later became a member of the Communist party] becomes inevitably an international question and will in the future become more and more international, as the nations draw together. In this great attempt to find common ground and to maintain peace, it is therefore, fitting and proper that the thirteen million American citizens of Negro descent should appeal to the United Nations and ask that organization in the proper way to take cognizance of a situation which deprives this group of their rights as men and citizens, and by so doing makes the functioning of the United Nations more difficult, if not in many cases impossible.

The United Nations surely will not forget that the population of this group makes it in size one of the considerable *nations* of the world. . . . and while we rejoice that *other smaller nations* can stand and make their wants known in the United Nations, we maintain equally that our voice should not be suppressed or ignored.[17] (italics added)

According to the New York *Journal-American* of July 1, 1964, page eight, Malcolm X warned that "if necessary, he would take the plight of the U.S. Negro to the United Nations."

You will recall that on July 12 Malcolm arrived in Cairo to attend a meeting of the council of ministers of the Organization for African Unity. What he said there, according to the New York *Times* of July 14, was, as we have seen, that he would acquaint the Africans "with the true plight of America's Negroes and to show them how our situation is as much a violation of the United Nations Human Rights Charter as the situation in South Africa or Angola."

You will also recall the famous rally at which Mr. Gray called for "guerrilla warfare." At that rally Mr. Gray announced yet another rally for the next day, to be held at the UN, to demand UN intervention "in the police terror in the United States." [18]

"I do believe police brutality in this city, Mississippi and other such places should be an issue placed before the United Nations," says James Farmer, national director of CORE.[19]

Because this is still a free country, it is perfectly possible for Mr. Farmer, and for Mr. X, Mr. Gray and even Mr. Patterson, to say whatever they like, even something this fantastic. But that's no proof we're going to get it.

Or is it?

On March 9, 1964, journalist Robert S. Allen reported:

> The same administration attorneys who drafted the civil rights program are engineering White House backing for an international court to enforce "civil rights" as stipulated under a treaty being prepared at the United Nations.
> A draft of this treaty to ban all forms of racial bias was presented to the UN by Morris B. Abram, former general counsel for the Peace Corps and now the U.S. member on a UN subcommission on Prevention of Discrimination and Protection of Minorities.

The sinister fact is that "the treaty and the international civil rights court are part of a backstage State Department plan to link the racial problem in the U.S. with that in Africa, and then put final jurisdiction under the UN." [20]

The Communists are busy in Puerto Rico, as they are everywhere else. On November 20, 1964, according to the New York *Times,* a UN committee took

> the first step toward forcing a United Nations discussion of independence for Puerto Rico.
> . . .
> The decision pushed by the committee majority was clearly a follow-up to action taken last month in Cairo by the conference of non-aligned countries.

That conference, mainly at Cuba's instigation, approved a report that deplored delay in giving some territories independence. It drew the United Nations' attention to the "case of Puerto Rico," with a request that its situation be studied.

Mr. Dwight Dickinson, the American member of the "Special Committee on Colonialism," told his colleagues that their decision was "shocking—I repeat, shocking." [21]

Dear me, Mr. Dickinson! Surely you aren't going to make any wild charges!

## NOTES

1. Leslie Morris, "National and Democratic Revolution in French Canada," *World Marxist Review*, vol. 7, no. 9 (September 1964), p. 19.

2. William L. Patterson, in *Negro Liberation, A Goal for All Americans* (New York, New Currents Publishers, July 1964), p. 51.

3. William Worthy, "The Red Chinese American Negro," *Esquire*, vol. 62, no. 4 (October 1964), p. 176.

4. Joseph Stalin, *Marxism and the National and Colonial Question*, p. 64. Speech delivered at the seventh all-Russian conference of the Russian Social Democratic Labor party (April 29, 1917).

5. James S. Allen, "Negro Liberation," International Pamphlets, no. 29 (New York, International Publishers, 1932), pp. 21-22.

6. *Investigation of Un-American Propaganda Activities in the United States*, appendix IX, Special Committee on Un-American Activities, House, 78th Congress, second session (Washington, D.C., Government Printing Office, 1944), pp. 1284-1295. Also, *Hearings Regarding Infiltration of Minority Groups*, vol. 3, House, 81st Congress, first session (Washington, D.C., Government Printing Office, 1949), p. 2148.

7. William A. Nolan, *Communism Versus the Negro* (Chicago, Henry Regnery Company, 1951), p. 134. See also *Hearings Regarding Infiltration*, p. 511, referred to in footnote 6 of this chapter.

8. Pamphlet, National Negro Congress (New York, May 1947).

9. Wilson Record, *The Negro and the Communist Party* (Chapel Hill, The University of North Carolina Press, 1951), pp. 189-190, 197-198.

10. Senator James O. Eastland (D., Miss.), speech, *Congressional Record* (July 22, 1964), pp. 16037-16038. Discussing a "human rights" march in San Francisco on July 12, 1964, Eastland said: "A man named Revels Cayton, who was a member of the California Communist Party State Committee back in 1946, was one of those active in organizing the march. Cayton has been identified in sworn testimony as one of the top Communists on the Pacific Coast in the trade union movement during the days of the maritime federation."

11. National Negro Congress, pamphlet, p. 8. See footnote 8, this chapter.

12. *Ibid.*, p. 5.

13. *Ibid.*, p. 7.

14. As quoted in "The Communist Position (1947)," pp. 14-16. See footnote 16, chapter 3.

15. *Report on the Civil Rights Congress,* House Committee on Un-American Activities (September 2, 1947).

16. *We Charge Genocide, The Historic Petition to the United Nations for Relief from a Crime of the United States Government Against the Negro People* (New York, Civil Rights Congress, 1951).

17. This position of Du Bois is contained in a pamphlet by the National Association for the Advancement of Colored People, "An Appeal to the World!" (New York, NAACP, 1947), pp. 13-14.

18. New York *News* (July 20, 1964), p. 18.

19. New York *Journal-American* (July 20, 1964), p. 4.

20. Marietta (Georgia) *Journal.*

21. New York *Times* (November 21, 1964), p. 2.

## CHAPTER IX

# Life Among the Eskimos

*[I am] sick and tired of people saying this movement has been infiltrated by Communists and Communist sympathizers.*

*There are as many Communists in this freedom movement as there are Eskimos in Florida.*[1] The Rev. Dr. Martin Luther King, Jr.

William Z. Foster and Gus Hall and other leading Communists have gone to great trouble to make clear not only that there is no contradiction between the two tactics the Communists in Moscow have developed for use in the United States—"self-determination" and "civil rights"—but that the two complement and reinforce each other and are in essence one and the same:

Let me sum up on this general point [says Foster], that is, the orientation of the Negro people is first, toward full participation and full equality in American life, and second, toward the development of their national consciousness. Comrade Ed Strong made a good contribution when he stressed the basic harmony between these two streams of courses of development. . . .[2]

. . . Each influences the other [says Gus Hall]. . . . Thus, the struggles for full equality of the Negro national minority and the struggle for national liberation of the oppressed nation are very closely interlinked.[3]

In the North the slogan for equal rights will be the basic slogan [explains Communist official William L. Patterson]. A major feature of the program in the North must be the struggle to destroy the ghetto. . . . We must smash the ghetto. *The ghetto is tied to the South and to the issue of the right of self-determination.*[4] (italics added)

How, one wonders?

". . . These are the people who are ready for revolution —any kind of revolution . . ." says Professor Lincoln about the Black Muslims. "Furthermore, in the segregated Black

Ghetto, the illusion of a 'Black Nation' within a surrounding and hostile 'white nation' takes on a semblance of reality. . . ." [5]

So what is the nature of "the basic harmony between these two streams of courses of development," as Foster so clearly puts it?

> The vast bulk of American Negroes merely aspire to precisely the same rights as other Americans [says C. L. Sulzberger]. . . . North American extremism is of real danger only if existing injustices are not rectified in time.
>
> However, should there be no prompt reform, the United States could see hideous racial quarrels on a scale hitherto unimaginable.[6]

". . . On fund-raising missions to corporate boards, Whitney Young, Jr., executive director of the National Urban League, poses these alternatives; invest in positive assistance —or risk hostility and growing strength for the Muslims. . . ." [7]

In 1963 he made the same prediction.

> "Unless we do something, the Negro in the future will no longer react with resignation but with bitterness and hostility."
>
> And those are the ingredients of trouble. "We're liable to get some real violence—in Chicago, in Detroit, in New York," Young predicts gloomily. . . .[8]

So what should we do?

> The white leadership must be honest enough to grant that throughout our history there has existed a special privileged class of citizens who received preferred treatment. That class was white. Now we're saying this: if two men, one Negro and one white, are equally qualified for a job, hire the Negro.[9]

> *"The fundamental policy of a Soviet Government with regard to the Negro generally would therefore be to create even relatively greater opportunities for advance and progress for the Negro than for the white. Special emphasis would be placed upon training more Negro skilled workers. . . . A Soviet Government must confer greater benefits upon the*

*Negroes than upon the whites, for the Negroes have started with less. . . ." *[10]

> As long as we are not allowed to establish a state or territory of our own [says Mr. Muhammad] we demand not only equal justice under the laws of the United States, but equal employment opportunities—NOW!
> . . . The United States government should provide, free, all necessary textbooks and equipment, schools and college buildings. . . .[11]

So what Mr. Muhammad wants is more and more civil rights, until he gets the "separation." In fact, once he gets the separation—*from a government that has been grabbed by civil rights*—". . . We believe that our former slave masters are obliged to maintain and supply our needs in this separate territory for the next 20 to 25 years—until we are able to produce and supply our own needs." [12]

*"Thirdly, there would be even greater aid from the Central Soviet Government of the United States. . . ." *[13] The Negroes in a Soviet America

So it turns out that even Mr. Muhammad isn't completely opposed to civil rights. *Muhammad Speaks* for January 31, 1964, hails the CORE attempt to "integrate" the staff of the Jefferson Bank and Trust Company in St. Louis.[14]

And in an editorial in July 1962, we read:

> Muslims certainly have no opposition to the program and policies of the NAACP. . . .
> There is much to be admired in the heroic struggle waged by the NAACP since the days of its formation against incalculable odds. Many NAACP leaders, nationally and locally, are men and women of high intelligence and integrity.[15]

"If one can't gain objectives through mediation, if one can't gain objectives after a riot," explains the Rev. Milton Galamison, leader of the New York school boycott, "then all these things may become a Sunday school picnic by comparison to what people are going to do in order to get their grievances remedied." [16]

And so the point is, as Professor Lincoln suggests, that "Muslim extremism may even rebound and actively assist the forces of integration. It may, for example, force a white reappraisal of other protest organizations, such as the NAACP, which are now widely resisted as 'too pushy' or 'radical.' . . ." [17]

Let's sum up: There are in the United States two kinds of "Negro Leaders": the violents, and the "nonviolents." The violents want to destroy the United States and set up their own nation on part of it. All the nonviolents want is integration.

Americans of all colors are going to get one or the other, they are told, so they'd better take the integration. If they don't, they'll get the self-determination, and that's bound to be unpleasant. In other words, if the violents make a riot, and the nonviolent Rev. Galamison doesn't get what he wants, the violents will probably make a bigger riot.

If you wanted to define it in one word you'd pick the word "extortion."

What is important to observe is that the two strategies advance like legs on the same man. Left to themselves, the violents would probably fall on their collective face just because they *are* violent, and it's therefore easier to tell what they are actually all about. And the nonviolents would collapse because they would lack the violence to back threats. But notice that when you put the two together, they both get progressively violent, or less and less nonviolent—but the nonviolents in comparison always look like moderates.

Roy Wilkins begins to sound like President McKinley, because a Malcolm X sounds like Attila the Hun.

And Jesse Gray begins to sound like Malcolm X.

On June 28, two weeks before he arrived in Cairo to attend that meeting of the Organization for African Unity, Malcolm formed a revolutionary group called the Organization of Afro-American Unity, with himself as chairman. As members of the OAAU braintrust, Malcolm named Rev. Albert Cleage, leader of the Michigan Freedom Now party; Gloria Richardson, leader of the Freedom Now movement in Cambridge, Maryland; Lawrence Landry, Chicago school boycott leader; John Lewis, head of the Student Nonviolent Coordinating Committee; and Jesse Gray—all practicing nonviolents.[18]

As we have seen, Malcolm X has become the leading symbol of the violents.

And the Rev. Dr. Martin Luther King, Jr. has become the leading symbol of the nonviolents.

In fact, we are told, the Rev. Dr. King is the only man who can save us from Malcolm X.

And so the question arises: What was the relationship, if any, between Malcolm and the Rev. Dr. King?

What sort of person is the Rev. Dr. Martin Luther King, Jr.?

In November of 1938 the Communist party formed an organization called the Southern Conference for Human Welfare.[19] Rob Hall, then secretary of the Alabama Communist party, tells how "our comrades . . . naturally watched the conference preparations closely and helped wherever possible." [20]

SCHW was what is known as a Communist front. Early in their movement, the Communists came boldly out as Communists—possibly because they assumed that other people could not wait to join up. However, it turned out that other people were not interested. In fact, it turned out that by far most people of every race and country are thoroughly decent and want no part of Criminal Communism. As *Political Affairs* said:

> To the extent that we aroused enthusiasm among the Negro people, it was largely in spite of, not because of our over-simplified presentation of the right of self-determination. Anyone who has worked in the South must realize that our presentation of this right for the most part had only the effect of puzzling and confusing the Negro people who followed our movement. They generally listened politely to our exposition of this right, but treated it as some strange idiosyncrasy to which we were addicted, but which could be forgiven in friends. The most damning thing of all was that those Negroes who took the trouble to ascertain

exactly what we were driving at generally voiced very decided opposition.[21]

So the Communists realized, as Jesse Gray reportedly remarked, that in order to put people to use, they would have to develop some sort of trick.

Consequently, they developed the strategy of the Communist "front." The front is operated in two ways: Either the Communists infiltrate an organization, work inside it (in Communist language, "bore from within"), and eventually capture it; or they form their own organization—and simply invite the gullible in. In either case, many unsuspecting Americans wind up working to further some specific Communist objective.

*"Comrades, you remember the ancient tale of the capture of Troy. Troy was inaccessible to the armies attacking her, thanks to her impregnable walls. And the attacking army, after suffering many sacrifices, was unable to achieve victory until with the aid of the famous Trojan horse it managed to penetrate the very heart of the enemy's camp.*

*"We revolutionary workers, it appears to me, should not be shy about using the same tactics with regard to our fascist foe. . . ."* [22]

But what is essential, in either case, is that since the overwhelming majority of people of any kind are thoroughly decent, the front must not only avoid mentioning, but actively deny, that it has anything at all to do with Communism.

Once the secret gets out, the Communist front has lost its value—*because* most people are decent.

*"Everything should be done to bring wide masses of Negroes into these partial struggles. This is important—and not to carry the various partial demands to such an ultra-radical point that the mass of working Negroes are no longer able to recognize them as* their own. *Without a real mobilization of the mass-movements . . . even the best Communist partial demands get hung up. . . ."* [23]

In other words, keep the Negroes under the impression that the campaign has something to do with what they want, when all along it has only to do with Communism.

But comrades let remarks slip. In speaking of the Southern Conference for Human Welfare and other southern fronts, Communist James W. Ford boasted in an article entitled "The Struggle for the Building of the Modern Liberation Movement of the Negro People," that "the Communists, through their pioneering work in the South, may justly claim to have laid the foundation for these great social movements." [24]

So the secret was out:

> Careful examination of its official publication and its activities will disclose that the conference is being used in devious ways to further basic Soviet and Communist policy. Decisive and key posts are in most instances controlled by persons whose record is faithful to the line of the Communist Party and the Soviet Union.[25]
>
> The Southern Conference for Human Welfare was conceived, financed, and set up by the Communist Party in 1938 as a mass organization to promote communism throughout the Southern States.[26]

And so the Communists abolished the Southern Conference for Human Welfare.

Immediately thereafter, there appeared on the scene an organization known as the Southern Conference Educational Fund. The Southern Conference Educational Fund's business address was 822 Perdido Street in New Orleans.[27] The Southern Conference for Human Welfare's business address had been 822 Perdido Street in New Orleans. The Southern Conference Educational Fund published—and continues to publish—a paper called the *Southern Patriot*. The paper published by the Southern Conference for Human Welfare had been called the *Southern Patriot*. Both organizations used the same telephone, and both had generally the same officers.

SCHW and SCEF, in short, are the same organization. Nothing has changed but the last two letters.

Who, exactly, is running SCHW-EF?

Mr. Carl Braden of Louisville, Kentucky, who serves as field director of SCEF, has been named under oath as a member of the Communist party.[28] Mrs. Anne Braden, also of Louisville, Kentucky, and editor of the *Southern Patriot,* has also been named under oath as a member of the Communist party: ". . . Alberta Ahearn . . . swore, both in Court and later before the Senate Internal Security Subcommittee that Carl and Anne Braden had recruited her into the Communist Party, and that she knew them as Communist Party members." [29]

Mr. Braden is a former convict. While in Louisville, he was convicted of a felony—a matter involving some dynamite. And Mrs. Braden was indicted for sedition.[30] It seems she doesn't like our form of government.

Carl Braden is also listed on its letterhead as one of the "national sponsors" of the Fair Play for Cuba Committee—which sponsored member Lee Harvey Oswald, the "lone fanatic"—and which is a Communist front. Braden was one of the main speakers at the FPCC dinner in New York on April 28, 1961.[31]

Benjamin E. Smith and his law partner, Bruce Waltzer, take part in the "overall management" of SCEF.[32] Both are under indictment "for multiple violations of the Louisiana Subversive Activities and Communist Control Act." [33]

At a closed meeting of the Southern Conference Educational Fund on February 3, 1964, at the Roosevelt Hotel in New York, Benjamin Smith, Treasurer of the Southern Conference Educational Fund, stated: "Come June, armies will take the field." "These armies are coming to strike. The Southern Conference Educational Fund is one of those armies." "The Southern Conference Educational Fund occupies a unique place in the South, it furnishes a staff organization supervising others." "There will be strikes, sitdowns, movements, we must play our part." . . . "Revolution is on its way." [34]

Mr. Aubrey Williams was president of SCEF until 1963, when he became so busy as chairman of the National Committee to Abolish HUAC—which is a Communist front—

that he decided to make himself president emeritus. As director of the National Youth Administration under President Roosevelt, Mr. Williams was Lyndon Johnson's boss. He also held other important jobs in the New Deal. ". . . In 1945, however, the U.S. Senate rejected his appointment as administrator of the Rural Electrification Administration, after his affiliations with the Communist apparatus had been placed in the record. . . ." [35]

On March 19, 1954, Mr. Williams testified before the Senate Internal Security Subcommittee that he had made the following statement in a speech in New York on September 11, 1947: ". . . It is my belief that it is precisely at this point that we take our stand and defend *the right of any Communist* to maintain his position as an employee of the Government of the United States. . . ." [36] (italics added)

Aubrey Williams in April of 1954 at Hearings held in New Orleans by the Senate Internal Security Subcommittee, was identified as a Communist Party member by one witness who had been in the Party, and was identified by another witness at the same time as one who had accepted Communist Party discipline. . . .[37]

Yet, note this carefully: President Johnson called on Aubrey Williams at his home just after the assassination of President Kennedy!

That's right. A man who has been authoritatively identified as a Communist agent, and whose goal therefore is the complete destruction of the United States, received a personal visit from the president of the United States.

The new president of SCEF is the Rev. Fred Shuttlesworth. Fred Shuttlesworth "has been affiliated with several communist-front organizations," [38] and is a former convict.[39]

The next document is a letter dated September 21, 1960, from Carl Braden to James A. Dombrowski. It shows that the Rev. Fred L. Shuttlesworth, ex-convict leader of the "Alabama Christian Movement for Human Rights" . . . was using the Bradens to write his news releases, obviously because the Bradens were, and are, highly skilled professional propagandists. . . . We offer the letter.[40]

Dr. James A. Dombrowski was executive director of SCHW. Dr. James A. Dombrowski is executive director of SCEF.

At the SISS Hearings in March of 1954, John Butler, former Alabama Communist party official, testified that in July 1942, he attended a meeting of Communist party leaders in the Thomas Jefferson Hotel, in Birmingham, Alabama, at which Alton Lawrence introduced James A. Dombrowski as a member of the Communist party.[41] Butler said this meeting of Communist party leaders was held in Dombrowski's own hotel room.

It seems that Dr. Dombrowski has many friends. In 1932, along with a man named Myles Horton, he was running an outfit called Commonwealth College in Mena, Arkansas. Commonwealth College was controlled by the People's Institute of Applied Religion, which had been organized by the Communist party.[42] The idea behind the college was that since Communism in the South couldn't beat religion, the Communists would *use* religion by, among other things, comparing texts taken from the *New Testament* and Karl Marx.

But the college—run by Dombrowski and Horton—was convicted under the laws of Arkansas of displaying the hammer and sickle and openly teaching Communism,[43] whereupon Arkansas levied a fine of $2,500. The college couldn't come up with the cash, so the state took over the property, sold it at public auction and used the money to cover the costs.

A detailed Communist plot to use the college as a chief instrument for Communist propaganda in the South is outlined in a secret report on Communism which was reprinted by the House Committee on Un-American Activities.[44] And on April 27, 1949, the U.S. attorney general cited Commonwealth as a Communist front.[45]

Commonwealth College lived on, however, for the faculty moved to the town of Monteagle, Tennessee, where, with the assistance of a man named Don West, they organized the Highlander Folk School.[46]

Don West was district director of the Communist party of North Carolina.[47] It was probably all right, though, because Aubrey Williams, President Johnson's friend, was also involved.[48]

Of course the Highlander Folk School was tax-exempt. A school leaflet advertising the 1949 winter term claims that the "purpose of Highlander Folk School is to promote the progressive labor movement in the South." Among the courses announced in the same leaflet is one in union problems that "deals with definite problems of the students as labor unionists. Methods of organizing, strike tactics, Labor Board procedure, education in unions, race relations are some of the things discussed. . . ." [49]

*". . . It is necessary . . . to go the whole length of any sacrifice, if need be, to resort to strategy and adroitness, illegal proceedings, reticence and subterfuge, to anything in order to penetrate into the Trade Unions, remain in them, and carry on Communist work inside them, at any cost. . . ."* [50] V. I. Lenin

What the school was actually doing was teaching the superiority of the Soviet form of government and advocating revolution to bring it about in the United States, and recruiting young students into the Young Communist League:

. . . I have seen these YCL cards in the possession of Ralph Tuffytaller, Myles Horton, James Dombrowski, and Bill Marlowe and have heard them all talk in favor of the Young Communists League. I have also heard all of the above mentioned people speak in favor of the Russian form of Government. I have heard Myles Horton and James Dombrowski make the following remarks ("Only a revolution will bring about a change from our present form of Government to the Russian form of Government"). I have heard them make this remark on several occasions and they would be in the Highlander Folk School building.

I have also heard Myles Horton talk about Commonwealth College with reference to the friendly relations between Highlander Folk School and this Commonwealth College. I also know that several students from Commonwealth College have visited the Highlander Folk School from time to time.[51]

And this disturbed the authorities of the American state of Tennessee. So in 1960, through court action, they succeeded in closing the organization known as the Highlander Folk School at Monteagle.

On August 30, 1961, an organization called the Highlander Research and Education Center of Knoxville, Tennessee, was incorporated, and immediately received tax-exempt status from the U.S. government, since the Internal Revenue Service had declared Highlander "a recognized educational institution with government approval."

The director of this new organization turns out to be Myles Horton. In a form letter dated May 15, 1963, Mr. Horton explained that: ". . . In the words of board of directors chairman, Dr. B. R. Brazeal, 'The Highlander idea, like a Phoenix rising from the ashes, has truly been born again in the Highlander Center.' "

Also of interest is the career of the Rev. Andrew Young, as recorded by the Atlanta *Constitution:*

> The administrator of the Dorchester Center in nearby Liberty County played a leading role in the desegregation activities of the Chatham County Crusade for Voters.
>
> The administrator, the Reverend Andrew Young . . . received training at the old Highlander Folk School at Monteagle, Tenn.
>
> Before its charter at Monteagle was revoked, the Highlander School received support from the International Union of Mine, Mill & Smelter Workers.
>
> An officer of the union, now under indictment on a charge of filing a false non-Communist affidavit, was one of the directors of the Highlander School.
>
> The Reverend Young has been headquartered rent-free in Savannah in the offices of the International Union of Mine, Mill & Smelter Workers. The Subversive Activities Control Board, an agency of the Federal Government, has found the union to be Communist infiltrated. The Mine-Mill Union has appealed the finding to a Federal court of appeals." [52]

Then there is the interesting case of a gentleman who is sometimes known as Mr. Hunter Pitts O'Dell:

> The Senate Internal Security Subcommittee declared today that "a smoothly coordinated" Communist underground was operat-

ing in New Orleans as late as last spring [1956]. The panel made public in support of its finding the transcripts of hearings held in that city in April.

The subcommittee said that American Communists

sought to infiltrate labor unions, churches, farmer organizations, parent-teacher organizations, channels of public opinion, and other streams of influence in our society.

. . .

Much of the Senate panel's case was built up at New Orleans from material found by New Orleans policemen in the abandoned apartment of one Hunter Pitts O'Dell. Mr. O'Dell had been identified in previous testimony as being the district organizer of the Communist party in New Orleans.[53]

On April 12, 1956, identifying himself as Hunter Pitts O'Dell, a New Orleans waiter, he testified before the Senate Internal Security Subcommittee. He invoked the Fifth Amendment and refused to say whether he was a southern district organizer for the Communist Party.

Robert Morris, counsel for the subcommittee, said information had been received that O'Dell was, in fact, a district organizer for the Communist Party in New Orleans; that O'Dell gave "directives to the professional group" in that city, and that he operated under three different names—the two other names being John Vesey and Ben Jones.[54]

In 1958, when O'Dell was living in Montgomery, he again declined to answer questions about his Communist party activity.

In 1962, the House Committee on Un-American Activities published a two-volume study entitled *Structure and Organization of the Communist Party of the United States.*

On page 576, there is a list of those elected to the national committee of the Communist Party, U.S.A., as known to the committee in November 1961.

Among the names was that of Hunter Pitts O'Dell.

Mr. O'Dell apparently also found time to do some work for the Dorchester Center, near Savannah, Georgia, which is operated out of Mine, Mill & Smelter by the Rev. Andrew Young, who is operated out of the Highlander School of Monteagle, Tennessee.

The name of Bayard Rustin has long struck fear into the heart of every segregationist.

> Mr. Rustin said that in 1938 or 1939 he had joined a Young Communist League group at City College in New York. But he insisted that he, like many members of the youth group, never became a member of the Communist party because the party was ultra-suspicious of young college students and had little confidence in their reliability.[55]

Mr. Rustin knows best of course, but the peculiar thing is that one of the major reasons for the existence of the YCL was to recruit young college students into the Communist party.

This record, based on FBI and police reports, is as follows:

> As a student at the College of the City of New York in 1936, Rustin joined the Young Communist League *and was active in its operations on the campus and elsewhere.*
>
> In World War II, he was arrested several times for making speeches advocating resistance to the conflict against Hitler and Mussolini. As a professed conscientious objector, he served 26 months in the federal prisons at Ashland, Ky., and Lewisburg, Pa.[56] (italics added)

He says he resigned from the YCL in 1941.

> . . . Rustin worked closely, often as an office holder, with: the War Resisters League, the World Peace Brigade, *Liberation* magazine, the Medical Aid to Cuba Committee, the second General Strike for Peace, the Monroe (N.C.) Defense Committee, the Committee for Non-Violent Action . . . the Greenwich Village Peace Center, and any number of other groups, ad hoc committees, petitions, etc., few of which are arrestingly wholesome. . . .[57]

> *". . . The Young Communist Leagues must strive in every way to unite the forces of all non-fascist mass organizations of the youth, including the formation of various kinds of common organizations for the struggle against fascism. . . .*[58]

Mr. Rustin has also been active in a group called the American Forum for Socialist Education, which is Communist dominated.[59]

Early in 1957, he spoke at the City College of New York to some four hundred students:

> The students . . . applauded heartily when Rustin appealed for a student campaign to ban the H-bomb.
>
> Other speakers were Joseph Clark, foreign editor of the *Daily Worker*; Eric Haas, of the Socialist Labor Party . . . and Myra Tanner Weiss, of the Socialist Workers Party.
>
> . . .
>
> Rustin strongly supported the non-violence tactics of the Montgomery movement. He contrasted the democratic reforms in Poland with the "retrogression to Stalinism in Hungary," and attributed the difference to the fact that in Poland the workers pursued non-violent tactics while in Hungary they resorted to violence. . . .[60]

Observe that Mr. Rustin believes that what happened in Poland was good—and somehow equates it with the Montgomery movement.

It is interesting to note that he was fresh from the sixteenth national convention of the Communist party of the United States, in which he participated, in February 1957, as an official "non-Communist" observer. The observers observed in a signed statement

> that the sessions of the convention were democratically conducted with vigorous discussion of all matters brought to the floor. There were many indications that no individual or group was in a position to control the convention.
>
> . . .
>
> Finally, we wish to protest vigorously against the continuance by Senator Eastland's Senate Internal Security subcommittee of the un-American practice of governmental inquisition into political opinions and activities, as instanced by the summons to Eugene Dennis [a Communist official] to appear next Monday before the subcommittee. . . .[61]

In 1958, Mr. Rustin was one of five Americans who went to Russia under the sponsorship of a group known as the Nonviolent Action Committee Against Nuclear Weapons.[62]

The January 1963, issue of *Fellowship* reveals Mr. Rustin

to be a "friend" of Kwame Nkrumah, the Communist dictator of Ghana. In the same issue Rustin is credited with having worked to establish a center for nonviolence at Dar es Salaam, Tanganyika, where, as we have seen, Communist troops are now in training.

In September of that year, he was in Richmond, Virginia, where he suggested "that more bloody Negro suffering should be encouraged so that squeamish Northern Negroes would be horrified into line. . . ." [63]

He was fresh from the march on Washington, which he conducted on August 28, for the ostensible purpose of helping to pass the civil rights bill, the day after which he urged that the only hope for Negroes was to "go left." [64]

On February 3, 1964, Mr. Rustin successfully conducted the New York City school boycott.

On the next day, photographers recorded his departure from a cocktail party at the Russian mission to the United Nations.

"Rustin said his presence stemmed from his activities in the Committee for Non-Violent Action, a civil rights group, and his pre-occupation with artistic freedom in Russia." [65]

"He has denied ever having been a member of the Communist Party. . . ."

## NOTES

1. New York *World-Telegram* (July 23, 1964), p. 2.

2. As quoted in "The Communist Position (1947)," pp. 14-16. See footnote 16, chapter 3.

3. Gus Hall, *Marxism and Negro Liberation* (New York, New Century Publishers, 1951), p. 19.

4. As quoted in "The Communist Position (1947)," p. 60.

5. C. Eric Lincoln, *The Black Muslims in America* (Boston, Beacon Press, 1961), p. 25.

6. New York *Times* (May 29, 1963), p. 32.

7. *Newsweek*, vol. 61 (May 6, 1963), pp. 27-28.

8. *Ibid.*

9. New York *Times* (August 1, 1963), p. 16.

Algerian Premier Ahmed Ben Bella meets Rev. Martin Luther King. The two are top leaders in a worldwide war of national liberation.

Martin Luther King is confident that "there are as many Communists in this freedom movement as there are Eskimos in Florida."

Hunter Pitts O'Dell was the district organizer in New Orleans for the Communist party. Later, while a concealed member of the central committee of the party, he was employed by Martin Luther King's Southern Christian Leadership Conference as executive director.

Martin Luther King addresses the assemblage at the 1957 Labor Day week-end meeting of the Highlander Folk School. King's second-in-command on many projects, the Reverend Ralph Abernathy, was also in attendance that weekend. The famous Communist folk singer Pete Seeger was another notable at these Highlander sessions.

This photograph of the audience during one speech at the Highlander 1957 Labor Day conference shows in the left foreground Abner W. Berry of the central committee of the Communist party. On the right, in the front row, is Martin Luther King. To King's right are Aubrey Williams, president of the Southern Conference Educational Fund, and Myles Horton, the director of the school.

Malcolm X, assassinated leader of the Black Nationalists, had claimed, "any Negro freedom movement not international in scope and perspective is foredoomed to failure. . . ." On another occasion he urged, "There ought to be a Mau Mau in the U.S."

*UPI photo*

Elijah Muhammad, leader of the Black Muslims, told a press conference in Los Angeles, according to United Press International, that the black race will rule the world by 1970. "The white men are the devils of the world. They have held the black man in slavery for hundreds of years," he added.

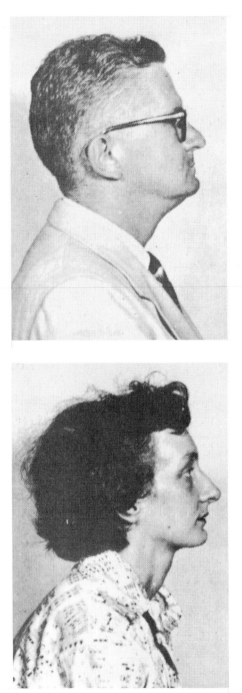

Carl and Anne Braden have been an active team in the Communist apparatus in the South. She is editor of the *Southern Patriot,* organ of the Southern Conference Educational Fund. He is field director for the SCEF.

James A. Dombrowski was at one time a Communist party leader. He served as executive director of the Southern Conference for Human Welfare, a Communist front. This group closed and in its place was formed the Southern Conference Educational Fund, today one of the leading powers in the civil rights movement. Its executive director is James Dombrowski.

Benjamin J. Davis, national secretary of the Communist party, has said that the conspiracy badly needs to stimulate a Negro youth movement in Harlem. He appointed Jesse Gray to do the job.

*UPI photo*

Jesse Gray is an identified Communist organizer, and a leader of New York rent strikes. His method of recruiting youth for the Communist movement: "you can trick them into this youth movement." He has urged guerrilla warfare by "black revolutionaries who are ready to die."

William Epton, right, a Communist and leader of rioting factions in Harlem in 1964, advocated violent overthrow of the government and assassination of policemen. Police have traced his source of funds to Communist China by way of Cuba.

*UPI photo*

Bayard Rustin was a member of the Young Communist League during his college days. In 1957 he was an "observer" at the national convention of the Communist party. Rustin, a leader of the 1963 march on Washington, has demanded that "more bloody Negro suffering should be encouraged so that squeamish Northern Negroes would be horrified into line. . . ."

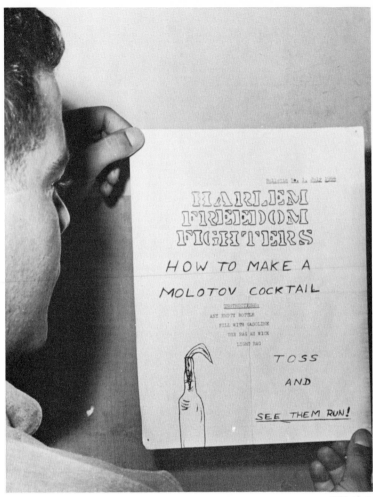

*UPI photo*

United States race riots in 1964 were not spontaneous affairs. Among many careful plans behind the actual events were instructions on making a deadly arsenal to use against police.

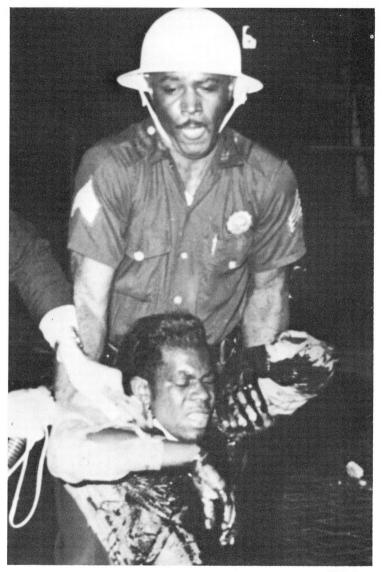

A Negro police sergeant in Jersey City, New Jersey, aids a badly wounded youth at the height of a second night of rioting in early August 1964.

A Brooklyn, New York, storekeeper sweeps up the broken glass early July 22, 1964, after rioters tore down the fence in front of his store and broke the windows. Massive violence was a common denominator of the 1964 and 1965 racial riots.

10. James S. Allen and James W. Ford, *The Negroes in a Soviet America* (New York, Workers Library Publishers, June 1935), pp. 37-38.

11. Elijah Muhammad, "The Muslim Program." See footnote 9, chapter 4.

12. *Ibid.*

13. Allen and Ford, p. 44.

14. *Muhammad Speaks,* vol. 3, no. 10 (January 31, 1964), p. 5.

15. *Ibid.* (July 1962), p. 16.

16. New York *News* (August 3, 1964), p. 5.

17. Lincoln, p. 251.

18. New York *Journal-American* (July 1, 1964), p. 8.

19. *Report 592 on the Southern Conference for Human Welfare,* House Committee on Un-American Activities, 80th Congress, first session (Washington, D.C., Government Printing Office, June 16, 1947). Also, *Testimony of Walter S. Steele, Hearings,* House Committee on Un-American Activities (July 21, 1947), pp. 136-141.

20. Rob F. Hall, "The Southern Conference for Human Welfare," *Communist,* vol. 18, no. 1 (January 1939), p. 61. Also see William A. Nolan, *Communism Versus the Negro* (Chicago, Henry Regnery Company, 1951), p. 115.

21. Francis Franklin, "The Status of the Negro People in the Black Belt and How to Fight for the Right of Self-Determination," *Political Affairs,* vol. 25, no. 5 (May 1946), p. 451. As quoted by Nolan, p. 55.

22. Georgi Dimitroff, *The United Front* (New York, International Publishers, 1938), p. 52. Also see Nolan, p. 12. Quoted from a report to seventh world congress (August 1935).

23. Resolutions of the Communist International on the Negro question in the United States (October 1930). As quoted in "The Communist Position (1934)," p. 54. See footnote 6, chapter 3.

24. James W. Ford, "The Struggle for the Building of the Modern Liberation Movement of the Negro People," *Communist,* vol. 18 (September 1939), p. 828. As quoted by Nolan, p. 115.

25. *Report 592,* p. 1. See footnote 19 of this chapter.

26. *Southern Conference Educational Fund, Inc.,* report of the Senate Internal Security Subcommittee (Washington, D.C., Government Printing Office, 1955), p. v.

27. *Activities of the Southern Conference Educational Fund, Inc. in Louisiana,* part 1 (November 19, 1963), p. 12. See footnote 14, chapter 6.

28. *Ibid.,* p. 13.

29. *Ibid.,* part 2 (April 13, 1964), p. 19.

30. New York *Times* (October 2, 1954), p. 6; also New York *Times* (December 14, 1954), p. 26.

31. *Activities of the Southern Conference Educational Fund, Inc. in Louisiana,* part 2, pp. 16-17.

32. *Ibid.,* part 1, p. 13.

33. *Ibid.,* part 2, p. 124.

34. *Ibid.,* p. 120.

35. J. B. Matthews, testimony before the Florida Legislation Investi-

gation Committee, vol. 1 (February 10, 1958, available in two volumes from Georgia Commission on Education, 19 Hunter Street, S.W., 220 Agriculture Building, Atlanta 3, Georgia), p. 21.

36. *Ibid.*, p. 22.

37. *Activities of the Southern Conference Educational Fund, Inc. in Louisiana*, part 1, pp. 13-14.

38. *Ibid.*

39. *Ibid.*

40. *Ibid.*, part 2, p. 85.

41. *Southern Conference Educational Fund, Inc.*, report of the Senate Internal Security Subcommittee, p. 45.

42. William A. Nolan, *Communism Versus the Negro* (Chicago, Henry Regnery Company, 1951), pp. 129-131.

43. *Activities of the Southern Conference Educational Fund, Inc. in Louisiana*, part 1, p. 25.

44. *Investigation of Un-American Propaganda Activities in the United States*, appendix IX, pp. 1466-1467.

45. New York *Times* (April 28, 1949), p. 6.

46. "I would like to mention in this connection that the Highlander Folk School at Monteagle, Tennessee, was a school organized by Myles Horton and Don West, and which Mr. Dombrowski shortly thereafter joined." *Testimony of Paul Crouch*, report of the House Committee on Un-American Activities (May 6, 1949), p. 193. Paul Crouch was the top Communist party official in the South. Also, *Activities of the Southern Conference Educational Fund, Inc. in Louisiana*, part 1, pp. 26-28.

47. *Testimony of Paul Crouch*, p. 191.

48. *Activities of the Southern Conference Educational Fund, Inc. in Louisiana*, part 1, p. 14.

49. *Tax Exempt Foundations*, report of the Special Committee to investigate Tax-Exempt Foundations and Comparable Organizations, House, 83rd Congress, second session (Washington, D.C., Government Printing Office, 1954), p. 399.

50. V. I. Lenin, *"Left-Wing" Communism*, published by "The Toiler" (no imprint and no date), p. 36.

51. *Activities of the Southern Conference Educational Fund, Inc. in Louisiana*, part 1, exhibit 9, affidavit of William Eldridge, p. 31.

52. Atlanta *Constitution* (July 24, 1963), pp. 1, 7.

53. New York *Times* (September 16, 1956), p. 54.

54. St. Louis *Globe-Democrat* (October 26, 1962).

55. New York *Times* (August 16, 1963), p. 10.

56. "Allen-Scott Report" (August 16, 1963).

57. *National Review* (August 20, 1963), p. 2.

58. Georgi Dimitroff, *The United Front* (New York, International Publishers, 1938), p. 66.

59. Annual report—1957, Senate Internal Security Subcommittee (Washington, D.C., Government Printing Office, 1958), pp. 36-40.

60. *Daily Worker* (April 12, 1957), p. 2.

61. *Ibid.* (February 25, 1957), p. 1.

62. Shreveport *Journal* (August 8, 1963), as inserted by Senator Strom

Thurmond (R., S.C.) in the *Congressional Record* (August 13, 1963), p. 14035.

  63. Richmond *News-Leader* (September 27, 1963), editorial.

  64. *Ibid.*

  65. Boston *Globe* (February 5, 1964).

## CHAPTER X

The King of the Eskimos

*Based on all available information from the FBI and other sources, we have no evidence that any of the top leaders of the major civil rights groups are Communists or Communist controlled. This is true as to Dr. Martin Luther King, Jr., about whom particular accusations were made, as well as other leaders.*[1] Former Attorney General of the United States Robert F. Kennedy

Okay. Fine. We've proved our point: This is quite a nasty crowd of people. But you are probably already asking: So what? What's it prove?

What's all this got to do with the Rev. Dr. King?

You will recall that on December 1, 1955, a nonviolent lady named Mrs. Rosa Parks, who is a Negro, refused to move to the back of a bus in Montgomery, Alabama, and thereby made the first move in what soon came to be the Montgomery bus boycott.[2] Mrs. Parks had no doubt been prepared for the adventure by a recent educational experience that included a course at an institution by the name of the Highlander Folk School, then located in the town of Monteagle, in the state of Tennessee.[3]

It was of course the Montgomery bus boycott, conducted by Dr. King, which thrust him suddenly from the shadows of obscurity into the dangerous glare of fame. Dr. King did his work at the head of an organization by the name of the Montgomery Improvement Association (MIA). The Montgomery Improvement Association had been formed by the Rev. Fred Shuttlesworth.[4]

*". . . Where possible we should build shop units and everywhere else units in the church youth organizations. Why? because in the South, especially for the Negro youth, the church is the center of all cultural and social activity. It is*

*here that we must work. By building our units in the church organizations, we can also improve our work under the illegal conditions, as it will be easier to work in the church organizations. In Alabama there are certain places in which we can in a short while take over the church organizations of youth, under our leadership, and these can become legal covers for our work in the South.*" [5] Communist official Gil Green, 1935

So the Rev. Fred Shuttlesworth and the Rev. Dr. King went about improving Montgomery. And in this they were joined by Bayard Rustin. For it happened that in this same year, 1955, Mr. Rustin had somehow managed to find employment as Dr. King's "secretary," and "adviser." [6]

Dr. King thinks very highly of Mr. Rustin. He describes him as "a brilliant, efficient and dedicated organizer and one of the best and most persuasive interpreters of nonviolence." [7] Indeed, he was even allowed to accompany Dr. King to Oslo, where Dr. King was awarded the Nobel Prize—for Peace.[8]

*"In the first place the communists, applying the tactics of the ultra-left period (1928-34), made the fatal error of alienating Negro ministers by such techniques as attacking religion and calling them 'social-fascist misleaders of the masses.' James Ford later admitted that this line proved to be a disastrous mistake. Time and again, the writer has been told in interviews that the leading force among the Negro lower class and part of the middle class is the ministers, and that no movement will succeed among the 'masses' which has not the approval of the Negro clergy. . . ."* [9]

So the three of them went ahead and improved Montgomery.

After they had improved Montgomery for more than a year, they held a meeting in Atlanta, in March of 1957, at which they formed the Southern Christian Leadership Conference (SCLC).

The meeting probably couldn't have been called in February because Mr. Rustin, Dr. King's "secretary," was then attending the sixteenth national convention of the Communist party.

The president of the Southern Christian Leadership Conference is the Rev. Dr. King.

The vice-president of the Southern Christian Leadership Conference is the Rev. Fred Shuttlesworth.[10] And the Rev. Fred Shuttlesworth is the new president of the Southern Conference Educational Fund[11] (also known as the Southern Conference for Human Welfare—they are the same organization), which is a Communist front, and whose field director, Carl Braden, is a national sponsor of the Fair Play for Cuba Committee, which is also a Communist front.

The program director for the Southern Christian Leadership Conference is the Rev. Andrew Young,[12] who is also administrator of the Dorchester Center near Savannah, Georgia, which is part of SCLC, and which uses the offices, rent free, of the Communist-infiltrated Mine, Mill & Smelter Workers. The Rev. Andrew Young was trained at the Highlander Folk School, then located in the town of Monteagle, in the state of Tennessee.

On the Labor Day weekend of this same year, 1957, at this same Highlander Folk School of Monteagle, Tennessee, many humanitarians gathered to discuss civil rights. A photograph of the events records the presence of Mrs. Rosa Parks. Charles Gomillion, dean of students at Tuskegee Institute, was there. Still another picture shows Fred Routh, an official of the Southern Regional Council, 63 Auburn Ave., N.E., Atlanta, Georgia, conducting a "workshop."

*"In addition to serving as a founder, vice president and principal organizer of the Southern Negro Youth Congress, he [James E. Jackson, Jr., national committee of the Communist party, editor of the* Worker] *participated in the formation and building of the Southern Conference for Human Welfare, the Southern Regional Council, and many other*

*movements which in any way challenged the status quo of*
*Negro oppression and Southern social backwardness."* [13]

The Rev. Dr. Martin Luther King, Jr. was there, of course,
with his close friend and associate, the Rev. Ralph Abernathy.
A photograph records Abernathy's presence. Another photograph shows the Rev. Dr. King addressing the assemblage
—perhaps at the very moment when he piled praise on
School Director Myles Horton, whose "noble purpose and
creative work," he has long admired, possibly because it has
included some cash to Dr. King. (See illustration section.)

Dr. King also mentioned Aubrey Williams, whom he
termed "one of the noble personalities of our times." [14]

Still another photograph shows the following individuals
enjoying a lecture: the Rev. Dr. King, who is of course a
nonviolent; Aubrey Williams, who is an identified Communist, was then president of the SCEF-HW, and is a probable
violent; Myles Horton, who is a friend of Communists and is
a teacher of Communists; and Abner W. Berry of the central
committee of the Communist party, a definite violent. (See
illustration section.)

Comrade Berry looks bored but the others seem to be enjoying the lecture very much. On the form letter of May 15,
1963, in which Director Horton explains that the Highlander idea has been "born again," the Rev. Dr. King is
listed as a Highlander sponsor.

"Need for this program became clear," the letter explained,
"as we developed the Citizenship Schools now being spread
throughout the South by Dr. Martin Luther King's Southern
Christian Leadership Conference and student civil rights
organization."

On October 7, 1959, the Rev. Dr. King wrote a letter to
Anne Braden—a definite violent—who, as you will recall, had
been indicted for sedition by the American state of Kentucky
and is the editor of the *Southern Patriot,* which is published
by the SCEF-HW, which also employs her husband Carl, an

ex-convict and also a violent, as field director. Louisiana Committee on Un-American Activities Counsel Jack Rogers explains at a hearing that

> in this [letter] *King urges Anne Braden and her husband, Carl, both Communist party members, to become permanently associated with the Southern Christian Leadership Conference. . . . Of course, the Bradens were well identified publicly as Communists long before the date of this letter.* We offer the letter.

The next document is a letter from Martin Luther King to James A. Dombrowski, dated August 16, 1960. It shows *the friendly personal relationship that had developed between these two men by that time.* It is very brief, I will read it to the Committee. It says: "Dear Jim: This is just a note to acknowledge receipt of your letters of recent date. *We, too, were more than happy to have you in our home,* the fellowship was very rewarding. I will expect to hear from you when Bishop Love returns to the country. At that time we can set the date for an Atlanta meeting. Very sincerely yours, Martin." [15] (italics added)

Dr. Dombrowski is executive director of SCEF-HW and is an identified Communist.

> King has cooperated closely with the Southern Conference Educational Fund since our last report [testified committee counsel Jack Rogers]. He filed a lengthy affidavit in the Federal Court in New Orleans strongly supporting James A. Dombrowski and the Southern Conference Educational Fund as "integrationists" of good character. When I saw this affidavit, I sent King three copies of our first report on the Southern Conference Educational Fund by air-mail, special delivery; and I sent him word through his attorney, Wiley A. Branton, Atlanta, Georgia, that he, King, could appear in Court in New Orleans and repudiate the affidavit if he so desired, on the basis of having been given evidence of the Communist connections and leadership of the Southern Conference Educational Fund. . . . If King were ever inclined to cleanse himself of the taint of Communism, this would have been a very excellent opportunity, well justified under the circumstances. I regret to inform the Committee that no answer, whatsoever, was received from Martin Luther King, and his affidavit still stands in the court record in New Orleans, in spite of his certain knowledge of the true character of the Communist leadership of the Southern Conference Educational Fund.[16]

Indeed, a photograph exists which shows the Rev. Dr. King along with Anne Braden, Carl Braden and James Dombrowski, the last three all identified Reds, the back of which reads as follows in Dombrowski's handwriting: "The 6th Annual Conference of the Southern Christian Leadership Conference, Birmingham, Alabama, September 25 to 28, 1962." [17]

In part two, page nine of the Louisiana report we read also of

> a check issued by the Southern Conference Educational Fund, Inc., signed by Benjamin E. Smith, and James A. Dombrowski, dated March 7, 1963, to the order of Dr. Martin Luther King, Jr., $167.74, with a notation on it, "New York expenses," and the endorsement of Dr. Martin Luther King, Jr., on the back. . . .

You will recall Robert F. Williams, who is a Communist and a violent. It seems that he, too, is on excellent terms with Carl Braden: "Dear Carl, We hope you and Anne are doing fine. We are all well. We were glad to see the review of NEGROES WITH GUNS in the *Southern Patriot.* . . ." [18] And so on.

Not long after, Dr. King traveled to Danville, Virginia, in the company of the Bradens.[19]

In 1960, "secretary" Rustin decided to quit. But Dr. King did not lose stride. Late in the year he hired a man named Hunter Pitts O'Dell.

You will recall that Mr. O'Dell was known in 1956 to be an important Communist official, and since 1961 to be a member of the national committee of the Communist party.

Newspapers pointed this out:

> A Communist has infiltrated to the top administrative post in the Rev. Martin Luther King's Southern Christian Leadership Conference.
>
> He is Jack H. O'Dell, acting executive director of conference activities in southeastern states, including Georgia, Alabama, Mississippi and Louisiana.[20]

So Dr. King fired O'Dell. He explains that O'Dell "may have had some connections in the past, but we were convinced that he had renounced them and had become committed to the Christian philosophy of non-violence in dealing with America's social injustices." [21]

". . . *Although as a Communist one is inwardly not religious—the statement continues—it is nevertheless of importance, and even vital for the expansion of Communism that one should pretend to believe in the purity and sublimity of religion.*" [22]

So O'Dell did some work at the Dorchester Center, which is run by the Rev. Young, and then as administrator of the New York office of SCLC, until pressure from the press forced Dr. King to fire him again.

"King said the Negro, Jack H. O'Dell of New York, left the SCLC the second time June 26 [1963] by 'mutual agreement' because of concern that his affiliation with the integration movement would be used against it by 'segregationists and race baiters.' " [23]

That ended it.

". . . *the Party is today engaged in a systematic program to infiltrate American religious groups. 'The Communist Party,' said the National Committee in 1954, 'declares that it seeks no conflict with any church or any American's religious belief. On the contrary, we stretch out our hand in the fellowship of common struggle for our mutual goal of peace, democracy and security to all regardless of religious belief.' Members are being told: 'Join churches and become involved in church work.'*" [24] J. Edgar Hoover, director, FBI

In fact, Dr. King

denied repeatedly a recently published report [in the Atlanta *Constitution*] that O'Dell was currently [July 1963] employed by the SCLC in any capacity.

The newspaper said he was director of the SCLC New York office. *A staff employee who answered the telephone Thursday morning told United Press International O'Dell was still with the office as administrator of the New York operation.* Later in the day the same office said he was not connected with the agency and had no knowledge of his whereabouts.

King told reporters he could not understand why anyone in his office would say O'Dell worked there when he doesn't. . . .

King said the O'Dell issue was being used in another attempt to forestall and hamper the true essence of today's civil rights struggle.

"It is another McCarthy-like tactic to destroy the movement," King said.[25] (italics added)

Dr. King becomes almost nauseated at even the thought of "McCarthy-like tactics," you see. If there's one thing he insists on, it's fair play:

". . . I think nothing threatens the health, the survival and the morality of our nation more than the possibility of Mr. Goldwater being elected President. . . . We see danger signs of *Hitlerism* in the candidacy of Mr. Goldwater." [26] (italics added)

"*. . . the increasing frequency with which communist terminology was being adopted to describe Negro events and problems in the Negro newspapers and other literature. For instance, it became commonplace to write about 'fascist police brutality,' 'fascist slave labor,' etc. . . .*" [27]

In fact, there are danger signs everywhere:

The subject of the real head-shaking is Rev. Martin Luther King. His influence is very great. His original dedication to non-violence can hardly be doubted. Yet he has accepted and is almost certainly still accepting Communist-collaboration and even Communist advice.

. . .

Official warnings have again been given to King about another, *even more important associate who is known to be a key figure in the covert apparatus of the Communist Party. After the warnings, King broke off his open connection with this man, but a second-hand connection none the less continues. . . .*[28] (italics added)

So when Communist official Benjamin J. Davis—a violent —describes Dr. King as "a brilliant and great practical leader who articulates the philosophy of the Negro people, for direct non-violent mass action" [29]—it should not be surprising.

When a *Worker* editorial praises him for giving "great inspirational leadership to the struggle of his people to bring down the wall of segregation and discrimination in the United States"; and describes him as "the foremost advocate of the solution of social problems through non-violent methods of mass action" [30]—*that* should not be surprising.

And it is not at all puzzling when the Rev. Dr. King says in a telegram to Jesse Gray, who is very violent and an associate of Malcolm X: "You have my *absolute* support in your righteous and courageous effort to expose the outrageous conditions that Negroes confront as a result of substandard housing conditions." [31] (italics added)

You see, Dr. King feels that

> This determination of Negro Americans to win freedom from all forms of oppression springs from the same deep longing that motivates oppressed peoples all over the world. The rumblings of discontent in Asia and Africa are expressions of a quest for freedom and human dignity by people who have long been the victims of colonialism and imperialism. So in a real sense *the racial crisis in America is a part of the larger world crisis.*" [32] (italics added)

That's why Dr. King's American Committee for Africa sponsored and financed the American tour of Communist Holden Roberto—a violent—leader of the Angolan "war of national liberation," which he began on the morning of March 15, 1961, with the killing and dismembering not only of a thousand whites but also of about eight thousand Africans.[33]

And that's probably also why, in October 1962, King turned up in a Harlem hotel suite with Communist bank bandit Ahmed Ben Bella—another violent—after which they joined in a statement that the two injustices of colonialism and American segregation were "linked." [34]

Dr. King does it, you see, because: "The Negro is shedding himself of fear, and my real worry is how we will keep this fearlessness from rising to violent proportions." [35]

## NOTES

1. United Press International story carried by the Jackson (Miss.) *Clarion-Ledger* (July 26, 1963), as inserted by Representative John Bell Williams (D., Miss.) in the *Congressional Record,* appendix (July 31, 1963), p. A4881.

2. For a study of the boycott, see Uriah J. Fields, *The Montgomery Story* (New York, The Exposition Press, Inc., 1959).

3. J. B. Matthews, testimony before the Florida Legislation Investigation Committee, vol. 1, p. 24. See footnote 35, chapter 9.

4. *Activities of the Southern Conference Educational Fund, Inc. in Louisiana,* part 1 (November 19, 1963), p. 13. See footnote 14, chapter 6.

5. Gilbert Green, *International of Youth* (Moscow, Young Communist International, March 1935), pp. 25-26. As quoted by Zygmund Dobbs, *Red Intrigue and Race Turmoil* (New York, The Alliance, 1958), pp. 52-53.

6. New York *Times* (August 10, 1964), p. 16.

7. Washington *Post* (August 11, 1963), as inserted by Senator Strom Thurmond (R., S.C.) in the *Congressional Record* (August 13, 1963), pp. 14033.

8. New York *Times* (December 10, 1964), p. 58.

9. William A. Nolan, *Communism Versus the Negro* (Chicago, Henry Regnery Company, 1951), p. 80.

10. *Activities of the Southern Conference Educational Fund, Inc. in Louisiana,* part 1, p. 13.

11. *Ibid.*

12. Atlanta *Constitution* (July 24, 1963), pp. 1, 7.

13. *Daily Worker* (December 1, 1954), p. 6.

14. *FACTS* (Pasadena, Calif., September-October 1964), p. 8.

15. *Activities of the Southern Conference Educational Fund, Inc. in Louisiana,* part 2, p. 84.

16. *Ibid.,* p. 85 ff.

17. *Ibid.,* part 1, pp. 99-100.

18. Letter dated April 23, 1963, as reproduced in *Activities of the Southern Conference Educational Fund, Inc. in Louisiana,* part 2, p. 30.

19. Richmond *News-Leader* (September 27, 1963), editorial.

20. St. Louis *Globe-Democrat* (October 26, 1962).

21. Richmond *News-Leader* (September 27, 1963), editorial.

22. Harry J. Benda and Ruth T. McVey, editors, *The Communist Uprisings of 1926-1927 in Indonesia: Key Documents* (Ithaca, N.Y., Cornell University, 1960), p. 17.

23. United Press International story carried by the Jackson (Miss.) *Clarion-Ledger* (July 26, 1963), as inserted by Representative John Bell Williams (D., Miss.) in the *Congressional Record,* appendix (July 31, 1963), p. A4881.

24. J. Edgar Hoover, *Masters of Deceit* (New York, Holt, Rinehart and Winston, Inc., 1958), p. 324.

25. United Press International story carried by the Jackson (Miss.) *Clarion-Ledger* (July 26, 1963), as inserted by Representative John Bell

Williams (D., Miss.) in the *Congressional Record,* appendix (July 31, 1963), pp. A4881-A4882.

26. Boston *Globe* (September 13, 1964).

27. Nolan, p. 235, footnote 51.

28. Boston *Globe* (April 15, 1964), p. 11.

29. *Worker* (November 10, 1963), p. 3.

30. *Ibid.* (September 15, 1964), p. 2.

31. *Ibid.* (June 2, 1964).

32. Martin Luther King, *Stride Toward Freedom* (New York, Harper & Row, Publishers, 1958), p. 191.

33. New York *Times* (March 20, 1961), p. 3. Intercepted instructions said "women and children should be singled out for attack to sow the greatest confusion and panic. . . ." Roberto was indoctrinated into Communism at an early age by Belgian Communists in the Congo, where in 1958 he formed the Angola People's Union, which absorbed the Angola Communist party. In 1960 Roberto was sent by the Russians to Moscow, and then to Prague and Leipzig where he was trained in guerrilla warfare. Of Roberto's "national liberation" activities, Brigadier General Frank L. Howley writes as follows in the *Reader's Digest* for November 1961: "It all adds up to a picture of primitive, hideous terror reminiscent of the Mau Mau outrages in Kenya at their worst; a picture replete with gruesome episodes of fetishist body-chopping, ritual cannibalism and tribal hatred. . . . Though its primary targets are whites and mulattoes, the vast majority of the murdered and maimed have been black Africans."

General Howley speaks of "a black girl of nine who had only just begun to open her eyes, after keeping them tightly shut since the horror struck her village. She had been forced to join in eating the flesh of her murdered mother. The shock had deprived her of speech and the ability to open her eyes."

34. New York *Times* (October 14, 1962), p. 20.

35. *Newsweek,* vol. 61 (May 6, 1963), p. 28.

## CHAPTER XI

The Rest of the Igloo

*[I am] sick and tired. . . .* The Rev. Dr. King

The activities of an organization of nonviolents known as the Congress of Racial Equality (CORE) have long puzzled rational men:

> . . . In San Francisco, a CORE group has attacked a chain of supermarkets by loading shopping carts with groceries, then dumping them on the floor around the cashiers' tables. In St. Louis, pickets have blocked access to a bank that had refused to hire Negroes. In Cleveland, CORE members have thrown themselves in front of a bulldozer working on the site for what would be a segregated school; one of them, a young white clergyman, was killed when the driver backed the bulldozer away, not knowing someone was behind him. In New York, CORE members have dumped garbage in the roadway to block a major bridge at rush hour, chained themselves to construction cranes, and jammed the stairs to a union office to keep the officers from going in or out. . . .[1]

The strategy is simple: "You do something that drastically inconveniences people, forcing them either to negotiate with you or to be violent against you. . . ." [2]

You expropriate a man's property, in short, so that he either has to divide it with you—because you are there—or forcibly throw you out.

If he does the latter, of course, he's morally wrong.

The Rev. Dr. King has been a member of the national advisory committee of CORE, and during the nineteen-forties Bayard Rustin was a field secretary.[3]

In fact: ". . . Some CORE chapters have been taken over by Black Nationalists and even Black Muslims; a few have come under strong Communist influence. . . ." [4]

But the man who makes CORE what it is, is its national

director, James Farmer; and though it is almost impossible to learn what Mr. Farmer really thinks—other than the fact that he is a specialist on police brutality—he seems to be some sort of moderate. After college, he went to work for the pacifistic Fellowship of Reconciliation, creating the job of race-relations secretary;[5] in 1946 he became a trade-union organizer and in 1959 the NAACP hired him as national program director.

> . . . Alone of all the major Negro leaders, Farmer refused to participate in the march on Washington in 1963. At leadership meetings, he had fought unsuccessfully for a demonstration *far more irritating* than a simple mass meeting. . . . His absence from Washington caused great offense among the other civil-rights leaders, as did CORE's refusal this summer to join the established Negro groups in calling for a suspension of demonstrations after the Harlem riots.[6] (italics added)

"CORE is the hard-cutting edge of the civil-rights movement," Mr. Farmer explains. "We're much more militant than Malcolm X—we're *activists*." [7]

And it seems he isn't kidding:

> According to an exclusive series of news stories in the Chicago American, based on many weeks of investigation, and printed in September of 1963, Communist efforts to infiltrate the Chicago organization of CORE had met with a substantial measure of success even by that date. Specific identification had been made of a number of Communists participating in CORE-sponsored picket lines and other demonstrations. Those included a former Daily Worker editor, Eugene Feldman, and the head of the 42d Ward Communist Club, Charles McCord. McCord has been for many years a close associate of Claude Lightfoot, vice chairman of the Communist Party of the U.S.A.; and Claude Lightfoot participated directly, in person, in the food-and-jobs demonstration at the Illinois Public Aid Commission in Chicago on January 31 of this year [1964]. Another participant in that demonstration was Theresa Ehrlich, identified as a "Stalinist" by the Worker, who participated in another demonstration in Chicago on May 14 of this year, when she tried to lead a hunger march on the Chicago office of Gov. Otto Kerner.
>
> Thirty-one persons who had been active in one or more sub-

versive organizations were among the so-called civil rights demonstrators in Cleveland in April of this year. This was disclosed when Mayor Locher, of Cleveland, gave a list of the 31 names to the Department of Justice. One of the names, according to the Cleveland press, was Eric Reinthaler. Reinthaler is not a casual hanger-on around the edges of the CORE organization. He is, or at least was in April, co-chairman of the finance committee of the CORE organization for the entire city of Cleveland, and according to police records he was one of the most active participants in the April demonstrations in Cleveland. Reinthaler has a long record of Communist activity. He presently claims that he is no longer a member of the Communist Party, and the party says the same thing through its current officers, both Reinthaler and the party stating that Reinthaler was expelled from the party for some unidentified violation of party discipline. The fact remains that Reinthaler was at one time secretary of the Communist Party for the entire Ohio Valley, and between April 1961 and July 1962, when he was released from Federal prison at Milan, Mich., he served 15 months on a conviction for filing a false non-Communist affidavit under the Taft-Hartley Act.[8]

*"But those who cannot coordinate illegal forms of the struggle with legal ones are very poor Revolutionists. . . ."*[9] V. I. Lenin

William S. Massingale, former vice chairman of the Communist Party of Missouri, and Communist candidate for alderman in St. Louis in 1943, is not a member of CORE; but he was extremely active in sit-in demonstrations at one of the major banks of St. Louis and at the St. Louis City Hall. These sit-ins were supposed to have been conducted by CORE, and their alleged purpose was to protest what CORE characterized as racially biased hiring practices at certain downtown St. Louis banks.

According to the St. Louis Globe Democrat, in spite of Massingale's Communist Party record, he not only denied membership in CORE but denied membership in the Communist Party as well.[10]

*". . . The only serious organizational principle the active workers of our movement can accept is: Strict secrecy. . . ."*[11] V. I. Lenin

On March 7, 1964, at the Sheraton-Palace Hotel in San Francisco, a woman named Tracy Sims conducted a demonstration in the hallowed tradition of nonviolence, in which the hotel was blockaded and no one was let in or out: "Her first arrest came last September, during sit-ins at a real estate office, organized by the Congress of Racial Equality. . . ." [12]

Tracy Sims "lives with Linda Carlson, daughter of Frank Carlson, a longtime Communist Party member in Los Angeles, and Rosanne Forest, daughter of Jim Forest, former Communist Party leader in St. Louis. . . ." [13]

She is the leader of an outfit known as the Ad Hoc Committee to End Discrimination, or the Ad Hoc Committee for the Sheraton Palace.

> The Ad Hoc Committee is composed of various pro-Communist youth and propaganda outfits from around the Bay, the major influence being exerted by the Dubois Clubs, Marxist-Leninist action groups. Ad Hoc Committee leader Tracy Sims was a guest of honor last January at the anniversary dinner of the *People's World,* West Coast Communist weekly. She is assisted by Mike Myerson, who is best remembered, however, for his part in running the "American" delegation to the 1962 Communist World Youth Festival at Helsinki.
>
> The cadres of the Dubois Clubs, and therefore the Ad Hoc Committee, are trained at a little-known Marxist academy, the San Francisco School of Social Science, located in a building owned by attorney and tireless Communist fellow traveler Vincent Hallinan. The school is run by a son, Terence Hallinan, and faculty members include former *Worker* Moscow correspondent John Pittman, former Castro employee J. P. Morray, and identified Communists (under oath) Holland Roberts, Irving Fromer, James Forest, and William Mandel. . . . Tracy Sims is a student there.
>
> Rev. King should examine the records of the 500 arrested [in the Sheraton-Palace and other demonstrations]. More than 200 have significant records in the CP, its fronts, or related activities. Intelligence agencies now know that at least eleven of those arrested are current CP members. Seventy-five of those arrested have Communist front records and, most important, 55 arrested demonstrators are the sons and daughters of long-time CP members. Some of the biggest names in American Communism are involved: the daughters of Mickey Lima, Joseph North, Herbert Aptheker, Louis Goldblatt, William Mandel, the sons of Mike Gold, Joseph Starobin, Frank Wilkinson and Albert E. Kahn. Two leaders, Marco Schneck and Beverly Radcliffe, declined to

testify before the House Committee on Un-American Activities about the Communist Youth Commission. . . .

. . .

. . . In mid-June San Francisco was the site of a convention called by Terence Hallinan, to found a new national "socialist youth organization." Signing the call to the convention were . . . *some Eastern CORE leaders,* and representatives of such exposed Communist youth enterprises as Advance, Progressive Youth Organizing Committee and New Horizons for Youth. . . .[14] (italics added)

On July 12 . . . a so-called human rights march in San Francisco had an identified Communist and a known leader of Communist fronts holding two top spots in the organizing group.

William H. Chester, vice president of a Communist front . . . and an officer of the International Longshoremen's and Warehousemen's Union, was coordinator of the march. . . .[15]

The other was Revels Cayton, who, as you will recall, was executive secretary of the National Negro Congress, and therefore had a hand in its petition to the United Nations.

. . . Half of CORE's $900,000 annual budget is spent in the South, and more than half its 40-odd paid "field staff" are there, setting up CORE's own voter-registration and desegregation drives in Louisiana, operating in uneasy alliance with the eager youngsters of the Student Nonviolent Coordinating Committee in Mississippi, working in somewhat happier collaboration with Martin Luther King's Southern Christian Leadership Council in Florida. . . .[16]

We have already learned something about SCLC. Let's have a look at the Student Nonviolent Coordinating Committee:

. . . Its close connections with the Southern Conference Educational Fund are demonstrated by the following documents. First, here are copies of eight checks from the Southern Conference Educational Fund payable to the Student Non-Violent Coordinating Committee. These are samples of a large number of such checks paid over the last two or three years. In one eighteen-month period, from December, 1961, to June of 1963, the Southern Conference Educational Fund gave the Student Non-Violent Coordinating Committee over ten thousand, three hundred dollars, ($10,300.00). . . .

The next document is a letter dated June 11, 1961, from Bob Zellner, an officer of the Student Non-Violent Coordinating Committee, addressed to James A. Dombrowski, showing that Zellner feared open identification with the Southern Conference Educational Fund, but was quite willing to cooperate with Dombrowski anyway. Note the stationery which is that of the Highlander Folk School in Monteagle, Tennessee. This has been previously well identified as a Communist Training School. Zellner comments in the letter that he would be at the Highlander Folk School for two or three months. We offer the letter.[17]

On February 28, 1962, James Forman, executive secretary of SNCC, sent a letter to Dr. Dombrowski:

We sincerely thank you for the last installment on the grant to Robert Zellner made by the Southern Conference Educational Fund.

May we take this opportunity to thank you for the other services rendered to the Student Nonviolent Coordinating Committee by SCEF. The cooperation we have received has made it possible to carry on a program despite the many obstacles we have encountered this past year.

Specifically, your efforts in raising bond money for the McComb students and members of our staff will long be remembered. The fact that SCEF has made available to us certain channels of communication has been vitally important to the movement in general.[18]

Committee Counsel Jack Rogers, of the Louisiana Joint Legislative Committee on Un-American Activities, concludes:

Without the help and backing of the Communist-led Southern Conference Educational Fund, the Student Non-Violent Coordinating Committee would collapse overnight. However it originally started, the Student Non-Violent Coordinating Committee is certainly now under the complete control of the Southern Conference Educational Fund through both money and leadership. . . .[19]

The Committee finds that the Southern Christian Leadership Conference and the Student Non-Violent Coordinating Committee are substantially under the control of the Communist Party through the influence of the Southern Conference Educational Fund and the Communists who manage it.[20]

Columnist Holmes Alexander speaks of

the cracking of the case, its documentation, its survival against Communist suppression attempts in the state and federal courts.

This report is no "McCarthyism," not a witch hunt, not a Redscare. It puts known Communists, those fingered by the FBI and by accredited witnesses, right in the agitation center of the Negro disturbance.

It links the Fair Play for Cuba Committee, a Castro front, by common membership to the Southern Christian Leadership Conference, the Student Non-Violent Coordinating Committee and the Southern Conference Educational Fund. *It ties Martin Luther King to Communist leaders like James Dombrowski, Benjamin Smith and Bruce Waltzer, all three under indictment for multiple violations of the Louisiana anti-Communist statutes.*

*. . . It traces the Communist-led race riots, which began in the South and moved to the North, through a maze of names like Bayard Rustin and King* which reappeared last summer in the march on Washington.[21] (italics added)

What it does in short is irrevocably to tie up the violents with the nonviolents.

What it does in fact is to show that *both are two legs on the same bug.*

The National Association for the Advancement of Colored People is of course to the Southern Conference Educational Fund as Tito is to Mao Tse-tung. It's a "moderate" organization, you see.

On February 10, 1958, at a public hearing of the Florida Legislation Investigation Committee in Tallahassee, Florida, Dr. J. B. Matthews testified as follows under oath:

Two examples of NAACP officials who are currently prominent in the affairs of Communist organizations will illustrate the interlocking of the NAACP and the Communist apparatus.

Andrew D. Weinberger, a national vice-president of the NAACP, is listed as treasurer on the 1957 letterhead of the Emergency Civil Liberties Committee, one of the most active Communist organizations in the United States at the present time.

John Wesley Dobbs, a national vice-president of the NAACP, is a member of the board of directors of the *Southern Conference Educational Fund,* the most influential Communist organization currently operating in the South. Mr. Dobbs was a guest of honor at a 1957 meeting of the Emergency Civil Liberties Committee. He was also a signer of the brief *amici curiae* submitted to the U.S. Supreme Court on behalf of the Communist Party in the fall of 1955.

It may be enlightening to give some totals which indicate the extent to which the top leadership of the NAACP has given aid and comfort to the Communist-front apparatus. Listed on the current letterheads of the NAACP are the names of 236 different national officers. One hundred forty-five (or more than 61 percent) of these individuals have been involved, in one way or another, with Communist enterprises, for a grand total of 2,200 affiliations of public record [an average of more than fifteen per name]. Forty-six of these NAACP national officers have had one or two Communist affiliations; 99 have had 3 or more such affiliations; 52 have had 10 or more; and 46 have had 15 or more.[22] (italics added)

The number of NAACP national officers who are affiliated —or at least were affiliated in 1958—with various Communist organizations we have already examined include: the Civil Rights Congress, 12; National Negro Congress, 20; Southern Conference Educational Fund, 23; Southern Conference for Human Welfare, 14.[23]

The *Congressional Record* of July 29, 1963, contains information from the files of the House Committee on Un-American Activities relating to fifty-nine of the officers, members of the board of directors, legal, health and other committees of the NAACP, as well as to certain members of the organization's executive staff. Between them, these individuals have been associated with more than 450 Communist fronts —cited as such by your government. Roy Wilkins, executive secretary, has seven citations; A. Philip Randolph, president of the AFL-CIO Brotherhood of Sleeping Car Porters, chairman of the 1963 March on Washington and national vice president of the NAACP in 1961, has twenty citations; John Haynes Holmes, national vice-president of the NAACP from 1954 to 1961, has thirty citations.[24]

And so on.

A founder and key official of the NAACP, the late W. E. B. Du Bois, had ninety-six Communist front affiliations, received the Lenin Peace Prize in 1959, and in 1961 finally announced his enrollment in the Communist party. He was responsible for the association's appeal to the United Nations.

*"The emergence of a powerful Left, anti-imperialist, anti-fascist current among the Negro people is unmistakable and is clearly discernible in the NAACP. This Left, anti-imperialist trend in the Association insists upon much greater attention by the organization to the pressing economic and political problems facing the Negro masses."* [25] Communist official Robert Thompson

It is important to remember that membership in a Communist *front* doesn't necessarily mean that a man is a member of the Communist *conspiracy*. As we have seen, the whole point to a front is to win the support for a specific, limited objective in the Communist program, of exactly those people who are not Communists, and thereby give that objective a good odor, or at least cover the smell.

You and I know this.

And of course, the gentlemen up at the NAACP—who are in the business of persuading people—know it.

So the most moderate position to take is that a civilian who belongs to a few Communist fronts may only have been victimized.

But for an official of the NAACP to belong to a dozen—that's reasonable grounds for suspicion.

Because he *knows* that an organization that promotes a Communist objective may very possibly be a Communist front —and that the whole point to a Communist front would be to cloak that objective with the "humane" reputation of the NAACP—simply because decent people won't support what the Communists support.

*"It is time, Comrades, that we salute the heroic leadership which the NAACP is giving to this far-flung struggle in the heartland of Dixiecrat racism. The NAACP in the South is leading a struggle against an implacable and ruthless enemy. We must support the NAACP in this struggle with every ounce of energy at our disposal."* [26] Political Affairs, official Communist magazine

## NOTES

1. Martin Mayer, "CORE: The Shock Troops of Revolt," *Saturday Evening Post* (November 21, 1964), pp. 79-80.

2. *Ibid.,* p. 79.

3. New York *Times* (August 10, 1964), p. 16.

4. Mayer, p. 82.

5. *Ibid.,* p. 81.

6. *Ibid.*

7. *Ibid.,* pp. 80-81.

8. Senator James O. Eastland (D., Miss.), speech, *Congressional Record* (July 22, 1964), p. 16037. See also, *Washington Report* (Chicago, American Security Council, July 20, 1964).

9. V. I. Lenin, *"Left-Wing" Communism,* published by "The Toiler" (no imprint and no date), p. 78.

10. Eastland, pp. 16037-16038.

11. V. I. Lenin, *What Is to Be Done?* (New York, International Publishers, 1929), p. 131.

12. San Francisco *Chronicle* (March 8, 1964), p. 1A.

13. Eastland, p. 16038.

14. M. M. Morton, "The Role of Communists in San Francisco 'Civil Rights' Agitation," *National Review,* vol. 16, no. 28 (July 14, 1964), p. 578.

15. Eastland, p. 16038.

16. Mayer, p. 80.

17. *Activities of the Southern Conference Educational Fund, Inc. in Louisiana,* part 2, p. 93. See footnote 14, chapter 6.

18. *Ibid.,* p. 105.

19. *Ibid.,* p. 110.

20. *Ibid.,* p. 126.

21. Beaumont (Tex.) *Enterprise* (April 27, 1964).

22. J. B. Matthews, testimony before the Florida Legislation Investigation Committee, vol. 1, pp. 41-42. See footnote 35, chapter 9.

23. *Ibid.,* pp. 44-46.

24. House Committee on Un-American Activities, file material, as inserted by Representative E. C. Gathings (D., Ark.) in the *Congressional Record,* appendix (July 29, 1963), pp. A4785-A4815.

25. *Political Affairs* (February 1950), p. 26.

26. *Ibid.* (January 1956), p. 17.

## CHAPTER XII

The Grand Alliance

*[I am] sick and tired. . . . The Rev. Dr. King*

Many Americans may now be saying—with characteristic generosity—that, look, the Rev. Dr. King is a *minister*. He has his head in the clouds, you see. He's all fired up with the fight for civil rights. And his good friend Bayard—who helped him accept the Prize—he's one of these "thinkers," you see. So what this is probably all about is just that they don't know what they're doing. Isn't that possible? Suppose they just couldn't tell the difference between a Communist and a thug in an alley—if there were any difference.

What if they're *naïve?*

Yes, it is possible. It is also possible that Dr. King is really Rip Van Winkle. So let's say no more about their party cards, and concentrate instead on their ideas.

As we have seen, the first step in the Communist program for the capture and communization of the United States is the manufacture of a "war of national liberation"—a suicidal attack upon "colonialist" whites, by Negro Americans who have been sold the idea that they are some sort of "oppressed nation." But this strategy is of course based on the idea of "race," and a Communist, as we all know, sees everything only in terms of economics: ". . . Political power is based not upon racial characteristics but upon classes. . . ." [1]

"*. . . the condition of the Negro has its roots primarily in the political and economic structure, not merely in the ignorance and prejudice of whites. . . .*" [2] The League for Industrial Democracy

So as is the case with all they touch, the Communists in the first step are *using* the idea of "race," and of course for

139

the usual purpose: to create division and promote hostility. And it is this hostility which will make the revolution.

The second step, as you will recall, is that after this hostility is well under way in the form of a "war of national liberation," the Communists will *turn* it, slowly, subtly,

*"The civil rights movement, which swelled so magnificently in the summer of 1963, was plunged into a new crisis the following winter. It had finally reached the Negro masses, but to hold and more fully involve them it had to transform itself, its leaders had to undergo a re-orientation, and new leaders had to be developed."* [3] The League for Industrial Democracy

so that after a while what people are mad at will not be whites—or blacks—but capitalism, because after all it isn't prejudice, or discrimination, that the Communists are so against—it's capitalism.

*"Rustin stressed that the Negroes' fight was shifting from a 'civil rights revolution' to what he termed 'a social and political revolution' in the United States. . . ."* [4]

Now, how would you do that?

Well, you would combine with your war of national liberation another strategy which—like equal rights and self-determination—may appear superficially contradictory: while Negroes and whites are killing each other in your war of national liberation, you begin to sell the idea that they should *unite,* form an alliance, against the *real* enemy—which of course is capitalism. You say that, yes, there is such a thing as racism, but somehow the cause of it is capitalism.

"The struggle for the further extension of democracy in the South," says Communist official Ray Hansborough in 1946,[5] "must be led by the working class, in alliance with the oppressed Negro people, the poor and middle class whites,

*"Rustin revealed"*—in 1964—*"that the civil rights organizations are seeking an alliance with what he termed the 'poor and unemployed whites'. . . ."* [6]

and the liberal bourgeoisie."

*"The Rev. Dr. Martin Luther King Jr. called today for a 'grand alliance' of American intellectuals, liberals and labor and religious leaders to fight the final battles in the civil rights struggle."* [7]

The main driving force [says Hansborough] must come from the working class in which the Negro workers constitute a sizable sector. The chief duty of the white and Negro Communist is to struggle for the unity of the Negro and white workers and for the unity of the labor movement in the South.

*"In order to assure that the work of democracy so well begun in the summer of 1963 will move forward steadily in the seasons to come," says Dr. King, "the Negro freedom movement will need to secure and extend its alliances with like-minded groups in the larger community.*

*"In the case of organized labor, an alliance with the Negro civil rights movement is not a matter of choice but a necessity. If Negroes have almost no rights in the South, labor has few more; if Negroes have inadequate political influence in Congress, labor is barely better off; if automation is a threat to Negroes, it is equally a menace to organized labor."* [8]

What are needed, writes Communist official John Pepper in 1928, are "campaigns to draw the white workers and the poor white farmers into the struggle for the support of the demands of the Negro workers and tenant farmers." [9]

*"In Chicago we have set up a pilot project to work among the poor whites in the tenement section," says Rustin, "and we are planning another in the poverty-stricken Appalachia area. We plan to organize these people into powerful groups."* [10]

". . . The Communist Party of America must emphasize in all its campaigns the solidarity of the white and black workers," says Pepper in 1928.

*Mr. Rustin believes "it is time to broaden the fight to include voter registration and economic issues and to seek alliances with liberal sources of power like labor unions."* [11]

Between the proletarian revolution and the revolution of the Negro people for land and freedom there is a living link [write Ford and Allen in 1935]. This is the working class. It is among the workers that solidarity first develops and is the strongest. In the cities and towns of the South and in the big industrial centers of the North this solidarity between white and Negro labor is forged. Here reposes the leadership of the two aspects of the revolution.[12]

*"An unusual factor in this strike is a strong link forged between the union and the civil rights movement.*

*"The Rev. Dr. Martin Luther King Jr., whose Ebenezer Baptist Church stands only two blocks from the Scripto plant, has set into motion a nationwide boycott of Scripto products by his civil rights organization.*

*"The Southern Christian Leadership Conference, headed by Dr. King, is distributing handbills saying 'Don't buy Scripto products.'*

*". . .*

*"In a television interview here [Atlanta] on Dec. 4, in commenting on the Scripto strike, Dr. King told a reporter:*

*"'We have decided that now is the time to identify our movement very closely with labor.'*

*"'Can we then assume that this is only the first?' Dr. King was asked.*

*"'That is right,' he replied. 'There will be many more to follow.' "* [13]

. . . one of our principal lines of activity [say Ford and Allen] has always been to develop now the solidarity of the white workers and Negro masses, to build this alliance in our daily life and struggles, to assure the combination of the two aspects of the American revolution.

The Highlander School's own leaflet claims that the "purpose of Highlander Folk School is to promote the progressive labor movement in the South," and announces a course in union problems which "deals with definite problems of the students as labor unionists. Methods of organizing, strike tactics, Labor Board procedure, education in unions, race relations are some of the things discussed. . . ."

The problem before all democrats [says Communist official Henry M. Winston in 1964] is to win the support of the white masses in the fight for equality. This is a struggle to raise the consciousness of the white workers, indeed of all white democratic Americans, as to the oneness of the needs of the nation in general and those of the Negro people in particular.

This is a struggle which should have a three-pronged aim. First, to enlist fully and on a higher level the active participation of the growing legions of white Americans who support the struggle for equality and freedom. Second, to assure at least the neutrality of the millions of white Americans who are rejecting in practice white supremacist ideologies, but are not yet prepared actively to support the struggle for equality and freedom. . . . Third, through the active participation of the first and the neutrality of the second, united with the labor and people's movement as a whole, to isolate the Dixiecrats and bring about bigger advances in the fight for civil rights.[14]

*As Bayard Rustin sums up: "We won in Birmingham and Washington only because we were able to split the white power structure. We must continue to do so. This is why I am advocating that we start now in winning the support of the poor whites in this country."* [15]

And as Gus Hall summed up in a recent, secret meeting in New York:

Gus Hall . . . told his fellow comrades the Red movement considers the Negro civil rights issue not as a racial problem but a part of the *class struggle leading to the eventual communization of America.*

Hence, the Communists regard the civil rights movement as the "link" the Reds can seize to create what they call Negro-white unity and class unity in the bigger fight against the so-called ruling class.

Hall ordered a concentration on the Negro struggle and outlined the tasks of the Communists. The picture, as sketched by Hall to the top Communist bosses, was to unite the Negro movement with the labor movement in a broad coalition. The party would play the leading or "vanguard" role to promote its own interests and move toward a Communist take-over in the U.S.[16] (italics added)

*"I can't resist telling you something I heard on the radio this morning. Bayard Rustin made a speech to an ADA*

*group in New Jersey last night and he said the Negro move-
ment is over—as a Negro movement. He said it's now going
to have to be a broad social movement, an alliance of all the
poor and organized labor as well as the civil rights groups."* [17]

Now, why is this alliance so important?

We have already had some dealings with the League for
Industrial Democracy. In August 1964, Mr. Rustin sent out a
form letter soliciting funds for it. He salutes the passage of
the civil rights bill. But: "You and I know that these are not
problems the Negro, however militant, can solve alone. Ultimately he needs white allies welded into a mass movement
for basic social change."

The point is that you can't get what Mr. Rustin calls "basic
social change," or "a social and political revolution," in the
United States, without black and white Americans being
"welded into a mass movement."

Neither the blacks nor the whites can do it alone.

*"The revolution for land and freedom in the South and
the proletarian revolution in the country as a whole will
develop hand in hand. Each will lend strength and support
to the other. The working class—both white and Negro—
will lead both.*

*"How does it come about that the white workers not only
will, but must lend their support to the struggle for Negro
liberation?*

*"First of all, because the workers will not be able to over-
throw capitalism unless they have the help of the Negro people. . . ."* [18] The Negroes in a Soviet America

I am a political actionist who believes that mass demonstrations
are among our most powerful weapons in the social and political
revolution [says Mr. Rustin], but we can't win unless we have the
wholehearted support of the trade unions, the unemployed and
the church groups.[19]

*"The Negro question in America must be treated in its
relation to the liberation struggle of the proletariat against
American imperialism.* The struggle against white oppression

of the Negro masses is a part of the proletarian revolution in America against capitalism. *The American working class cannot free itself from capitalist exploitation without freeing the Negro race from white oppression. . . ."* [20] John Pepper

So if black and white Americans want their "social and political revolution," there's nothing for it but to get "welded." Or as the Rev. Dr. King puts it:

The next step in the civil rights movement . . . would be "work in the field of political action and reform."

He said that American Negroes, by themselves, did not have sufficient power to take the struggle beyond the lunch counters, "and so the movement will have to depend on a constructive alliance." [21]

The question arises: Why will the white workers decide to join up? What's in it for them?

First, the movement has to put forward a broad social program for other deprived Americans as well as for Negroes [says the League for Industrial Democracy]. . . . And, since this broad program cannot be fulfilled by any ten percent of the population alone, Negroes have to seek as allies all who share their need for more jobs, better housing, better schools.[22]

"Certainly the Negro has been deprived," says the Rev. Dr. King.

Not all the wealth of this affluent society could provide an adequate compensation for the exploitation and humiliation of the Negro in America down through the centuries. Yet a price can be fixed for settling the debt. I am proposing that the United States launch a broad-based and gigantic Bill of Rights for the Disadvantaged.
    . . .
While Negroes form the vast majority of America's disadvantaged, there are millions of white poor who would also benefit from such a bill. . . .

It is a simple matter of justice that the U.S., in dealing creatively with the task of raising the Negro from backwardness, should also be rescuing a large stratum of the forgotten white poor. A Bill of Rights for the Disadvantaged could mark the rise of a new era, in which the full resources of the society would be used to attack the tenacious poverty which so paradoxically exists in the midst of plenty.[23]

And let's call this "Bill of Rights"—strictly for instance—a "war on poverty."

It's all a matter of the right tactics, says Michael Harrington:

> If you develop the right programs and tactics—like calling for more jobs for all, not for Negroes alone, better schools for all, not for Negroes alone, more housing for all—then you can make real allies among the white workers, the poor whites, and the liberals. What has to be done is to build large grass roots organizations in the Negro community to press for concrete social reforms related to the war on poverty—you'll see many white allies come in on these issues.[24]

*"For the revolutionist, the Revolution is everything, and 'reforms' are only a means to an end. What we are concerned with are not the reforms, but the uses they can be put to. A revolutionist may sponsor a 'reform' because he sees in it a means for linking up constitutional action with unconstitutional action—because he feels he can make use of it as a screen behind which he can strengthen his secret work."* [25]
Joseph Stalin

In April 1957, Bayard Rustin spoke at the City College of New York along with Eric Haas, of the Socialist Labor party, Myra Tanner Weiss, of the Socialist Workers party and Joseph Clark, foreign editor of the *Daily Worker*. Another speaker was Michael Harrington, who represented the Young Socialist League: "Harrington said a united socialist movement in this country must work primarily toward the establishment of a Labor Party." [26]

Mr. Harrington has since come far. In fact, he wrote a book called *The Other America*—which is all about the horror of life in America if you earn less than $3,000 a year—and which is now a big weapon in the war on "poverty":

> On June 24th and 25th, the organizing meeting of the Citizens Crusade Against Poverty was held in Washington, D.C. under the chairmanship of Walter Reuther. Labor, Civil Rights, religious

and social agency leaders determined to proceed with establishing a nation-wide coalition in support of the abolition of poverty in America. . . . Representing the LID and giving one of the three reports which opened the meeting, was Michael Harrington, who was also named to the Temporary Steering Committee.[27]

The way it worked, says Mr. Rustin, was that the Negro workers "stimulated Mike's book, they stimulated Johnson's program, which was in part stimulated by Mike's book, et cetera. It has an accumulative effect." [28]

There are a few kinks, of course, and these must come out:

In place of these youth training camps, Rustin proposed a multi-billion-dollar federal education program under which all students from the first through the 12th grades would be paid to go to school.

"This is done in the Soviet Union; why not here?" challenged Rustin. . . .[29]

## NOTES

1. James S. Allen and James W. Ford, *The Negroes in a Soviet America* (New York, Workers Library Publishers, June 1935), p. 40.

2. *LID News Bulletin,* vol. 5, no. 1 (Summer 1964), p. 1.

3. *Ibid.*

4. "Allen-Scott Report," *Human Events* (November 28, 1964), p. 6.

5. "The Communist Position (1947)," p. 46. See footnote 16, chapter 3.

6. "Allen-Scott Report," *Human Events* (November 28, 1964), p. 6.

7. New York *Times* (December 10, 1964), p. 58.

8. *Life* (May 15, 1964), p. 101.

9. John Pepper, "American Negro Problems," *Communist,* vol. 17, no. 10 (October 1928), p. 635.

10. "Allen-Scott Report," *Human Events* (November 28, 1964), p. 6.

11. New York *Times* (August 10, 1964), p. 16.

12. Allen and Ford, pp. 28-29.

13. New York *Times* (December 17, 1964), p. 46.

14. Henry M. Winston, in *Negro Liberation, A Goal for All Americans* (New York, New Currents Publishers, July 1964), p. 4.

15. "Allen-Scott Report," *Human Events* (November 28, 1964), p. 6.

16. Jack Lotto, Jackson (Miss.) *News* (November 9, 1963).

17. *LID News Bulletin,* vol. 5, no. 1 (Summer 1964), p. 4.

18. Allen and Ford, p. 28.

19. "Allen-Scott Report," *Human Events* (November 28, 1964), p. 6.

20. Pepper, p. 628.

21. New York *Times* (December 10, 1964), p. 58.

22. *LID News Bulletin,* vol. 5, no. 1 (Summer 1964), p. 1.

23. *Life* (May 15, 1964), p. 98.

24. *LID News Bulletin,* vol. 5, no. 1 (Summer 1964), p. 7.

25. From the Stalin archives of the National War College in Washington, D.C., as quoted in *Coronet,* vol. 29, no. 3 (January 1951), pp. 23-24.

26. *Daily Worker* (April 12, 1957).

27. *LID News Bulletin,* vol. 5, no. 1 (Summer 1964), p. 5.

28. Bayard Rustin, in "The Negro Movement: Where Shall It Go Now? —A Discussion," *Dissent,* vol. 11, no. 3 (Summer 1964), p. 285.

29. "Allen-Scott Report," *Human Events* (November 28, 1964), p. 6.

CHAPTER XIII **What Negroes Need**

*Money is the root of all these problems. Go down to skid row and you will find penniless men of every race standing up, sitting down, talking to each other and sleeping together in alleys—but give one of them a far greater share of money power and I guarantee you he won't associate with his old buddies until his money is gone.*

*If everyone had the same amount of money and opportunity, there would be no problem. Money is the problem.*[1] Letter from a white reader in Muhammad Speaks

Suppose you have to work for a living. Suppose you're an American who happens to be a Negro trying to earn a living, and you want to make it possible for yourself to advance—which of course would also make it possible for *all* Negroes to advance.

What do you need?

The question is no sooner posed than the answer becomes obvious. You realize that you need what *all* Americans, and all men everywhere, need. You need the newest, most revolutionary, most productive economic idea ever thought—which alone has given the average American the wealth of an ancient king.

We call it capitalism.

Even the Communists admit it.

. . . there is a rapid development of a Negro petit-bourgeoisie, a Negro intelligentsia and even a Negro bourgeoisie [Pepper complains as early as 1928!]. The very fact of segregation of the Negro masses creates the basis for the development of a stratum of small merchants, lawyers, physicians, preachers, brokers, who try to attract the Negro workers and farmers as consumers. . . .

. . . There were in 1924, 73 Negro banks, carrying an annual volume of business of over 100,000,000 dollars. There are 25 Negro insurance companies; 14 of these have assets totalling 6,000,-000 dollars and during 1926 alone paid over 3,000,000 dollars in

149

claims. *This Negro bourgeoisie is closely tied up with the white bourgeoisie; is often the agent of the white capitalists. . . .*[2]

Very interesting, isn't it? And remember that this is not the National Association of Manufacturers talking—it's the Communist International.

Even today—forty years later—blacks in Africa do not run businesses which do $100 million of volume a year, yet we know, of course, that blacks are blacks. So the reason cannot be that African blacks are "inferior" to American blacks.

The reason can only be that in America—in 1924—the capitalism was there which made it possible for blacks—and whites—to advance.

> From among the American Negroes in industry must come the leadership of their race in its struggle for freedom in the colonial countries [writes Communist official William F. Dunne in 1925]. *In spite of the denial of equal opportunity to the Negro under American capitalism, his advantages are so far superior to those of the subject colonial Negroes in the educational, political and industrial fields* that he is alone able to furnish the agitational and organizational ability that the situation demands.[3] (italics added)

And if this was already the case *forty years ago,* imagine what it would be today if, instead of less and less capitalism, we had gotten *more and more.*

Indeed, even though we *have* been getting less and less capitalism, American Negroes in 1963 had a total income—after taxes—of $21.9 billion—and they don't have this in Ghana. By 1960, they owned 1,974,000 homes, and today probably half a million more. ". . . Tens of thousands of these are worth over $35,000, and many of the latter are in Southern States." Negroes own 2,278,000 cars. In big, industrial areas their pay *"runs even higher than that of executives in England and continental Europe. . . ."*[4] (italics added)

Why is this?

Capitalism—unlike any form of collectivism: racial, religious or political—is based on the principle of individualism, on the idea, that is, that a man is an end in himself. Capitalism says that man is not a means to some mysterious end—such, for instance, as racial integrity—but that man himself is the end. It says that that is good. It says that that is what human life is all about. It says that that is what this country is all about—the schools, the theaters, the subways and the stores—Man.

*That's all.*

But racism is based on the opposite principle of collectivism, on the idea that a man is *not* an end in himself. Racism says that it is not the purpose of a man's life to live, but to play out some role in a genetic drama. It says in fact that if necessary a man should be *forced* to play it—*because* he isn't an end in himself. So racism can prosper only in an economic system based on the same principle: the principle of collectivism.

Racism, in short, can prosper *only* if the government can *force* a man to do what it likes—only under some sort of socialism.

It was the socialism of pre-revolutionary, czarist Russia that made possible all its racism. It is the socialism of Soviet Russia that makes possible all the racism there today.

The point is that capitalism discourages racism.

Capitalism not only discourages racism—it punishes it, by means of the very profit motive which has been so much maligned. A man who wants to make a profit—in his own interest, because he is an end in himself—has no time to worry about the shape of the next man's nose. He spends his time trying to hire the best man. He knows that *he has no choice* —no economic choice—because if he doesn't, the best man will go to work for somebody else.

A man who wants to make a profit does not refuse to do business—limit his market—because he isn't entirely pleased with the next man's nose. He knows that there is always someone else who is eager to do business.

So the point in short is that even if a man does decide to be a racist in a system of capitalism—real capitalism—he can't *force* his ideas on others, simply because—since in real capitalism the government stays out of business and business stays out of the government—he just hasn't the *force* to do it. His private neurosis remains a private neurosis.

It doesn't become government policy.

So if you are an individualist who happens to be a Negro —luckily living in capitalism—you simply feel for a moment that most unwholesome of emotions: pity—*for the racist*— and promptly bid him goodbye, with the sure knowledge that since you *are* an individualist, he, as a racist, does not deserve to know you.

The results are there for those who will see, and as we have observed, even the Communists see them.

They of course are against capitalism and have no real interest in seeing Negroes advance:

> . . . The communists must not forget for a moment that *the struggle for the national liberation of the Negroes includes the relentless struggle against the Negro bourgeoisie and the struggle against the influence of the petit-bourgeoisie over the Negro proletariat. . . .*[5]

In fact, says Manning Johnson, a Negro who spent ten years in the Communist party and was at one time a candidate for the politburo:

> The Negro business man has always been a chief target of the reds. They despise him because of his conservatism. They label him "a tool of the white imperialists" and an "enemy of the Negro masses." Such labels are reserved for those the reds plan to liquidate and since the Negro business man is an inspiration and example to other Negroes to take advantage of the countless opportunities of the free enterprise system, he is therefore an object of derision by Communists. An enthusiastic response of the Negro to the appeal and opportunities for Negro business is a cardinal bulwark against Communism. Consequently, the reds seek to discredit, discourage and liquidate Negro business.[6]

So it would be interesting, would it not, to see what our Negro leaders have to say about capitalism. This, unfortunately, is not so easy. As we have seen, they spend most of their time talking about police brutality and some sort of revolution, so they don't ever get to say exactly *what* sort they have in mind:

> In November, 1963, Rustin had spoken at the fourth annual conference in Washington of the Student Non-violent Coordinating Committee. He told those battle-seasoned activists: "Heroism and ability to go to jail should not be substituted for *an over-all social and political reform program* that will not only help the Negroes but one that will help all Americans. Only then can we win." His advice to the S.N.C.C. field workers, therefore, was: "Study. Read. Understand *the social changes which must take place* if there are to be integrated schools and jobs." [7] (italics added)

Mr. Rustin does not tell us what these "social changes" are. And he does not describe in detail his "over-all social and political reform program."

But there are indications:

The Leadership Training Institute for Civil Rights Activists, for instance, is conducted under the auspices of the League for Industrial Democracy, and according to Nat Hentoff has "partly been the product of Bayard Rustin." [8]

". . . The student body consisted of 25 of the most militant members of CORE in New York and four equally committed youngsters from HARYOU (Harlem Youth Opportunities Unlimited). . . ."

CORE is of course the organization conducted by James Farmer, who according to himself is "more militant than Malcolm X."

HARYOU is entirely paid for by public money.

Hentoff says the institute was held in Nyack, New York, at "Shadowcliff, the national headquarters and conference center of the Fellowship of Reconciliation." Pasadena Police Department arrest record No. 33914, which in 1953 described Mr. Rustin's qualifications as a sexual pervert, said he was then employed by the Fellowship of Reconciliation.

As we have seen, Mr. Farmer also worked for the Fellowship of Reconciliation and, as it happens, in the same position of race-relations secretary.

"At 11:30, all the students assembled in Shadowcliff's

sunny, first-floor conference room. *Norman Hill, national program director of CORE,* rose to start the Institute. . . ." (italics added)

A CORE member from East Harlem is reported to have explained: "You can't explain segregation, unless you point out that a 'nigger' is needed to keep up the capitalistic system." [9]

> In another workshop, a slim, intense, soft-voiced member of HARYOU was trying to explain his objections to capitalism. "What I'm saying," he spoke very slowly, "is that the ghetto is there because there's an economic need for it to be there. Capitalism is based on having a group you can exploit, and so long as you keep that lower class stabilized, you can go on exploiting the white as well as the black poor by encouraging the whites to use up their energies to KEEP the 'niggers' down."

You will recall that, according to Hentoff, this is "partly the product of Bayard Rustin."

This same HARYOU man tells us:

> . . . We've already divided Harlem into ten basic districts with a coordinator for each. And then each block has its indigenous captain. He contacts his friends in the various apartments and then we have house captains. When we really establish this kind of organization throughout the community, can you conceive of the things we can do? . . .[10]

The national program director of CORE, Mr. Norman Hill, was much in evidence at the institute. Mr. Farmer himself, the national director of CORE, once served as field secretary for the Student League for Industrial Democracy (SLID), according to a Texas legislative report, in which capacity he visited many college campuses. According to the SLID publication *Revolt:*

> The League for Industrial Democracy is a militant educational movement which challenges those who would think and act for a "new social order based on production for use and not for profit." That is a revolutionary slogan. It means that members think and work for the elimination of capitalism and the substitution of a new order.[11]

And what would you guess that new order might be?

The Rev. Wyatt Tee Walker is Dr. Martin Luther King's chief-of-staff and friend. According to the Rev. Walker: "If the Negro is to be given equality, our whole economy will have to be changed—probably to some sort of Socialism." [12]

In socialism you are "given" everything: food, housing, clothing and medical treatment—just as you were if you happened to be a slave on the Old Plantation. And all you have to do in return, of course, is the work—without any chance to make a profit—just as you did if you happened to be a slave on the Old Plantation.

But in capitalism you are "given" absolutely nothing. The whole point to capitalism is not that a man is disgusting, incompetent and by nature a slave, but simply that if the government does what it should—keep the criminals under control—he will create everything he needs *by himself*, because he is by nature a *creator*.

And as we have seen, it happens to work. The Jews came here and nobody liked the Jews—they were all shylocks—but then it turned out that they weren't all shylocks and that they weren't after all such bad fellows—and there was no need to install "some sort of Socialism." The Italians and the Germans came and nobody liked the Italians and Germans because of course the Italians were all gigolos and the Germans ate sauerkraut, but then it turned out that they weren't all gigolos and that sauerkraut is pretty good, and that they weren't after all such bad fellows—and there was no need for "some sort of Socialism." The Swedes and the Poles, the Greeks and the Chinese, all came here, all turned out to be not such bad fellows—and there was no need for any "sort of Socialism." The Irish came and, according to an Irish-American who wrote a pamphlet called *A Nation of Immigrants,* were warned in employment circulars that "No Irish need apply." No "sort of Socialism" was necessary, but in 1960 that Irish-American—John F. Kennedy—was elected president of the United States.

All prospered because they were free to prosper; because, that is, they had the benefit of the free economy of capitalism; because they were not automatically frozen into serfdom by some bureaucrat's whim.

All prospered because, since they *did* have capitalism, *it didn't make any difference* whether somebody else didn't like sauerkraut or didn't like Greeks, because *nobody else had the force*—the government—to do anything about it—*as in socialism.*

Yet here are the next *economic* newcomers, the Negroes, who would prosper just as much, but who, according to the Rev. Walker, need instead "some sort of Socialism."

Why?

Could it be that Rev. Walker has developed the idea that if just left to themselves, Negroes—unlike all other men— would be unable to create their own wealth—that Negroes are somehow inferior?

Could it be in fact that the Rev. Walker—chief-of-staff for Dr. Martin Luther King—is less interested in the Negroes than he is in the socialism?

What about the Rev. Dr. King?

William Worthy speaks of

> the correlation between the birth locally of nationalist groups dissatisfied with the "moderate" Negro organizations and the purchase by these groups' youthful members of the basic works of Karl Marx. . . .
>
> . . . the likely successors to Wilkins, King and Farmer are openly seeking intellectual, ideological and strategic guidance from the Chinese revolution. . . .[13]

And as we have seen, this creates the impression that Dr. King is in favor of "civil rights" but against "self-determination"; that what King & Co. want is somehow moderate; that they *don't* buy Marx.

In *Stride Toward Freedom,* Dr. King reveals that

> in spite of the shortcomings of his analysis, Marx had raised some basic questions. I was deeply concerned from my early teen days about the gulf between *superfluous* wealth and abject poverty, and my reading of Marx made me even more conscious of this gulf. Although modern American capitalism has greatly reduced the gap through social reforms, there was still need for a *better*

distribution of the wealth. Moreover, Marx had revealed *the danger of the profit motive* as the sole basis of an economic system. . . .

In short, I read Marx as I read all of the influential historical thinkers—*from a dialectical point of view,* combining a partial yea and a partial no. . . . My readings of Marx convinced me that truth is found neither in Marxism nor in traditional capitalism. Each represents a partial truth. Historically capitalism failed to see truth in collective enterprise and Marxism failed to see the truth in individual enterprise. . . . The Kingdom of God is neither the thesis of individual enterprise nor the antithesis of collective enterprise, but a synthesis which reconciles the truths of both.[14] (italics added)

Dr. King says here that he has been concerned about superfluous wealth. He doesn't say *whose* superfluous wealth worries him, or *how much* wealth is superfluous. He doesn't say *who* gets to decide—he doesn't have to. All he says is that this superfluous wealth makes a gulf and that "modern American capitalism has greatly reduced the gap through social reforms. . . ."

He doesn't say why it is that the more social reforms that are carried out, the poorer and poorer the Negroes become—according to the Negro leaders themselves.

*"The revolutionist will accept a reform in order to use it as a means wherewith to link legal work with illegal work, in order to use it as a screen behind which his illegal activities for the revolutionary preparation of the masses for the overthrow of the bourgeoisie may be intensified."* [15] Joseph Stalin

But he does say that what Negroes need is *more* social reforms and an even *"better* distribution of the wealth." He doesn't say *who* gets to decide what's "better." And he doesn't say, since his social reforms are what's keeping Negroes down—he doesn't say why Negroes need more of them.

But he does say that Marx showed up "the danger of the profit motive as the sole basis of an economic system. . . ."

He doesn't say why the profit motive is so dangerous. He doesn't say how wonderful it would be for Negroes to make profit. He doesn't say that if he stops the next man from making profit he stops Negroes from making profit, too. He doesn't say how Negroes can advance if they *don't* make profit.

But he does say that he does his reading "from a dialectical point of view." In other words he says he's thinking like Marx. And Lenin and Stalin and Mao Tse-tung. Because "dialectical materialism," the next logical step, is the theory "implying social transformation through socialism toward a classless society, which was advanced by Karl Marx and Friedrich Engels and adopted as the official Soviet philosophy." [16]

All Dr. King says is that he combines "a partial yea and a partial no."

In other words, he straddles the fence.

But he does say that "truth is found neither in Marxism nor in traditional capitalism. . . ." And he says that "The Kingdom of God is neither the thesis of individual enterprise nor the antithesis of collective enterprise, but a synthesis which reconciles the truths of both."

Now of course he doesn't say that there is simply no way to synthesize individualism and collectivism even a little bit without getting collectivism. He doesn't say that a little synthesizing makes nothing *new*—that all it makes is collectivism; that when you mix slavery and freedom all you get is more slavery; and that if a man is only half-free he is also all slave. He doesn't say that collectivism—and therefore Marxism—is nothing else but this synthesis and that there is and can be no such thing as pure collectivism—simply because, like it or not, a man *is* an individual, and the source of all enterprise is always one man's mind—so that if you start out with Marxism, you must end up with a "mixed economy."

*"Spurring what now appears to be an irresistible movement for the introduction of Western management techniques into Soviet economic life are the confusion and disarray of the Soviet economy that former Premier Khrushchev's successors inherited from him.*

". . .

"... *Western observers had noted that in 1963 Soviet agriculture suffered a disastrous grain harvest, while in recent years the growth rate of Soviet industrial production has slowed down steadily."* [17]

Dr. King doesn't say this.

He doesn't say that since the most pressing problem in this country was caused by collectivism—racial collectivism —it's collectivism that Negroes, and all Americans, have to get away from.

He doesn't say that in the context of his program to think in terms of "theses," "antitheses" and new "syntheses"—is nothing else but dialectical materialism.

And he doesn't say that—according to dialectical materialism—what is supposed, as he puts it, to "reconcile the truths of both" the thesis of Marxism and the antithesis of capitalism is of course a *revolution*—and that what's supposed to come out is Communism.

But he knows it.

## NOTES

1. *Muhammad Speaks,* vol. 4, no. 3 (October 23, 1964), p. 10.

2. John Pepper, "American Negro Problems," *Communist,* vol. 17, no. 10 (October 1928), pp. 630-631.

3. William F. Dunne, "Negroes in American Industries," *Workers Monthly,* vol. 4, no. 6 (April 1925), p. 260.

4. Victor Riesel, article, as inserted by Senator Strom Thurmond (R., S.C.) in the *Congressional Record,* appendix (July 20, 1964), p. A3752.

5. Pepper, p. 636.

6. Manning Johnson, *Color, Communism and Common Sense* (New York, Alliance, Inc., 1958), p. 58.

7. *LID News Bulletin,* vol. 5, no. 1 (Summer 1964), p. 2.

8. *Ibid.*

9. *Ibid.,* p. 3.

10. *Ibid.,* p. 6.

11. This quotation and this information about Mr. Farmer was reported by the Senate Committee on the Judiciary. The committee report was quoted in the Nashville *Banner* (July 26, 1963), as inserted by Senator Strom Thurmond (R., S.C.) in the *Congressional Record,* appendix (August 13, 1963), p. A14034.

12. Wyatt Tee Walker, remark made on television program "The Ameri-

can Experience," Richard D. Heffner, moderator (June 16, 1963), television channel 5, New York City.

13. William Worthy, "The Red Chinese American Negro," *Esquire,* vol. 62, no. 4 (October 1964), p. 175.

14. Martin Luther King, *Stride Toward Freedom* (New York, Harper & Row, Publishers, 1958), pp. 94-95.

15. Joseph Stalin, *Foundations of Leninism* (New York, International Publishers, 1932), p. 101.

16. *Webster's New Collegiate Dictionary* (Springfield, Mass., G. & C. Merriam Company, 1951), p. 228.

17. New York *Times* (November 22, 1964), sec. 3, p 1.

## CHAPTER XIV

# Equal Rights

> Another necessary alliance is with the federal government. It is the obligation of government to move resolutely to the side of the freedom movement. There is a right and a wrong side in this conflict and the government does not belong in the middle.[1] The Rev. Dr. Martin Luther King, Jr.

> Our task is to assign party members to the key points in the State apparatus, and to see to it that the apparatus is thus subjected to party leadership.[2] Joseph Stalin

Now that we have seen the men behind the Negro revolution —who they know, and what they think—the question arises: What are they doing? Let's give them still another chance to explain themselves by asking whether or not the struggle for equal rights and the struggle for self-determination are being used—as the Communists have planned—to communize the country.

Well, the struggle for equal rights consists so far of two elements: the civil rights act and the war on poverty.

So let's have a look at the civil rights act.

The Communists have always wanted one: *"Any act of discrimination or of prejudice against a Negro will become a crime under the revolutionary law,"* said Ford and Allen in italics in 1935.[3]

And so it was natural that the Communists supported such a revolutionary law in 1963: ". . . it is necessary first, to mobilize all possible support for the Administration's civil rights legislation. Its passage will place the role of the federal government in a new light and will thus constitute a major advance. . . ." [4]

How?

". . . Communists believe," says Communist official Benjamin J. Davis, that *"the achievement of this program* [legislation, etc.] will lay an *indispensable basis* not only for the further social progress of the country, but for its *socialist and communist future. . . ."* [5] (italics added)

Why?

The Communists have long been worried about the structure of our form of government. For example, Communist official Claude Lightfoot wrote:

> The structure of our form of government is a tremendous obstacle to any rapid advance. Our government is divided into three power structures (Legislative, Judicial and Executive). All three branches have certain powers which enable a canceling out process. This so-called equal distribution of power is nothing more than a built-in safeguard for reactionary policies.[6]

This is known of course as the famous system of checks and balances devised by James Madison and others for our protection, and taken in part from the "diffusion of power" principle—in Cicero's phrase—of the early Roman republic.

The idea—as Lightfoot is well aware—was to divide the federal government against itself, so that no one in it had too much power—and furthermore to separate it from the states, to balance the power of the federal government against the power of the states—also so that no one anywhere could collect too much power.

Why was this—and is this—so important?

> The states, which had stubbornly maintained their separate powers throughout German history, were the first to fall [writes William L. Shirer of an event in 1933]. On the evening of March 9, two weeks before the passage of the Enabling Act, General von Epp, on orders from Hitler and Frick and with the help of a few storm troopers, turned out the government of Bavaria and set up a Nazi regime. Within a week Reich Commissars were appointed to take over in the other states, with the exception of Prussia, where Goering was already firmly in the saddle. . . . The Chancellor, working at feverish haste, issued a new law on April 7, appointing Reich Governors (*Reichsstaathaelter*) in all the states and empowering them to appoint and remove local governments, dissolve the diets, and appoint and dismiss state officials and judges. Each of the new governors was a Nazi and they were "required" to carry out "the general policy laid down by the Reich Chancellor."

Thus, within a fortnight of receiving full powers from the Reichstag, *Hitler had achieved what Bismarck, Wilhelm II and the Weimar Republic had never dared to attempt: he had abolished the separate powers of the historic states and made them subject to the central authority of the Reich, which was in his hands. He had, for the first time in German history, really unified the Reich by destroying its age-old federal character.* On January 30, 1934, the first anniversary of his becoming Chancellor, Hitler would formally complete the task by means of a Law for the Reconstruction of the Reich. "Popular assemblies" of the states were abolished, the sovereign powers of the states were transferred to the Reich, all state governments were placed under the Reich government and the state governors put under the administration of the Reich Minister of the Interior. As this Minister, Frick, explained it, "The state governments from now on are merely administrative bodies of the Reich." [7] (italics added)

The point is that *the fewer reins of power there are, the easier they are to grab.*

Now of course, in the United States power is dispersed. So what you would have to do—if you were a Communist, of course—is to destroy those checks and balances—destroy the power of the states, as Hitler did, and concentrate all the power in one place, as Hitler did.

Let's have a look at the civil rights act:

It is 10% civil rights and 90% extension of Federal executive power. If this legislation becomes law and is upheld by the Courts—

—It will, in fact, extend Federal control over business, industry and over individuals (with a corresponding destruction of State power) in a degree that exceeds *the total of such extensions* of power by all judicial decisions and all Congressional actions since the Constitution of the United States was adopted.

*"The measures for strengthening socialism are: State monopoly of foreign trade, agricultural taxes, State purchase and sale of agricultural production, and an all-embracing plan for nationalization of industry, transport, and credit."* [8] Joseph Stalin

—It will, in fact, destroy the Constitutional checks and balances between the Federal Government and the States; and

—It will, in fact, destroy the Constitutional checks and balances between the Executive branch of the Federal Government and the Legislative and Judicial branches.

—*The "civil rights" aspect of this Legislation is but a cloak; uncontrolled Federal Executive power is the body.*

The authors of this remark, both past presidents of the American Bar Association, are Loyd Wright and John C. Satterfield, who continue:

If it is enacted, the states will be little more than local governmental agencies, existing as appendages of the central government and largely subject to its control.[9]

"*. . . At the present time this Negro zone—precisely for the purpose of facilitating national oppression—is artificially split up and divided into a number of various states which include distant localities having a majority of white population. If the right of self-determination of the Negroes is to be put into force, it is necessary wherever possible to bring together into one governmental unit all districts of the South where the majority of the settled population consists of Negroes. . . .*"[10] The Communist International

This legislation [continue Wright and Satterfield] assumes a totally powerful National Government with unending authority to intervene in all private affairs among men, and to control and adjust property relationships, in accordance with the judgment of Government personnel.

"*. . . The revolution will disfranchise and expropriate the present exploiting and ruling class. This, of course, will be done on the basis of class distinction and not race distinction. . . .*"[11]

It is impossible [they go on] to prevent Federal intervention from becoming an institutionalization of special privilege for political pressure groups.

"*. . . Thus, there are three basic demands to be kept in mind in the Black Belt, namely, the following:*

"*(a) Confiscation of the landed property of the white land-*

*owners and capitalists for the benefit of the Negro farm-
ers. . . ."* [12]

This must lead eventually [conclude these two past presidents
of the American Bar Association], not to greater human freedom,
but to an ever-diminishing freedom.

*". . . Within the limits of this state there will of course
remain a fairly significant white minority which must submit
to the right of self-determination of the Negro majority.
There is no other possible way of carrying out in a democratic manner the right of self-determination of the Negroes. . . ."* [13]

How does the act actually work?

The answer is in a minority report signed by six members
of the House Committee on the Judiciary:[14]

. . . In the language of the bill, "The President is authorized to
take such action as may be appropriate to prevent * * *" (sec.
711 (b) ), and "Each Federal department and agency * * * shall
take action to effectuate * * *" (sec. 602). This vests, of course,
almost unlimited authority by the President and his appointees
to do whatever they desire.

It is, in the most literal sense, revolutionary, destructive of the
very essence of life as it has been lived in this country since the
adoption of our Constitution. . . .

Let's consider the case of farmers:

The agencies required to police farmers, under the directions of
the Attorney General and the Commission on Civil Rights, are
all (1) Banks for Cooperatives, (2) Federal Land Banks, (3) Federal Intermediate Credit Banks, (4) Production Credit Associations, (5) the Agricultural Stabilization and Conservation Service, (6) the Commodity Credit Corporation, (7) the Federal
Crop Insurance Corporation, (8) the Agricultural Marketing Service, (9) the Farmers' Home Administration, (10) the Soil Conservation Service, and *all other* agencies or departments having
to do with Federal financial assistance in the field of agriculture.

*". . . All cotton will be sold directly to government agen-
cies either from the collective or state farms or by the cooperatives of the individual owners. Government credit will*

*be made available, on easy terms, to the poorest section of the farming population and to the collectives. . . ."* [15] The Negroes in a Soviet America

The various definitions contained in the bill, particularly titles II and VII, would extend "interstate commerce" so as to encompass substantially all intrastate commerce and thus bring under Federal control all phases of commerce, whether interstate or intrastate. . . .

The reported bill creates an Equal Employment Opportunity Commission to police and control the hiring, discharge, and terms of compensation, conditions and privileges of employment of all persons employed by any business or industry "affecting commerce" and which has 25 or more employees (title VII). . . .

The reported bill draws under Federal control inns, hotels, motels and other lodging houses, restaurants, cafeterias, lunchrooms, soda fountains, gasoline stations, motion picture houses, concert halls, theaters, sports arenas, stadiums, and other places of exhibition and entertainment. It also includes *any other* establishment located within the premises of a covered establishment or on the premises of which a covered establishment is located (title II). . . .

The banking system will be affected like this:

If a bank under this bill were to deny employment, a loan, a line of credit or a sales contract to a person, it would have to prove its decision was based on facts that did not, in any way, discriminate against the rejected applicant because of his race. Among the penalties that could be imposed on the bank would be the *cancellation of the bank's Federal deposit insurance and its right to handle GI, FHA, and other Government-insured money*. . . . If a small businessman . . . has been held in violation of the Federal civil rights law, under the provisions of this bill *the bank can be required to cease doing business with the culprit,* or else lose its FDIC protection for all its customers.
. . .

The agencies *required* to police banks and bankers, under the direction of the Attorney General and the Commission on Civil Rights, are all national banks, the Federal Deposit Insurance Corporation, the Federal Reserve System, the Federal Housing Administration, FNMA, and all similar agencies.

Among the institutions and agencies which would be required to conform to the act and police business and professional establishments are all banks, savings and loan associations, and other financial institutions served by the FDIC or the Federal Reserve System, the agencies administering GI, FHA, FNMA, SBA, and all other loans and programs involving Federal financial assistance. Withdrawal of protection of credit, foreclosure of loans, blacklisting, and similar sanctions may be expected.

If you own your own home you may also have trouble:

The right of homeowners in the United States to freely build, occupy, rent, lease, and sell their homes will be destroyed by this bill. . . .

Federal personnel (*not* the homeowner or his wife) will make decisions as to the personnel building the home, the renting of a single room or several rooms, as well as the rental, leasing, or sale of the home whenever race, color, or national origin is concerned. Federal personnel will also dictate the actions of realtors, developers, attorneys, and the lending institutions.

What of the right of property? What if the person who seeks to rent a room, lease or buy a home, is not, in the eyes of the homeowner, trustworthy or desirable? If race, color, or national origin is involved—and, by the nature of things, these *must* be involved—the Federal inspector (not the homeowner or his wife) makes the decision. The alternative—foreclosure, blacklisting, cancellation of any Federal benefits under any program.

*You may recall that soon after the Communists captured the government of Russia, they issued a decree, which decreed —to the centimeter—how much living space a man "needs," and if you happened to have more, they sent some "masses" to move in. The "masses" they sent were not Negroes. But that wasn't the point.*

*The point was that they had installed the principle that a man's home isn't his castle.*

The chickens of federal aid to education will also come home to roost:

The proposed legislation ultimately would result in total Federal control of the education processes in the United States.

Under provisions of this bill, the President and his appointees in Federal agencies would have the right to dictate pupil assignments in local schools and to approve the faculties (secs. 601, 602, 711 (b), title IV). The alternative would be the loss of all Federal aid (sec. 602). The child who is given lunch through Federal grant must also study under a federally approved faculty. This applies to every school, public or private, benefiting from programs involving Federal aid.

This despite the most solemn promises and assurances at the time the federal school lunch program was inaugurated that the federal government would *never* try to exercise any control of any kind over the schools because of this subsidy.

Even the unalienable right of freedom of speech would be affected:

> Title II, section 203, says: "No person shall * * * incite or aid or abet any person to do any of the foregoing," i.e., deny or attempt to deny any person any right or privilege described in the title.
>
> Read that language as you will, if this becomes the law it means that no editor could with impunity editorialize in opposition to its provisions.
>
> If a citizen takes a position in direct opposition to some provision of this title and a newspaper writes an editorial in support of that position, indeed, urges others to take similar stands, is that newspaper inciting, or aiding, or abetting? It would seem so (sec. 203 (a) (e) ).

The six dissenting members of the House Judiciary Committee conclude:

> The destruction of individual liberty and freedom of choice resulting from the almost limitless extension of Federal Government control over individuals and business, rather than being in support of the Bill of Rights, is directly contrary to the spirit and intent thereof.
>
> . . .
>
> In all the years Congress has pondered the equities of civil rights legislation, no committee has ever suggested for the executive such totality of power as is embodied in this package of legislation. Grant it, and our fire ball of liberty will spin into darkness, suffocate. For our Republic cannot live without breath and the breath of our Republic is personal liberty and personal responsibility.

Let's have one look at civil rights at work:

> Edward Rehm, a barber, was acquitted yesterday of charges that he had refused to cut the hair of two customers because they were Negroes.

He had been charged under the Illinois Public Accommodations Act, which forbids discrimination because of race, creed or color by operators of public services. Mr. Rehm could have been sent to jail for six months and fined $1,000 if convicted.[16]

So in the United States of America—the land of the free— a man can be sent to jail for six months, for refusing to cut somebody's hair.

According to the Rev. Dr. King, what we have to worry about is slavery. It was slavery that made the problem. And it is the "vestiges" of slavery that keep the problem alive. It's slavery that we have to get away from.

What is slavery?

A slave is officially defined as: "One whose person and *services* are under the control of another as owner or master." [17] (italics added) The point on the Old Plantation, according to Dr. King, was that some men's services were under the control of other men as masters.

And according to Dr. King this was wrong. It was slavery.

But according to Dr. King it's perfectly all right for the services of a man in Illinois to be under the control of another man as master. It's perfectly fine that a man can be sent to jail for six months for refusing to cut another man's hair. That's wonderful, that's okay.

That isn't slavery.

It's civil rights.

Yet the whole point to slavery, isn't it, is that a slave can't quit. Negro slaves couldn't quit the Old Plantation—and Mr. Rehm apparently can't quit in Illinois.

Those Americans of all colors who have endorsed this legislation in the belief that it has something to do with justice, should consider that a principle is "color blind"; that it *always* is applied *abstractly*—to *all* the specific people and things that give it life—because it *is* an abstraction; so the question of which side of it you're on is totally irrelevant.

If the government can say who must be hired, it can also say where you must work—because the principle you have installed is government control of employment.

If a man is forced to hire you to improve his "racial balance," you can be forced to work somewhere else, to improve someone else's—as a matter of principle.

If the government can say to whom you must rent, it can also say where you must live—because the principle you have installed is government control of housing.

But according to Dr. King—that's all right.

The fact remains, however, that it is irrational not to do business with a man for the sole reason that you aren't entirely pleased with his complexion. So the question arises: Suppose Mr. Rehm is wrong—in principle?

The answer, as James Madison labored long to make clear, is that Mr. Rehm has the right—the "unalienable right"—to be wrong.

If Mr. Rehm wants to be wrong—that's none of your business and none of mine, and none of Dr. King's. The whole point to this country, isn't it, is that you have the "unalienable" right to be wrongheaded *with your own property*.

The whole point to this country is that—since you *can* be wrongheaded with your own property *only*—you can't force anyone else to join you. Since all the government should properly do is not to issue welfare or to make morality but to protect the citizens—it doesn't make any difference whether someone happens to think Negroes are "inferior."

What does matter is that he has no way to force Negroes to believe it.

The point is that what some faceless integer thinks of you is of total unimportance. What counts is what you think.

If someone irrationally decides that you are "inferior"—that's not your problem.

It's his.

So a *man* doesn't prove him right by breaking into his store with a government gun.

What the *man* does is build his own store.

## NOTES

1. *Life* (May 15, 1964), p. 102.

2. From the Stalin archives of the National War College in Washington, D.C., as quoted in *Coronet*, vol. 29, no. 3 (January 1951), p. 23.

3. James S. Allen and James W. Ford, *The Negroes in a Soviet America* (New York, Workers Library Publishers, June 1935), p. 38.

4. "Peace and Civil Rights," an editorial, *Political Affairs*, vol. 42, no. 7 (July 1963), p. 7.

5. "The Time Is Now," *Political Affairs*, vol. 42, no. 8 (August 1963), pp. 30, 32.

6. Claude Lightfoot, "Turningpoint in Freedom Road" (New York, New Era Books, October 1962).

7. William L. Shirer, *The Rise and Fall of the Third Reich* (New York, Simon and Schuster, 1960), p. 200.

8. From the Stalin archives of the National War College in Washington, D.C., as quoted in *Coronet*, vol. 29, no. 3 (January 1951), p. 24.

9. John C. Satterfield and Loyd Wright, "Blueprint for Total Federal Regimentation" (Washington, D.C., The Co-ordinating Committee for Fundamental Freedom, n.d.).

10. Resolutions of the Communist International on the Negro Question in the United States (October 1930), as quoted in "The Communist Position (1934)," p. 47. See footnote 6, chapter 3.

11. Allen and Ford, p. 41.

12. "The Communist Position (1932)," p. 47. Last sentence is in italics in the original.

13. *Ibid.*

14. Document no. 914, Committee on the Judiciary, House, 88th Congress, first session, pp. 62-94.

15. Allen and Ford, p. 44.

16. New York *Times* (October 16, 1964), p. 4.

17. *Webster's New Collegiate Dictionary* (Springfield, Mass., G. & C. Merriam Company, 1951), p. 795.

## CHAPTER XV

The War on Poverty

*We do not know, and we cannot know, which of the inflammable sparks . . . will be the one to start the conflagration . . . we are, therefore, bound to utilize our new Communist principles in the cultivation of all and every field of endeavor, no matter how old, rotten and seemingly hopeless. . . .*[1]
V. I. Lenin

Soon after he was sworn in, President Johnson made a horrifying discovery: east side, west side, all around the town, in fact everywhere you turned in the land of the free—men were poor. Panhandlers blockaded every street. Toiling masses raised skinny arms as sneering industrialists barreled by, the bloated beasts. Behind every unwashed door stood an unkempt youth, unloved in an unswept room, belligerent because of his unemployed old man, who blamed it all on *his* unemployable old man, who howled and swore at the unmade bed—in which there was of course an unwed mother. Crazed with poverty as they were, many no doubt decided to emigrate —for a better life—to India. Even President Johnson himself was up against it. In all his underpaid years of government service he had managed to put together only five or ten million dollars.

It was horrible.

Humanitarians everywhere were delighted of course, for the existence of suffering was their chance to solve it, and at the same time they were worried. The problem was that, crazed with poverty though they were, many Americans might begin to wonder why, since they were crazed with poverty, it was necessary to send a few billion dollars a year of foreign aid to foreign countries; and why, after exactly thirty years of reforms designed to destroy poverty, they find themselves today even more overcome by poverty.

But President Johnson wasn't worried.

He decided to act.

He did act.

He declared war—on poverty.

The point was, as President Johnson loves to repeat, that

> The ancient enemies of mankind—disease, intolerance, illiteracy and ignorance—are not always going to prevail. There is going to be a revolution. There is going to be a rising up and a throwing off of these chains. If a peaceful improvement is not possible, if a peaceful revolution is not possible, a violent adjustment is inevitable.[2]

The president does not say what this revolution is all about. He does not even hint. All he says, as we have seen, is that one way or another we're going to get it.

The point is that if the people are not given what Bayard Rustin says they want, they will get crazed with poverty and make the revolution violent—just as they did last summer. But President Johnson—who is of course a nonviolent—says that he would prefer it to be nonviolent—so much so that he is even willing to sacrifice himself and lead it.

So President Johnson declared war on poverty:

> Those who exist within the ghetto are aware that officials in each of the riot cities have taken steps to participate in the Federal Government's newly enacted antipoverty bill, which will soon provide $861,500,000 for projects to help the poor. The problems of the poor are, for the most part, the problems of the Northern urban Negro.[3]

The principle behind it is as follows:

> We are going to try to take all the money that we think is unnecessarily being spent and take it from the "haves" and give it to the "have nots" that need it so much.
>
> [Because] strength and solvency alone don't quicken the heartbeat. The thing that really makes a great nation is compassion. . . .[4]

Remember that the author of this remark is the president of the United States.

Suppose you were the president of the United States, and

you made the decision to destroy poverty. What would you do?

If you were the president of the United States you would know that in a free society one man's fortune isn't the next man's handicap. In a free society it's the next man's opportunity to get a job and to make his own fortune.

You would know that it is only the man who "has" who can hire the man who "has not."

You would know that if you take from the "haves" (in a free society the people who because of their productive activities deserve the wealth) and give to the "have nots" (the people who don't), then the "have nots" will benefit only temporarily. They will consume what they have been given and will be much worse off than before because the men who "have" will no longer have the accumulated capital to make jobs.

You would know that the only way to enjoy consumption is to concentrate instead on production, and that every society that trades not in gold but in envy—that takes from the "haves" to win the votes of the "have nots"—always ends up by impoverishing all.

You would know that it is only in an economy where men are free to plan, to produce, to create, to accumulate capital, to make fortunes—so that they can make jobs—that men can best fulfill their economic drives.

And you would know that it was such a society that James Madison and his fellows had in mind.

You would know that Patrick Henry didn't go to all his trouble because he thought the purpose of the presidency would be to show how magnanimous you could be with the next man's money.

So what you would do, isn't it—if you really wanted to destroy poverty—would *not* be to take from the "haves" and give to the "have nots." What you would do is to make it possible for all to produce. You would begin removing the restrictions on creative men, on trade, on business and industry; you would begin to talk not about security, but about adventure, and not about open wounds but about skyscrapers; and you would realize that if you simply keep the criminals off a man's back—he will be perfectly able to produce what is needed to pay *your* wages.

But President Johnson didn't do this.

Instead he invented the war on poverty.

He set up to administer it an Office of Economic Opportunity.

He named as its director Mr. R. Sargent Shriver. And:

> Shriver sent for Michael Harrington, the young New York reformer whose book, "The Other America," first attracted widespread attention to the cycle of poverty that shuts millions of families out of any meaningful stake in this country's unparalleled general prosperity.
>
> "Now you tell me how I abolish poverty," was Shriver's blunt challenge as they sat down at lunch for the start of what turned out to be a two-week round of talks.[5]

We have already met the ubiquitous Mr. Harrington. He is the new chairman of the board of the League for Industrial Democracy,[6] which as you will recall is dedicated to the abolition of capitalism. Mr. Harrington is a socialist. As we have seen, he appears in the company of Joseph Clark of the *Worker*—the country's leading socialist newspaper. He is apparently a close associate of Bayard Rustin. In August 1964, Mr. Rustin sent out a form letter soliciting funds for LID. The Leadership Training Institute for Civil Rights Activists, which was "partly the product of Bayard Rustin," was "under the auspices of LID," and Mr. Harrington was one of the "intellectuals and activists from LID" involved.

He said:

> If you develop the right programs and tactics—like calling for more jobs for all, not for Negroes alone, better schools for all, not for Negroes alone, more housing for all—then you can make real allies among the white workers, the poor whites, and the liberals. What has to be done is to build large grass roots organizations in the Negro community to press for concrete social reforms related to the war on poverty—you'll see many white allies come in on these issues.

In fact it was he, apparently, who solved the problem of how humanitarians could declare war on poverty, when no one in this country really knew what real poverty was actually about; when—because of capitalism, of course—the poverty of even the poor people of Harlan County, Kentucky, includes their own automobiles, their own television sets and their own washing machines. It was Mr. Harrington, you see, who solved the problem of why American poverty is so unseen —apparently by saying that automobiles, television sets and washing machines *are poverty*.[7]

So Mr. Shriver made him a consultant.

Mull this over. An important official in the American government, who is said to have some experience in business, calls in a socialist, who is of course trying—as did Lenin— to destroy capitalism, the system that gave this country wealth, and asks him how to solve the problem of poverty.

Black, white, yellow or red, you have worked hard all week creating wealth, and Mr. Shriver calls in a socialist to help him spend it, to help him spend almost a billion dollars of your money.

As we have seen, the war on poverty has something to do with civil rights: "Sources in Washington," reports the New York *Times* on November 6, 1964, page twenty-six, "said yesterday that there was a good deal of high-level discussion at the White House on the future of the movement. 'It's being talked about more in terms of the poverty program than anything else,' one observer said."

The point of course, according to Mr. Harrington, is that the war on poverty will be the flypaper with which to catch some white allies.

The NAACP is naturally in on it: "The National Association for the Advancement of Colored People will put its major emphasis on efforts to involve Negro youths and adults in the Federal antipoverty program, Roy Wilkins, the executive director, said yesterday."[8]

In fact, says William Strickland, executive director of the

Northern Student movement—an arm of the Student Non-violent Coordinating Committee:

> . . . integration is no longer the issue. The issue is poverty. . . .
> Ultimately the problem of poverty is a political problem, and
> it can only be dealt with by the political organization of the
> poor. . . .[9]

And this of course raises the question of what the war on poverty is actually about. A moment's reflection reminds us that generous Americans already spend billions of dollars to fight poverty—so what's the point of this billion dollar federal program? We know that it is designed to produce the peaceful revolution Mr. Johnson so much desires, but the question remains of what sort of revolution it is actually to be.

Let's have a look at the war on poverty.

Mobilization for Youth is an outfit in New York designed to mobilize for youth. It is "an example of the action programs envisioned in the Antipoverty Act . . ." according to the New York *Times*.[10] Mobilization for Youth is in effect a government agency—since almost all of its money comes from the government: "Three Federal agencies have committed $8 million to its work, and the Ford Foundation has pledged $2 million. The city government provided $2.8 million through July 1 [1964], and has since allotted about $150,000 a month on a month-to-month basis. . . ."[11]

Which means that whether you are black, white, yellow or red, and wherever you are in the country, whatever mobilizing Mobilization for Youth has done—you have paid for.

On August 16, 1964, when Americans were still wondering about the recent riots, and only four days before President Johnson signed the antipoverty act, the New York *News* said that an investigation "indicated that left-wingers by the score have infiltrated Mobilization for Youth and diverted its funds and even its mimeograph machines to disruptive agitation." [12]

Two nights later, a "spokesman" for the agency itself "revealed," according to a front page story in the New York *Times*, August 19, 1964, that "Nine of the 300 staff members of Mobilization for Youth were members of the Communist party or of Communist-front organizations in the nineteen-thirties and nineteen-forties, a Federal Bureau of Investigation loyalty check has shown."

That check had been made a year earlier, in 1963, and "according to officials of Mobilization for Youth, showed that 14 members of the agency had been associated with leftist organizations. Nine of the 14 are still on the staff. None were dismissed as a result of the check." [13]

But humanitarians everywhere were not dismayed: On August 20, while President Johnson was signing the anti-poverty act in Washington, MFY chairman Winslow Carlton, at City Hall in New York,

> categorically denied a charge published in The Daily News that Communists had "taken over" the $12.9 million project. . . .
> Of course it is "possible," Mr. Carlton said, that some members of the 300-man staff may be Communists. He added that the agency had never investigated the political beliefs of its members and that up to now it had been concerned solely with their professional abilities.[14]

And so of course when the FBI checked again on August 23, soon after the trouble started, it found "that the staff of 380 included two present members of the Communist party, three other hard-core leftists and *at least* 32 persons with former links to leftists." [15] (italics added) That is of course to say, with "Communist or Communist-front organizations . . ." [16] which adds up to "at least" thirty-seven staff members who have been busy with Communist activity.

Mr. Carlton said on August 25 that he knew nothing about it—that he had not seen the report.

" 'There is absolutely no indication of Communist infiltration or of a Communist take-over of MFY at this time,' Mr. Carlton said." [17]

The New York *Times,* which also shows absolutely no indication of Communist infiltration, took a position on August 21, just before the new FBI findings were announced:

. . . Mobilization for Youth finds itself under attack on a basis long familiar to agencies dealing with the problems of the poor. It is accused of being honeycombed with Reds—a charge for which the only substantiation thus far is a Federal Bureau of Investigation report that nine of its 300 staff members were members of the Communist party or of Communist-front organizations in the 1930's and 1940's.

[The *Times* speaks of] the thinness of the evidence adduced up to now and the regularity with which such accusations have been made against administrators of home and work relief, unemployment insurance and every other newly established program for aiding New York's jobless. . . .[18]

An FBI report that several staff members of MFY have also been members of a gang of criminals—this, says the *Times,* is "thin evidence."

We learn in fact, in the same issue of the *Times,* that

Social workers fear that the attack on Mobilization for Youth may develop into a "witch hunt" involving all social agencies that receive Federal, state or local funds. They are concerned lest the city, frightened by right-wing criticism of the agency . . . may demand control over the agency's program.[19]

They are concerned, in short, that he who pays the piper will want to call the tune.

On the next day, the *Times* contained the following remarks:

Bertram Beck, associate executive director of the National Association of Social Workers, estimated that 50 per cent of the organization's 40,000 members have at one time belonged to groups that some would consider left-wing.

"I would hope," he said, "that every social worker at some time engaged in some social action that was non-conformist." [20]

And being a member of a band of criminals—why, that's very nonconformist.

Local 1701, Community and Social Agency Employees Union, the recognized bargaining agent for Mobilization of Youth employees, also issued a statement yesterday assailing the attack on the agency as McCarthyism.

"It is now apparent that the charges have been grossly exaggerated," the statement said.

"If a few zealous young employees have exceeded propriety in their dedication to the fight against the grinding poverty with which they are surrounded on the Lower East Side, this does not constitute prima facie evidence that they are subversives. . . ." [21]

Just because a few zealous young employees have joined the Communist party—why, that doesn't prove anything. Sure, it shows that they've exceeded propriety, that they're nonconformist, but just because you're a Communist doesn't prove you're a subversive.

All it may mean is that you're crazed with poverty.

"The American Civil Liberties Union and its local affiliate, the New York Civil Liberties Union, charged yesterday that the public airing of accusations of Communist infiltration of Mobilization for Youth was 'a throwback to the discredited era of McCarthyism.' " [22] The agencies hinted in a statement that City Council President Paul Screvane, who had the temerity to wonder whether public money should be used to employ Communists, "lacked both courage and the guidance of an elemental sense of justice," which "can only damage individual lives unfairly. . . ." The statement speaks of "rumors and unsubstantiated charges," and "guilt by association."

We learn on the same page of the *Times* of the charge by MFY staff workers that the attacks have been made by "deliberately irresponsible political elements."

We can be sure in short that even if some staff workers do turn out to be Communists, why, that's perfectly okay, because that isn't what's worrying "Federal officials." ". . . the presence of a few Communists in the lower echelons of the staff bother them much less than the mounting Republican attack on the social philosophy behind Mobilization for Youth." [23]

What's bothering them isn't the possible presence of a band of criminals in the pay of a foreign power—but criticism from some American citizens who are members of the opposition party.

In fact, Mobilization for Youth went out of its way to get square. On Monday, August 24, it was announced that MFY would investigate itself, and to do this MFY had hired an attorney named Philip W. Haberman, Jr.

But the directors were nevertheless still worried:

> Some of the directors . . . were reported disturbed by Mr. Haberman's comment Monday that the agency must discharge any employees who might be guilty of "the promotion of civil disorder or illegal activity."
>
> It apparently sounded to them as though Mr. Haberman had already decided on a purge. . . .[24]

In other words the directors seem perfectly willing to employ people engaged in illegal activity.

Mr. Haberman's later experiences, in fact, are worth recording:

> . . . Friends have told The News that Haberman was thwarted by MFY, with the agency withholding information from its own investigator.
>
> In fact, the situation became so tense that 10 days ago the MFY administrative staff tried to force Haberman to resign, according to information given The News. His attempts to learn the political leanings and backgrounds of MFY personnel have brought the reply that such information would violate the employees' civil rights.[25]

It is important to record that Mr. Haberman is not opposed to the work of MFY: "He said that he could find nothing wrong with the agency's support of rent strikes and protest marches, such as the march on Washington." [26]

The question persists: What was MFY actually doing? If it really is controlled by the Communists, that control will naturally show up in its programs. So what are those programs?

Well, as we have just seen, in 1963 MFY supported the march on Washington:

> . . . When Bayard Rustin, a pacifist, former Young Communist and convicted sex offender, organized the March on Washington, MFY recruited 500 marchers for him. . . . MFY also lent its enthusiastic support to Milton Galamison's school boycott. . . .
>
> . . . Another beneficiary was the neighborhood Reform Dem-

ocratic group, which printed campaign material on MFY facilities. . . .[27]

The explanation is simple:

Mobilization for Youth officials believe that Title II [of the anti-poverty act] gives them a mandate to support "legitimate" movements of social protest, such as rent strikes and school boycotts.[28]
. . . To the question of whether such programs can be carried on without alienating established community leaders, George Brager, a director of Mobilization for Youth, had this answer:
"It can't be done. These programs involve shifts in power and prestige. If somebody's gaining something, somebody else is giving something up!" [29]

Consider the plight of a citizen who owns some property, and another citizen who rents it, when the government that is supposed to defend them both decides to take from one and give to the other, to engineer a shift in power, that is to say, a peaceful revolution.
Mobilization For Youth

operates, in competition with private jobbers, a luncheonette, a service station, a woodworking shop, an auto repair shop and two espresso houses, and also provides workers for public housing construction; it provides all sorts of services—legal, psychological, tutorial, remedial, printing, secretarial, etc., and maintains a "narcotics program" and a "mental hygiene clinic," whatever they are. In July President Johnson described MFY as "one of the most promising in a variety of efforts to bring opportunity to neighborhoods where it has long been absent." [30]

You will recall the riots in the same month in the city of New York and that one of the demands then put forth was for a civilian complaint review board to investigate charges of police brutality. Mobilization for Youth was naturally in favor.[31]

You will also recall that posters then appeared in the streets, bearing the legend: "Wanted for Murder—Gilligan the Cop," referring to the police officer involved in the incident which was used as the excuse for the riots, and obviously designed to provoke hatred.

Note carefully where other printed items charging police brutality were prepared:

".  . . Mr. Haberman said he was still investigating the origin of a leaflet charging police brutality that had been printed on Mobilization equipment." [32]

In fact, on August 22, we read as follows in the New York *Times:*

> The police disclosed last night that two electric typewriters were stolen from the agency's offices at 214 East Second Street last weekend [that is, of course, as soon as the story broke].
>
> A department spokesman indicated that the typewriters might have been used to prepare inflammatory appeals during the Harlem and Brooklyn race riots, and that they were stolen to remove incriminating evidence.
>
> The police said no evidence was found of forced entry, indicating that the typewriters might have been stolen by an employee. . . .[33]

But the most fascinating of Mobilization's mobilizations is of course the rent strike.

Suppose you decided to conduct a rent strike.

Guess whom you'd call in:

"Among the beneficiaries of MFY assistance was Jesse Gray . . . who was offered 'a meeting place, staff guidance, mimeograph machines and postage' for organizing the Lower East Side rent strikes. . . ." [34]

Who else?

In fact, according to the New York *Times,* whose journalism in the case apparently consisted of a careful reading of the *News:*

> The Daily News, in stories charging Communist infiltration into Mobilization for Youth, gave prominent mention to Mr. Gray. The News said Mr. Gray "could be reached at any time through ORegon 7-0400," the phone number of the youth agency, and quoted a Mobilization for Youth spokesman as admitting that Mr. Gray had served the agency as "a rent strike expert consultant." [35]

So a man who has been identified as a Communist agent is invited into a government agency—and given what he needs to make his revolution.

Let's have a look at an MFY report entitled *The Community Organization Housing Program*. It describes the court system as "real-estate controlled and a tool for landlords." It continues: "A fighting, direct action program to organize low-income tenants is needed now." The purpose of the MFY housing program is

To organize tenants as a political force. . . .

In terms of MFY as a time-limited program, political organization is seen both as a means of effectuating change and as an end in itself.

We are drawing together and staffing a committee which will coordinate direct action campaigns in a militant manner.

This organization is an organization of organizations, contains the kind of fighting, sophisticated, politicalized organizations who are just itching to play out the "Jesse Gray" role and bring to the lower East Side what Harlem has begun.

[Mention is made of] coordination so that dozens of buildings are involved. Only massive rent strikes are effective in obtaining publicity, embarrassing the establishment, etc.[36]

*"The Negro miners' relief committee and the Harlem Tenants League are examples of united front organizations which may be set up as a means of drawing the Negro masses into struggle. But these organizations can be considered only as a beginning. The communists working within these organizations should try to broaden them, and similar committees should be organized in other Negro centers. . . ."*[37]

Now, how could Mr. Gray get so much influence? Well, on October 19, the *Times* described an MFY staff member named "Leroy McRae, who ran as a Socialist Workers party candidate for State Attorney General in 1962. The party is a dissident Communist group whose members are followers of Leon Trotsky."[38]

Which would mean that Mr. McRae is a Communist. You will recall that in June the Socialist Workers party "threw in with Malcolm X . . ."[39] who was of course an old pal of

Jesse Gray's, whom the Socialist Workers party also supports.

"Mr. McRae was hired nine months ago by Mobilization and was assigned to assist the rent strike on the Lower East Side. He was said to have worked earlier with Jesse Gray, the Harlem rent strike leader." [40]

So you would guess, wouldn't you, that by the date of this New York *Times* story, two months after the scandal broke, this Communist, who has worked earlier with an identified Communist, would long since have been fired. But of course, you'd be wrong:

"Last night, a Mobilization official said that Mr. McRae was still with the organization and had been through two hearings on subversive activities." [41]

You see, explains George Brager, who on that day was "action program director of Mobilization": "To my knowledge he fulfilled the functions of his job intelligently." [42]

Another leader of the rent strike sponsored by MFY was

named by the FBI in 1960 as a spy courier for the Soviet Union. . . .

Mrs. Esther Rand, 57, of 87 E. 4th st., executive secretary of the East Side Tenants Council, admitted to the New York Journal-American that she is the same woman accused as a co-conspirator in the case of Soviet spy Dr. Robert Soblen.

Mrs. Rand attended rent strike meetings at MFY headquarters, 215 E. 2d st., every other week for about six months from January to June of this year, said a spokesman for the youth agency.

Her tenants council, said Mrs. Rand, "performed several small services" for MFY, "such as submitting lists of slumlords."
. . .

Mrs. Rand staunchly defended MFY for doing "a splendid job," and charged that:

"I think there is someone behind this smear who is trying to destroy a very necessary part of the war against poverty. I think this scandal stinks!" [43]

Another lady whose salary you supplied is the "wife of a member of the U.S. Communist Party's national committee," and "an officer of the Brooklyn party organization in her own right. . . ." [44] She "was employed as a secretary by

Mobilization for Youth until recently . . ." the *News* reported as late as November 5.

> This latest example of Red infiltration of the scandal-ridden social service organization came to light as she and her husband took off from Kennedy Airport—along with four other U.S. Communist officials and the wives of two of them—on a pilgrimage to Moscow.
>
> The former MFY staffer is Mrs. Constance Bart, 101 Lafayette Ave., Brooklyn, whose husband, Philip, was general manager of the Worker when the party newspaper was a daily, and later was national organizational secretary of the party.

The *Times* also reported the departure for Moscow of Mr. and Mrs. Bart, but it said not a word about MFY—probably just wasn't fit to print.[45]

Well, several separate investigations tackled the whole mess. On October 18, 1964, in an interim report, Mr. Haberman—MFY's own investigator—urged the agency "to purge itself of subversives, tighten its fiscal controls"—oh, yes, it seems there had also been some freeloading—"and review its policy of supporting social protest activities." [46]

Mr. Haberman emphasized that he was " 'against loyalty oaths,' " but he thinks that "Mobilization should review its personnel hiring policy. . . ."

The *News* reported on November 6 that since it had revealed the results of its own investigation "there have been more than 50 staff resignations, both voluntary and at the 'suggestion' of the directors." [47]

The New York City report was unfortunately delayed for quite some time: "Findings have been so explosive that the report has been rewritten three times, each time in an effort to tone down the scandal—and phrasing acceptable to city authorities has not yet been devised." [48]

But early in November, it was finally released—the toned down version.

The toned down version, prepared under Council President Screvane,

> noted that Investigation Commissioner Fischel had received from the FBI nine names of MFY employees who allegedly had pres-

ent or past Communist affiliations or had engaged in subversive activity.

The Anti-Poverty Board also had received from confidential sources another list of 11 MFY help who allegedly had recent or present subversive affiliations.

Mr. Screvane explains—in the toned down version—that

> On a number of occasions . . . the Investigation Department had requested George Brager, present MFY administrative head, and Winslow Carlton, chairman of the MFY directorate, to direct certain MFY personnel to appear for questioning.
>
> "MFY," Screvane continued, "refused to honor such request unless the interrogation by the department were limited to such person's activities as an employee of MFY. Such limitation made it impossible to inquire properly into the alleged subversive or Communist affiliations of such MFY employees, which might be linked to their activities as MFY employees."

Mr. Screvane makes the point "that MFY had 'readily admitted' its activities in school boycotts and rent strikes, but had defended them as 'legitimate and consistent with the goals of the organization.' " [49]

It should be noted carefully that Mr. Screvane, like attorney Haberman, is not opposed to the idea of MFY. In addition to serving as council president, he is also chairman of the mayor's Anti-Poverty Operations Board, and says that the city " 'remains committed' to the original principles laid down for MFY, which are to help school dropouts and other disadvantaged youth find their way into productive activity." [50]

And on December 29, 1964, the New York State Senate Committee on the Affairs of the City of New York, under chairman John J. Marchi, issued its report.[51]

The committee identified seven MFY staff members by name: Mrs. Esther Gollobin—who is a member of the executive committee at MFY and a member of the New York county committee for the Communist party; good old Mrs. Bart—who it now turns out was administrative secretary of the World of Work program at MFY and is the Brooklyn educational director of the Communist party; Calvin Hicks—who is a group worker in MFY's Youth Action Program and in 1962, according to the report, became "a member of the lower Manhattan youth club of the Communist Party"; Archie Shepp—who worked in MFY's Coffee House Program, whatever that is, and was identified as "a member of the party's lower Manhattan youth club in 1962. In the summer of 1962, Shepp was a delegate to the Communist Youth Festival in Helsinki, Finland"; Carole Pina—who on June 12, 1964, "arrived in Cuba on a Castro-financed trip for students organized by Progressive Labor Movement," which is conducted, as you will recall, by Communist William Epton. "On her return from Cuba, Miss Pina received a second MFY grant from Aug. 1, 1964, to Jan. 31, 1965"; Marc Schleifer—who resigned when the going got rough. ". . . Schleifer was editor of . . . 'Negroes With Guns,' written by Robert Williams. . . . Schleifer spoke Dec. 14 at a rally of the 'May 2d Movement,' which was created with support of the PLM to organize on behalf of the Viet Cong (Communists) in South Viet Nam"; and our old friend Leroy McRae—whose Socialist Workers party is "on the attorney general's subversive list . . . ."

Marchi lists by letter only—H through W—16 persons "about whom the committee obtained *similar information* from sources of a confidential nature."

These include present and past employees who attended Communist-sponsored youth conferences in Helsinki, went to Cuba despite State Department ban, belong or belonged to the Communist Party, the PLM or the Socialist Workers Party.

Said Marchi: "The staff has additional information concerning more than 30 individuals connected with the MFY who have some alleged association with extremist or leftwing activities. Time has not permitted any evaluation of this material."

Addition at this point reveals in short, that as many as 53 members of Mobilization's staff may actually be professional Communist criminals.

Haryou-Act is another outfit all wrapped up in the war on poverty.

You will recall the Leadership Training Institute for Civil Rights Activists, which is under the auspices of LID, and which has "partly been the product of Bayard Rustin." You will also recall that the student body "consisted of 25 of the most militant members of CORE in New York and four equally committed youngsters from HARYOU. . . ."

You will recall that at the institute, a "slim, intense, soft-voiced member of HARYOU" carefully explained his objections to capitalism:

> What I'm saying is that the ghetto is there because there's an economic need for it to be there. Capitalism is based on having a group you can exploit, and so long as you keep that lower class stabilized, you can go on exploiting the white as well as the black poor by encouraging the whites to use up their energies to KEEP the "niggers" down.

And you will remember him explaining that:

> . . . We've already divided Harlem into ten basic districts with a coordinator for each. And then each block has its indigenous captain. He contacts his friends in the various apartments and then we have house captains. When we really establish this kind of organization throughout the community, can you conceive of the things we can do? . . .

Well, one of the things, according to the *Times,* is the establishment of a group known as the Haryou Cadets:

> The cadets, for instance, will offer uniforms to boys 9 years old and older. Military discipline will be instilled in the youngsters, who will drill with dummy rifles. Remedial schoolwork will be disguised in the form of military manuals. And the boys will have the chance to build pride in themselves by advancing rank by rank.
>
> Even now 106 cadets are being marched by Negro instructors into and out of P.S. 175, *fearing the discipline of simulated courts-martial* conducted by fellow cadets and preparing to teach other youngsters.

Kenneth Marshall, Haryou-Act program director, explains that in Harlem the Boy Scouts are considered "square and middle class." [52] (italics added)

Remember the Blood Brothers? "The gang leader is training a group of 17 juniors living in his block. His methods and the respect he commands from his 10-to-15-year-olds are not unlike those of a Marine Corps drill instructor." [53]

So you will be delighted to learn that on September 10, 1964: "The three-year Haryou-Act program that will pour $118 millions in federal and city funds into a self-help, anti-poverty drive in Harlem got under way . . . as Mayor Wagner signed an authorization granting the first city appropriation, $3,400,000." [54]

But a question arises which must be answered to insure justice:

Could it not be that what has happened in MFY, and what appears to have happened in HARYOU, is simply a fluke? Couldn't it be that it's all a mistake—an isolated mistake—and that as soon as it's corrected the war on poverty will proceed as it should—however that is?

How can we be sure we're not being unfair?

Well, Mr. Screvane, head of the antipoverty program in New York, says that Haryou-Act "has nationwide significance because 'what is done here, what works here, will be copied throughout the United States.' " [55]

The New York *News* says that MFY "was the pilot project in the anti-poverty campaign." [56]

And we can be absolutely sure that this is true, because according to the New York *Times*: "The organization is regarded as the prototype for the community action programs envisioned in Title II of the anti-poverty bill. . . ." [57]

Now, what would you guess our various national leaders would say about all this?

Well, the Committee for Community Action Against Poverty and Delinquency, which includes Alexander J. Allen, of the Urban League of Greater New York, James Farmer, national director of CORE, Dr. Edward S. Lewis and Dr. Arthur C. Logan, member and chairman of the board of directors of Haryou-Act, and Roy Wilkins, executive director of the NAACP, complained in an ad about "the campaign to destroy Mobilization for Youth, and to cripple or abort other efforts to deal creatively with these problems in the city, for self-help social action by slum dwellers inevitably arouses the hostility of those who see their interests threatened by it." [58]

The New York *Times* made its position clear in an editorial. Sure, Mobilization for Youth "has made mistakes." But that's just because it's a "pioneering project." What is important is that it "has broken important new ground . . . to restore the poor's sense of hope and purpose," and this "has been undermined by the ill-digested" Screvane report.

> . . . The real disservice in the Screvane report lies in its use of innuendo and repetition of accusations without supporting evidence. . . .
> . . .
> Mr. Screvane acknowledges that most of the expenditures by M.F.Y. have been worth while, but he challenges one of the most important aspects of its entire program when he casts doubt on the worth of its community action projects. If Mobilization for Youth is to do more than merely ameliorate the lot of the poorest elements of the community, it must teach them to help themselves by concerted efforts.
> Participation in such activities as rent strikes, school boycotts and last year's civil rights march on Washington has made powerful enemies for M.F.Y., some of whom are seeking to take advantage of its current difficulties to destroy it. . . .[59]

The New York state senate committee report is, according to another *Times* editorial, "a shocking way to conduct an investigation, a throwback to McCarthyism at its worst." [60]

But the response of your government, the government of all the people—that should stump you.

On November 18, long after the revelation that MFY had worked closely with Jesse Gray, an identified Communist, and with Esther Rand, named by the FBI as a Soviet agent, long after the revelation that MFY may actually have helped incite the New York race riots, long after the revelation that MFY paid the salaries of a Communist official and other Communists, long after it was known that more than fifty persons had quit their jobs since the story broke—and soon after its own investigator and an official agency of the city of New York had strongly criticized its employment of subversives and its social-action programs—Acting Attorney General Nicholas DeB. Katzenbach, a member of the cabinet of the president of the United States, in the approving company of Secretary of Labor W. Willard Wirtz, another member of the cabinet of the president of the United States, announced as follows as a spokesman for the federal government:

> I think the Community-action program is an important part of the whole program. And it has been endorsed by Congress.
>
> You never get anything done without someone jumping up and hollering. It's happened to Mobilization. It may well happen to Haryou.
>
> The important thing is to get in and get something done. From what I have seen today, this is true here. Things are being done.[61]

And you know—you can't argue with him. Things *are* being done.

## Notes

1. V. I. Lenin, *"Left-Wing" Communism,* published by "The Toiler," (no imprint and no date), p. 80.
2. New York *Times* (October 2, 1964), p. 20.
3. *Ibid.* (November 7, 1964), p. 56.
4. White House press release, as inserted by Representative William C. Cramer (R., Fla.) in the *Congressional Record* (February 6, 1964), p. 2227.
5. New York *Times Magazine* (November 22, 1964), p. 39.
6. New York *Times* (November 19, 1964), p. 27.
7. Michael Harrington, *The Other America* (New York, The Macmillan Company, 1962), p. 3. ". . . The other America, the America of poverty, is hidden today in a way that it never was before. Its millions are socially invisible to the rest of us. . . .
"Poverty is off the beaten track. It always has been. . . ."
8. New York *Times* (November 7, 1964), p. 56.
9. Chicago *Tribune* (November 17, 1964).
10. New York *Times* (August 21, 1964), p. 56.
11. *Ibid.* (November 11, 1964), p. 35.
12. New York *News* (August 16, 1964), pp. 2, 6.
13. New York *Times* (August 21, 1964), p. 56.
14. *Ibid.*
15. *Ibid.* (August 26, 1964), p. 18.
16. *Ibid.* (August 24, 1964), p. 12.
17. *Ibid.* (August 26, 1964), p. 18.
18. "Seeing Red on Youth Aid," an editorial, New York *Times* (August 21, 1964), p. 28.
19. New York *Times* (August 21, 1964), p. 56.

20. *Ibid.* (August 22, 1964), p. 22.
21. *Ibid.* (August 27, 1964), p. 30.
22. *Ibid.* (August 26, 1964), p. 18.
23. *Ibid.* (August 22, 1964), p. 22.
24. *Ibid.* (August 26, 1964), p. 18.
25. New York *News* (November 10, 1964), p. 3.
26. New York *Times* (October 19, 1964), p. 64.
27. *National Review* (September 15, 1964), p. 2.
28. New York *Times* (August 18, 1964), p. 15.
29. *Ibid.* (August 22, 1964), p. 22.
30. *National Review* (September 15, 1964), p. 2.
31. New York *Times* (August 22, 1964), p. 22.
32. *Ibid.* (October 19, 1964), p. 64.
33. *Ibid.* (August 22, 1964), p. 22.
34. *National Review* (September 15, 1964), p. 2.
35. New York *Times* (August 19, 1964), p. 26.
36. New York *News* (October 23, 1964), p. 5.
37. John Pepper, "American Negro Problems," *Communist,* vol. 7, no. 10 (October 1928), pp. 636-637.
38. New York *Times* (October 19, 1964), p. 64.
39. New York *News* (July 22, 1964), p. 13.
40. New York *Times* (October 19, 1964), p. 64.
41. *Ibid.*
42. *Ibid.* (August 27, 1964), p. 30.
43. New York *Journal-American* (August 21, 1964), p. 3.
44. New York *News* (November 5, 1964), p. 6.
45. New York *Times* (November 6, 1964), p. 3.
46. *Ibid.* (October 19, 1964), p. 1.
47. New York *News* (November 6, 1964), p. 2.
48. *Ibid.* (October 25, 1964), p. 3.
49. *Ibid.* (November 10, 1964), p. 3.
50. New York *Journal-American* (August 21, 1964), p. 4.
51. New York *News* (December 30, 1964), pp. 3, 12.
52. New York *Times* (August 27, 1964), p. 30.
53. *Ibid.* (May 29, 1964), p. 13.
54. New York *News* (September 11, 1964), p. 4.
55. *Ibid.*
56. *Ibid.* (October 25, 1964), p. 3.
57. New York *Times* (August 18, 1964), p. 15.
58. *Ibid.* (November 6, 1964), p. 28.
59. *Ibid.* (November 11, 1964), p. 42.
60. *Ibid.* (December 31, 1964), p. 18.
61. *Ibid.* (November 19, 1964), p. 1.

CHAPTER XVI  The Revolution in

the South

> First of all, we must consider the compact Negro farming
> masses of the "black belt" as the potential basis for a national
> liberation movement of the Negroes and as the basis for
> the realization of the right of self-determination of a Negro
> state. . . . *It is unquestionable that first of all the Negro
> farmers can be the basis of a Negro national liberation move-
> ment of the future. . . .*[1] John Pepper, 1928

In the fall of 1963, an outfit by the name of the Council of
Federated Organizations suddenly materialized in the state of
Mississippi. The organizations that got themselves federated
were the Congress of Racial Equality, the Southern Christian
Leadership Conference, the Student Nonviolent Coordinating
Committee and the National Association for the Advance-
ment of Colored People.

In fact, says Roy Wilkins, "the council was organized by the
N.A.A.C.P. . . . to coordinate civil rights activities in the
state. . . ."[2]

A gentleman by the name of Aaron Henry, of Clarksdale,
who is state president of the NAACP, is also president of the
Council of Federated Organizations.[3]

But, says Mr. Wilkins, COFO has since been "taken over"
by the Student Nonviolent Coordinating Committee,[4] which,
says Mr. Wilkins, "proceeds on most matters unilaterally without consultation with other groups."

You will recall that it was discovered by the Joint Legislative Committee on Un-American Activities of the State of
Louisiana that in one eighteen-month period, the Student
Nonviolent Coordinating Committee accepted more than $10,-
000 from the Southern Conference Educational Fund, which
is a Communist front.

You will also recall that in a letter dated June 11, 1961, on stationery of the Highlander Folk School in Monteagle, Tennessee, Mr. Bob Zellner, an official of SNCC, expressed to Dr. James A. Dombrowski, an identified Communist and an official of the SCEF, his complete willingness to cooperate.

You may have read the account by Carl Braden, who is an identified Communist and an official of the Fair Play for Cuba Committee and SCEF—which are both fronts of the Communist party—of his trip with Mr. Robert Moses, who is of course an official of SNCC and project director for COFO:

"Bob Moses and I traveled about 925 miles up and down and across the state in a period of six days. . . . We conducted workshops on civil liberties, nonviolence and the First Amendment." [5]

And you should definitely recall the conclusion of Louisiana Committee Counsel Jack Rogers that, "Without the help and backing of the Communist-led Southern Conference Educational Fund, the Student Non-Violent Coordinating Committee would collapse overnight," and the conclusion of the committee that SNCC is "substantially under the control of the Communist Party through the influence of the Southern Conference Educational Fund and the Communists who manage it."

In September 1963, SNCC sent a communiqué to the Southern Christian Leadership Conference, in which it called for "a massive, uniformed non-violent army of some 25,000 youngsters and adults in the Deep South."

The army would operate "under its own flag." [6]

". . . *It is incorrect and harmful to interpret the Communist standpoint to mean that the Communists stand for the right of self-determination of the Negroes only up to a certain point but not beyond this, to, for example, the right of separation. It is also incorrect to say that the Communists are only to carry on propaganda or agitation for the right of self-determination, but not to develop any activity to bring this about. No, it is of the utmost importance for the Communist*

*Party to reject any such limitation of its struggle for this slogan. . . ."* [7]

In the opinion of the Boston *Globe,* "known Communists have also begun to play a certain role in SNICK [SNCC]." And, the national chairman of the Student Nonviolent Coordinating Committee is John Lewis, who "quite frankly believes in quasi-insurrectionary tactics. . . ." [8]

Mr. Lewis feels that "the possibility of violence is justified . . . because 'out of this conflict, this division and chaos, will come something positive.' " [9]

And you know, it's a remarkable coincidence of course, but Marx felt the same way. In fact, Mr. Lewis's remark is nothing but a dramatic illustration of dialectical thinking.

What Marx thought would come out, of course, was Communism.

Mr. Lewis played an important part in the march on Washington. In fact at the Lincoln Memorial he made a speech, which unfortunately was marred when he was forced to delete the ripest passages. All Mr. Lewis wanted to say was

> "We will march through the South, through the heart of Dixie, the way Sherman did. We shall pursue our own 'scorched earth' policy and burn Jim Crow to the ground—non-violently."
>
> . . . Lewis went even further in a speech Feb. 20 of this year at a "freedom rally" in Nashville. He called for action ("non-violent" of course) that "would turn this Southland *upside down*" to rid it of "the evil of segregation." [10] (italics added)

*". . . This means complete and unlimited right of the Negro majority to exercise governmental authority in the entire territory of the Black Belt. . . . It would not be right of self-determination in our sense of the word if the Negroes in the Black Belt had the right of self-determination only in cases which concerned* exclusively *the Negroes and did not affect the whites, because the most important cases arising here are bound to affect the whites as well as Negroes. First of all, true right to self-determination means that the Negro majority and*

*not the white minority in the entire territory of the adminis-
tratively united Black Belt exercises the right of administering
governmental, legislative, and judicial authority.* . . ." [11] The
Communist Position on the Negro Question

> He urged "those of us involved in the freedom fight to bring
> about confrontations between the federal government and the
> state governments of the South." [12]

". . . *Only in this way, only if the Negro population of the
Black Belt wins its freedom from American imperialism even
to the point of deciding* itself *the relations between its country
and other governments, especially the United States, will it
win real and complete self-determination.* . . ." [13] The Communist Position on the Negro Question

What Mr. Lewis wants to do is "to precipitate a crisis in
Mississippi of such magnitude that 'the Federal Government
will have to take over the State.' . . ." [14]

Now of course, on first reading this seems a bit contradictory, doesn't it? If self-determination is what this is all
about, then why get the federal government to take over the
state? If what is wanted is separation from the United States,
then why call in the United States government?

Well, this *would* be a contradiction—if the United States
government were opposed to self-determination.

Self-determination usually takes place in a country the government of which is opposed to it—as, for instance, in the
Congo. As we have seen, the central government in the capital
of Leopoldville has been trying to put down a Communist
"liberation" movement in the provinces.

But you will of course recall the case of Algeria. The good
people of Algeria, Christian—*and Moslem*—wanted no part
of self-determination. They were, and wanted to remain,
French. It was in fact for this very reason, as you will of course
recall, that in 1958 the French army returned General de
Gaulle to power—because they were under the interesting im-

pression that he wanted to remain French. Unlike the American army in the United States, the French army in Algeria lived on an intimate basis with the people of Algeria, ran schools, and built roads, so that in its closeness to the people it was akin in a way to our national guard—and its leaders somehow developed the droll idea that General de Gaulle was a general of France.

But as "liberated" Algerians will bitterly recall, soon after General de Gaulle captured the central government, he used it to turn the army *against* the people, so that to its dismay it eventually wound up protecting not the people, but the forces of Ahmed Ben Bella, the Communist bank bandit who was *killing* the people. So that what de Gaulle did in effect to this "national guard"—to coin a word—was to "federalize" it.

Then he began to negotiate with the Communists, as if they were just another legitimate government—as if they had the right to as much authority in the French province of Algeria, as the provincial government in Algiers.

So that what de Gaulle had done in short, hadn't he, was to prepare the province of Algeria for self-determination by taking over the central government in Paris—and then, in effect, invading Algeria.

You may also remember—and if you are Polish you probably cannot forget—the story of what happened in Poland. During the Second World War, Stalin established in Moscow an outfit he called the Polish government-in-exile—which later came to be known among honest men as "the Lublin gang." Of course, the Lublin gang had nothing in common with the real government of Poland, which had been assured in Washington that we would not let it down. The Lublin gang was nothing more than a rival, a parallel, "government," solely designed to cloak with legitimacy the coming Russification and made possible in return only when the Red army actually took control of the ground.

You will recall that at Yalta the president of the United

States acquiesced to all this while under the influence of Joseph Stalin.

You are aware that we are still confronted with Communist control of Poland, in the person of the much admired moderate Wladyslaw Gomulka—who was a charter member of the Lublin gang.[15]

You will remember that in 1957, on the floor of the Senate, Senator John F. Kennedy announced his support of the Algerian rebels,[16] and after Kennedy became president he received Ben Bella as a guest in your White House.[17]

And you are of course also aware that we are still supporting Ben Bella in the form of food for those unfortunate Algerians who are starving as the inevitable result of Ben Bella's Communism.[18]

The point to self-determination is of course to create a parallel power structure—in the phrase beloved of Negro leaders—a phony government to rival the real one and claim to be legitimate, while awaiting the arrival of the power to sustain it.

You will remember that in 1957 President Eisenhower federalized the Arkansas national guard—and sent it into Little Rock.

And in 1962, President Kennedy sent still more federal troops to Mississippi.

So what we have to ask is whether or not what's happening in the South now has anything in common with what happened in Algeria.

Well, soon after COFO got started in the fall of 1963, it got to work on a remarkable idea. While the state of Mississippi conducted an election, COFO conducted its own election. It did not enter a candidate in the regular race; it simply conducted its own race—as if it were the proper authority in the state—in which eighty thousand individuals not legally qualified to vote cast counterfeit, and therefore officially uncounted, ballots for Aaron Henry for governor of Mississippi. That Mr. Henry did not win wasn't the point. No one ex-

pected him to win. The point was that here had been established the rudiments of a rival government in the state.

*"We have . . . avoided the errors we committed in the past.
For one thing, we did not enter into an academic debate or
fruitless speculation on when or how this right will be realized,
or precisely in what form. . . ."* [19] Eugene Dennis, general secretary, Communist party, 1947

The next thing COFO did was to found, in April 1964, the
Freedom Democratic party. At the Democratic national convention in August, two of the party's delegates actually were
seated when they challenged the regular Mississippi delegation, and the twenty-one regulars walked out in protest. So it
had been established, hadn't it, that the Freedom Democratic
party had as much legitimacy—or more—as the regular Democratic organization.

*"Further, in contradistinction to the past, we do not pre-
sent the slogan of self-determination as an immediate slogan
of action, but as the affirmation of a historic right which
guides and establishes the direction of all our work in the
South. . . ."* [20] Eugene Dennis

On December 23 in the House of Representatives of the
American congress, seventeen Democrats joined "in supporting
a plan to bar the seating of all five members of Mississippi's
delegation . . . on Jan. 4."

The plan, if adopted, "would prevent the Mississippians
from taking their seats pending the settlement of challenges
filed earlier this month by the Freedom Democratic party." [21]

*". . . The term 'Soviet Negro Republic,' therefore, does not
mean a Republic or a government composed exclusively of
Negroes. Whites as well as Negroes will participate in the new
power. . . . But the name 'Soviet Negro Republic' does express the fact that complete democracy, and the important role
played by Negroes in the revolution itself, have placed the Ne-*

groes in the bodies of government in accordance with their real majority." [22]

In February 1964, John Lewis announced in a brochure the forthcoming Mississippi summer project. The idea was

> This summer, SNCC, in cooperation with COFO, is launching a massive Peace Corps type operation in Mississippi. Students, teachers, technicians, nurses, artists and legal advisors will be recruited to come to Mississippi to staff a wide range of programs that include voter registration, freedom schools, community centers and special projects.

> *"In the institutions progress has been made by radical leaders parading as advocates of 'free milk, food and school books' for the student, better pay or better conditions for teachers, peace, unemployment and old age insurance, government control and ownership, and other 'appealing' doctrines; these schools are now the centers of strikes, riots, red meetings and graduating schools for new red leaders."* [23]

Because of course the point was that

> The struggle for freedom in Mississippi can only be won by a combination of action within the state and a heightened awareness throughout the country of the need for *massive federal intervention* to ensure the voting rights of Negroes. This summer's project will work toward both objectives. (italics added)

Also on hand was an outfit known as SDS (Students for a Democratic Society). Students for a Democratic Society was, until 1960, a part of the League for Industrial Democracy, now headed by Michael Harrington, the socialist who is advising your government how to spend your money.

*"Certain leagues and societies under the camouflage of 'debate' and so-called 'open-forums' have been established in every institution, and lead in the discussion of controversial subjects of a subversive nature. A certain organization specializing in this field has reached into 445 high schools, with propositions such as 'Recognition of Russia,' 'Capitalism Is a*

*Failure,' 'World Communism Will Supplant World Capital-
ism,' 'Communism Should Be Adopted in the United States,'
and so on.* Others bring to the front such subjects as doles,
social insurance, and other socialist and communist doctrines." [24]

"In the South," we read in an SDS leaflet, "we seek to build
informal groups . . . forming a 'counter-community' outside
the authority structure of their immediate environment."

*"I have already pointed out the role which the drawing of
the youth into the fascist organizations played in the victory
of fascism. . . ."*

*". . . The main task of the Communist youth movement in
capitalist countries is to advance boldly in the direction of
bringing about the* united front, *along the path of organizing
and uniting the young generation of working people. . . ."* [25]
Georgi Dimitroff

"Our sympathies lie most closely with the Student Non-
violent Coordinating Committee. . . . SDS groups carry on
fund-raising and serve as a northern liaison for its efforts."

At the same time, in February 1964, the National Council
of Churches decided to conduct a Delta project among the
residents of the Delta counties of Mississippi, where Negroes
comprise sixty-five to seventy percent of the population: "The
Delta area of the State of Mississippi manifests in full display
the total complexities of the problem of racial injustice and
persistent poverty . . ." you see.

"The main problem at this point," says the NCC, "is the
concentration of wealth among the few, e.g., on an average
5% of the farms control 50% of all farmland," which of
course is nothing that couldn't be cured by some "agrarian
reform."

*"The white masses on the land will support this new gov-
ernment for it will mean that their right to land is also recognized, that for the first time they, too, will have the benefits*

*of free public school education, freedom from usury, etc. The old South will no longer remain. The Negroes will come into their own."* [26]

Now as everyone knows, human life in Mississippi is simply impossible—especially if you're a Negro or an intellectual from New York. In fact, we learn from John Pratt, counsel for the Commission on Religion and Race of the National Council of Churches, it's a "police state."

"The truth in Mississippi is so unbelievable to one who has never been there that it is almost impossible to put into words." [27]

*"The Communist policy for the Communist infiltration of religion is a matter of tactics in the war against capitalism and religion . . . for enlisting their support for Soviet Russia and for the various campaigns in which the Communists were interested."* [28] Communist leader Benjamin Gitlow

A California preacher's daughter who was on the scene did put it in words: "This is Mississippi. It is hard to believe and maybe you don't. . . . Mississippi and our lives are measured by the sound of bombs in the night. Measured by how long it will take to get back from Sunflower to home and how long out of Natchez to safety. . . ." [29]

Now really! No humanitarian should send an untrained youngster into an inferno like that.

So the NCC went to work to train some youngsters. On the campus of the Western College for Women in Oxford, Ohio, under the sponsorship of the National Council of Churches, some seven hundred COFO recruits were thoroughly trained to expect hostility.

Now, suppose you wanted to establish, administer and pay for[30] a training center that would teach seven hundred freedom fighters about civil rights.

Guess whom you'd call in:

". . . Myles Horton, former head of the notorious High-

lander Folk School in Monteagle and now head of the Highlander Center at Knoxville, has been an active leader." [31]

Who else?

You couldn't even get started without also calling in Bayard Rustin, who "spoke to approximately 400 collegians at
the Civil Rights Training School at Oxford, Ohio, last
week." [32]

M. G. Lowman, executive secretary of Circuit Riders, Inc.,
"told the Enquirer that 'several groups co-operating in this
movement were founded by Communists—that is, with Communists in the background.' He said James E. Jackson, Jr.,
editor of the Daily Worker, is a behind-the-scenes man in
much of the summer project." [33]

*"Jim Jackson's constructive role in these movements stands
as an effective refutation of the imperialist lie that the Communists join popular mass organizations to 'use' them for
some ulterior motives. Throughout the South there are numerous leaders who could testify—and some day they will—
that Jim Jackson's contributions to the organization in which
they shared with him the labor 'in the heat of the day' were
always positive, helpful, and principled, whatever their dif-
ferences on the fundamental questions of class struggle and
the basic organization of society."* [34] Daily Worker

So it was no surprise that everything went according to
plan:

In a television interview seen in Meridian, Mississippi, on
September 21, a white COFO worker from New York explained: "We think the land should be redistributed."

And COFO workers cordially distributed the works of
Robert Williams,[35] who as you will recall is a close friend of
Mao Tse-tung.

In fact, soon after Mr. Williams explained in the May-June
issue of the *Crusader* that "Gasoline fire bombs (Molotov
cocktails), lye or acid bombs (made by injecting lye or acid in
the metal end of light bulbs) can be used extensively," "a

roadblock in Louisiana, searching cars for contraband, uncovered a substantial number of such 'lye bombs.' . . ." [36]

However, a couple of things did go wrong:

The New York *Times* reported the arrest for vagrancy in Moss Point, Mississippi, of "Ronald Ridenour of Dennis, Calif., a 24-year-old worker for the Student Nonviolent Coordinating Committee. . . ." [37]

What went wrong was that the *Times* forgot to mention that Mr. Ridenour

> was kicked out of Costa Rica in 1964 for carrying Communist literature into that country. The arrest was made after a riot in Costa Rica which resulted in the killing of four persons. Costa Rican authorities said Ridenour was an agent of international communism. When arrested in Costa Rica, Ridenour and a comrade had in their possession a large quantity of Communist literature, knives, and an automatic pistol. . . .[38]

Another thing went wrong when the San Francisco *Examiner* "printed an article on July 10 . . . about the desperate plight of what was described as a civil rights worker who had been jailed in Gulfport, Mississippi. The article was accompanied by photographs of the allegedly worried parents of the poor boy."

What went wrong was that the *Examiner* apparently forgot to mention that the parents were "Hugh B. Miller and Helen Schnedzler Miller, both identified as Communists in sworn testimony in 1957. . . ." [39]

Bob and Lisa Mandel, who, according to *Newsweek*, showed "a surprising tolerance even for the bitterest opposition," are described as

> 20-year-olds married at Reed College a bare three weeks earlier. [They] were picked up by police their second day in the delta. Trying openly to provoke Mandel to anger, one cop spat the filthiest of obscenities at Lisa. It didn't work. "You understand why this happens," she said later. "The community is afraid of us. They think we're here to hurt them. Well, I'm not backing down, but I do understand." [40]

The Mandels were not arrested, but what went wrong was that *Newsweek* apparently forgot to mention that "this particular Bob Mandel is the son of William M. Mandel, a Communist commentator with a long record of party activity." [41]

But you have to admit it was wonderful the way *Newsweek* happened to be on the scene.

Those who did happen to get locked up were well represented by counsel. Counsel for demonstrators arrested in Drew, Mississippi, for instance, were Frank Pestana, and Maynard Omerberg. The 1959 report of the California Committee on Un-American Activities states that Pestana was "repeatedly identified by witnesses" as a member of the Communist party. Maynard Omerberg was identified by the 1961 report of this same committee as, among other things, a lecturer in 1944 at the Communist school in Los Angeles. In 1951 he spoke and wrote for the Civil Rights Congress, which, as you will recall, was interested in transferring our sovereignty to the United Nations.

The National Lawyers Guild is also sending members to Mississippi to defend "rights workers." ". . . The National Lawyers Guild was first cited as a Communist front in 1944, and was described by HUAC in 1950 as 'the foremost legal bulwark of the Communist Party, its front organizations, and controlled unions.' . . ." [42]

George Crockett is

a member of the National Lawyers Guild, and the attorney who represented the chairman of the Michigan Communist Party in the New York City Smith Act trial. He was one of those placed in contempt of court by Judge Medina at the conclusion of that famous trial of Communist leaders, for his arrogant, provocative, and flagrantly contumacious conduct during the course of the trial.

Crockett was accompanied, in setting up his Mississippi headquarters for the legal defense of the invaders, by Mr. Benjamin Smith, of New Orleans. This Benjamin Smith has long been associated with the Southern Conference Educational Fund, with Mr. James Dombrowski and with Carl and Anne Braden, whose associations and activities are well known. This Benjamin Smith

. . . is registered under the Foreign Agents Registration Act as an agent of Fidel Castro.[43]

Martin Popper, counsel for the family of Michael Schwerner, one of the three "rights workers" murdered on June twenty-first, the first day of the COFO, is a guild official [44] and "a long-time Communist legal eagle, identified as such in December 1955. . . ." [45]

What really went wrong, we learn from a report in the New Orleans *Times-Picayune,* was that since, like all other people, all but a tiny handful of Negroes are thoroughly decent and want nothing to do with criminals, many of them became disillusioned with COFO because it did not screen out persons with Communist ties.

> The report said the Federal Bureau of Investigation had kept a check on persons involved in the council's project. "It found that two of every seven volunteers who came into the project had references to organizations on the bureau's subversive list," the report added. "Some were well-known figures in the Communist party." [46]

Makes you wonder, doesn't it?

". . . At present the group is spending $1,000 a week for such expenses as office rental, telephones and gasoline. COFO has 35 automobiles, 30 of which are equipped to communicate with field offices by radio. . . ." [47]

Makes you wonder what kind of war they are actually about.

## NOTES

1. John Pepper, "American Negro Problems," *Communist,* vol. 7, no. 10 (October 1928), pp. 632-633.
2. New York *Times* (December 1, 1964), p. 44.
3. *Ibid.*
4. *Ibid.*
5. Jackson (Miss.) *News* (August 31, 1962).
6. San Francisco *Chronicle* (September 24, 1963), p. 8.
7. "The Communist Position (1934)," p. 49. See footnote 6, chapter 3.

8. Boston *Globe* (April 15, 1964), p. 11.

9. San Francisco *Chronicle* (December 7, 1963), p. 4.

10. Shreveport *Journal* (July 1, 1964).

11. "The Communist Position (1934)," pp. 47-49.

12. Shreveport *Journal* (July 1, 1964).

13. "The Communist Position (1934)," pp. 47-49.

14. San Francisco *Chronicle* (December 7, 1963), p. 4.

15. *Current Biography* (New York, H. W. Wilson Company, 1957), p. 216.

16. New York *Times* (July 3, 1957), p. 1.

17. *Ibid.* (October 16, 1962), pp. 1, 3.

18. *Ibid.*, p. 3: "The United States has distributed about 11,000 tents and 210,000 metric tons of surplus food, mostly wheat. In addition, a 25-man medical team has been serving in an Algiers hospital since July."

19. "The Communist Position (1947)," pp. 24-25. See footnote 16, chapter 3.

20. *Ibid.*

21. New York *Times* (December 24, 1964), p. 17.

22. James S. Allen and James W. Ford, *The Negroes in a Soviet America* (New York, Workers Library Publishers, June 1935), p. 41.

23. Walter S. Steele, "Reds Train Youth to Revolt," *National Republic,* vol. 20, no. 2 (June 1932), p. 36.

24. *Ibid.*

25. Georgi Dimitroff, *The United Front* (New York, International Publishers, 1938), pp. 64, 66.

26. Allen and Ford, p. 27.

27. New York *Times* (December 9, 1964), p. 43.

28. As quoted by Carl McIntire, "Communist Influence in the Baptist World Alliance," *American Mercury,* vol. 91, no. 441 (October 1960), p. 93.

29. San Francisco *Chronicle* (August 2, 1964), magazine section, p. 22.

30. "The NCC is assuming the cost of running the training school for 'civil rights workers' . . . .

"The NCC furnished the administrative staff and the director, D. Bruce Hanson. . . ." Chattanooga *News-Free Press* (June 30, 1964).

31. Chattanooga *News-Free Press* (June 30, 1964).

32. Cincinnati *Enquirer* (June 30, 1964).

33. *Ibid.*

34. *Daily Worker* (December 1, 1954), p. 6.

35. Richmond *News-Leader* (September 4, 1964), editorial.

36. Senator James O. Eastland (D., Miss.), speech, *Congressional Record* (July 22, 1964), p. 16040.

37. New York *Times* (June 25, 1964), p. 19.

38. Eastland, p. 16038.

39. *Ibid.*, p. 16039.

40. *Newsweek*, vol. 64, no. 2 (July 13, 1964), p. 19.

41. Eastland, p. 16039.

42. *National Review* (August 18, 1964), p. 2.

43. Eastland, p. 16039.

44. *National Review* (August 18, 1964), p. 2.
45. Eastland, p. 16039.
46. New York *Times* (November 30, 1964), p. 28.
47. *Wall Street Journal* (November 6, 1964), p. 14.

## CHAPTER XVII

The Agent Provocateur

> . . . *Always we have a clear and precise aim towards which we strive, for one of the great merits of communism is that nothing is left to chance.*[1] Joseph Stalin

In the summer of 1963, four Negro girls were blown up by a bomb in a church in Birmingham, Alabama. And as you may recall, it was established in the public mind—long before anything substantial was definitely known—that the act had something or other to do with "right-wing extremists."

> Birmingham—The mangled bodies of the 4 Negro Sunday School girls are now buried and in their Birmingham graves [we read in *Muhammad Speaks*], but the spirit of the *Nazi-minded* murders goes marching on.
>
> "The Thunderbolt," a monthly KKK-type newspaper . . . and which describes itself proudly as the "Official white racial organ" of the Negro-hating National States Rights Party, must be given some credit, along with Gov. Wallace for maintaining the lynch-climate which made the murders probable.
> . . .
> Governor Wallace's most ardent allies has been the KKK, the organized White Citizens and the *crypto-Nazi* States Rights Party." [2] (italics added)

It was a crime so horrible that if you are an honest American—of any color—you may well have wanted nothing better at the time than to be locked in a room with the person who did it. You probably wondered what sort of person would deliberately murder, in so horrible a way, four little girls who probably didn't even yet know the meaning of "politics."

It is time to discuss a Communist tactic so incredible, so twisted, that to the normal American mind it will probably seem almost impossible. As it is absolutely imperative that you now observe, however—it isn't.

What sort of man *would* commit such an act?

You will recall that according to the "science" of Marxism-Leninism, all human life is lived in the following way: There is an onrushing "thesis," which is opposed by an immovable "antithesis"; there is a clash, and from "out of this conflict, this division and chaos," as John Lewis of SNCC likes to put it, there comes a "synthesis." And this just keeps rolling merrily on—like a billiard tournament that has been fixed—until we get the final synthesis, which—of course—is Communism.

Or to put it a different way—in terms of specific tactics for specific problems—there is an action, which is advanced by the Communists; there is a reaction, which of course is advanced by the *reactionaries;* there is a clash; and from "out of this conflict, this division and chaos" there comes a synthesis, which is the particular result—test ban treaty or bushels of wheat—that the Communists wanted.

Marxism-Leninism teaches in fact that no revolution can hope to succeed unless there is an effective counter-revolution. It teaches that the Communists cannot hope to win until the "anti-Communists" have been organized.

Why is this?

The Communists are fully aware, of course, that as they move to capture a country, they will meet with opposition. They are also fully aware that if the matter were decided in an open battle they would meet with a devastating defeat, simply because, since most people have an aversion to criminals, the Communists will always be hopelessly outnumbered.

So the only way the Communists can win is, as we have seen, with guile.

The only way they can beat the opposition, in fact, is to control the opposition.

Now, how would they do that?

. . . Under Czarism, until 1905 [we read in Lenin], we had no "legal possibilities," but when Zubatov, the secret service agent, organized Black Hundred workers' meetings and workmen's societies for the purpose of ferreting out revolutionists and fighting them, *we sent members of our Party into these meetings and societies.* . . . They put us in touch with the masses, acquired much skill in conducting propaganda, and *succeeded in wresting the workers from under the influence of Zubatov's agents.* . . .[3]

Americans are by now familiar with the Communist tactic of infiltrating—and creating—"left-wing" groups, or "fronts." They must now become familiar with the Communist tactic of infiltrating—and creating—"right-wing" groups. For here was a situation, was it not, in which a right-wing organization was actually being run by the Communists.

But a question at once arises:

How can it be that while the Communists secretly controlled the Black Hundreds, as we have seen, it was this very same Black Hundreds that the Communists openly denounced —for "committing crimes against the people of Russia"; for conducting pogroms against the Jews; for being, in short, the 1905 model of what we know today as a "right-wing extremist" organization with "fascist overtones"?

Isn't this some sort of contradiction?

Not at all—it's dialectical materialism. It's what Stalin meant when he said that Communism "leaves nothing to chance." It's making your "inevitable" victory inevitable— by controlling both sides of the conflict.

By controlling the opposition the Communists are able to confuse, divide and neutralize it; to keep it busy at meaningless work; to cause it to strike before it is ready; to find out who is in it and wipe them out a few at a time. But most important, by conducting their own opposition the Communists can create the problems they say they solve—and then blame their opposition for creating them.

You will recall that the reason for the riots in 1964 was of course police brutality.

"An official of the Central Intelligence Agency," we read in the New York *Times,* "has testified that *infiltration of police forces and efforts to turn the public against them* were favorite Communist tactics." [4] (italics added)

In other words, the police brutality actually exists. The

Communists infiltrate the police, create their own police brutality—by being brutal—and then cause a riot to condemn it. It is an interesting fact that according to the testimony of this CIA official, inspector general Lyman B. Kirkpatrick, Jr., the instructions for how to do the infiltration, and for how to run the riot, are contained in the same captured Communist handbook.

The New York *News* reports that in those same riots the agitators represented both the "extreme left" and "extreme right."

> Significantly, through the FBI, the police also established that funds from white racist groups—who want New York to get a taste of Negro violence—have been pouring into Harlem.
>
> In an unholy alliance, one high source disclosed, both the Commies and extreme Southern right wingers have been supporting the Black Muslims because they are the most violent muscle unit. In fact, the Muslims have bragged of receiving money from a Texas millionaire whom they don't hesitate to identify.[5]

Now, ask yourself. Suppose you're a *real* "extreme Southern right-winger." In the first place, you're short of cash. And in the second, you're trying to defend your home—*the South* —against Communism. Are you really going to be "pouring" cash into Harlem—to help the Communists capture New York?

Remember when Henry Wallace ran for president in 1948 as the candidate of the Communist controlled Progressive party?

> When Henry Wallace ran into a shower of vegetables during his early appearances in North Carolina, nearly all commentators expressed surprise, since that state was presumed to be highly tolerant. Only a *Life* reporter and a columnist on a Negro newspaper seemed to have sensed what probably took place. The Communist leaders desired maximum publicity for everything that Wallace did and said in the South, not merely for domestic consumption, but mainly for its export value in the field of world propaganda. It became essential, therefore, that trouble should occur at the beginning of his tour, not when it was half over. As the *Life* reporter seems to have suspected, capable Communist organizers probably stirred up some of their arrogant, neurotic

followers in the tobacco regions *to provoke disorders on the part of Dixiecrats. . . .*[6] (italics added)

And so the man who does the provoking has come to be known as—the "agent provocateur."

The Vietcong leadership has intensified its program lately to smuggle agents provocateurs into Saigon [we read in the New York *Times*] and mobilize sympathizers to exploit unrest and demonstrations. . . .

. . .

Cadres are instructed to mingle among the people, whenever a crowd gathers, and to shout inflammatory slogans to whip up excitement.[7]

In British Guiana, we read:

Until recent years, the Guianese Indians and Africans had lived side by side in integrated communities with a minimum of friction. This situation began to change when Jagan, the undisputed leader of the Indian faction, reached power.

The record shows that each time Jagan's Communist policies produced reactions endangering his position, he whipped the Indian community, many of whose members are prosperous merchants and successful farmers, solidly into line behind him by raising the specter of an African menace. . . .[8]

In November 1963, Jagan tried to win control of the sugar industry, by replacing the workers' union with his own.

The Progressive Youth Organization, a Communist-dominated unit of Jagan's political party, went into action. Sugar fields were burned with a 2-million-dollar loss to the colony's crop. *Indian workers who opposed joining the new union were killed by hooded raiders. Their homes were burned, their wives and daughters raped and their cattle slaughtered. Word was passed that the masked raiders were Africans.*

After some *Indians were intimidated* and walked off the plantations, sugar growers brought in Africans to take their places. With denunciations of "scab" labor, Jagan's tactics of racial violence began in earnest. People were shot from ambush. Beatings and burnings of homes increased. A bomb tossed into a school bus killed one white child and injured eight others. Police, most of whom are Africans, were shot from behind. (italics added)

Now, what had Jagan done here? As we have seen, he came upon a situation in which Guianese Indians and Africans had for years "lived side by side in integrated communities with a minimum of friction."

This he didn't like.

So this Communist dictator called in his Communist gang—the Progressive Youth Organization—and sent it to work.

But an interesting paradox at once arises: Jagan is of course an Indian, and claims to be defending the Indian community. Yet, as we have seen, the people whose homes were burned, whose wives and daughters were raped and whose cattle was slaughtered—by Jagan's followers—were *these very Indians* Jagan claims to represent.

Why?

Well of course, the reason Jagan the Communist did it was simply to make trouble—to *provoke* trouble. Jagan the Communist was serving here as the *agent provocateur*—as the "agent of the provocation."

Because, as we have seen, Jagan didn't tell his Indian victims that the fact that he is also an Indian means nothing, and that the fact that he is a Communist means everything.

As we have seen, the men he blamed for his own crimes were the Africans. He committed the crimes himself and then framed the Africans.

In short: He created the problem, and then—with an air of perfect innocence—he *denounced* the problem.

Furthermore, this Communist dictator next sent his Communist gang to terrorize the *Africans:* "People were shot from ambush. Beatings and burnings of homes increased." A bomb was tossed into a school bus, and so on.

And this time, as we have seen, the *Indians*—who were supposed to have committed these new crimes by way of "retaliation"—got the blame.

In short: Jagan the Communist not only created the problem and then denounced the problem; as we have seen, he also *controlled* the problem—both sides of it. He controlled both the spurious attacks by Africans and the spurious retaliation by Indians.

Eventually, of course, the problem really does become real —after both sides are sufficiently provoked—and then it begins to run by itself.

Let's sum up: What we have seen here is a textbook demonstration of how a Communist dictator divides and conquers. We have seen how with crimes, frame-ups and an innocent air, he sets people who have been living in peace against each other and thereby creates the chaos he needs to take over.

In America the idea has been created that our country's major problem is race. The *phony* idea has been created that the problem is between black Americans and white Americans.

As we have seen, the fact has been obscured that the real problem is between Americans of all colors and Communists of all colors.

". . . there is a well known axiom that revolution begets counterrevolution," says comrade Claude Lightfoot, who has obviously read his Marx. "These acts of terror against Negroes, these frantic efforts to demonstrate white opposition are part of a great upsurge of pro-fascist developments. . . ." [9]

You will recall that according to *Muhammad Speaks,* the National States Rights party is a "crypto-Nazi," "Negro-hating" outfit, which "must be given some credit . . . for maintaining the lynch-climate which made the murders probable."

Isn't it interesting how no matter what happens the States Righters turn up?

> Professional pickets and agitators, some with Communist ties, have been attracted to the Cleveland Negro rights protest.
>     The demonstrations have also attracted observers from the *radical-right* National States Rights Party, a dedicated segregationist group. . . . In the crowded, tension-filled halls of the school board building Monday, two members of the National States Rights Party appeared.[10] (italics added)

Now of course, if a crypto-nazi, Negro-hating outfit is opposed to the Negro "rights protest," then the Negro "rights protest" is probably okay, isn't it?

And since no good American of any color wants to have the slightest thing of any kind to do with a crypto-Nazi, Negro-hating outfit—*and since that outfit is said to be a part of the "radical right"*—why then, no good American of any color should want to have anything to do with the "radical right," should he?

The radical right probably *isn't* okay.

It goes without saying that since the National States Rights party is so obviously in favor of "states' rights"—then states' rights *definitely* isn't okay.

Remember the racial troubles in 1964 in St. Augustine, Florida?

. . . a Marxist-Leninist non-violent demonstration cannot be transformed into a situation of anarchy and chaos by riot unless the resistance is crystallized. Then all that is needed is the agent provocateur. At the right moment this also appeared as if by magic. A lawyer, J. B. Stoner, from Atlanta, Ga., and a California preacher, Connie Lynch, materialized to harangue the restless crowd. These men are well schooled in agitational techniques; and, although theoretically well educated, speak in the rhetoric of the mass. They merchandize a doctrine of hate only. Their sole objective seemed designed to divide the community into quarreling factions and to agitate the more volatile elements of the Whites to overt aggression against the Blacks. They proved to be one of the most helpful factors in Martin Luther King's invasion. Without their appearance it is quite probable that Martin Luther King would have met total failure—even with the other pressures that were brought to bear. This must be noted. In analyzing the situation as it occurred in St. Augustine, King's appearances and Stoner's appearances were always perfectly co-ordinated. Whenever King was in town, Stoner was almost certain to be. Martin Luther King divided the Negroes and whites; Lynch and Stoner successfully divided the whites. These two, by operating under an organization with the high sounding name, National States Rights Party, sought to gain an aura of respectability. The literature of this party can serve but one purpose: fragmentation of the community and discreditation of worthwhile patriotic organizations. Furthermore, by this activity of Stoner and Lynch and the literature of their organization, a large segment of the community is paralyzed and repulsed from any action in its own defense. So well do the activities of

Martin Luther King and those of Lynch and Stoner complement each other—and with such coordination—*one can not but help entertain the idea of a single control.*[11] (italics added)

Next, on January 18, 1965, while conducting a "civil rights" demonstration in the town of Selma, Alabama, Dr. King was punched in the face and kicked.

It should be no surprise who his attacker turned out to be:

"Dr. King's attacker was identified as Jerry Robinson, a member of the National States Rights Party, who had been watching King closely all day." [12]

And throughout the country, honest men of all colors came to the conclusion that there is something terribly wrong with the "radical right."

You will remember that the Black Muslims don't like Nazis. It was the "crypto-Nazi" States Rights party that made the murders of the four little girls "probable." In fact, in a story headlined "Says Nazis Plan Death for Negroes," we learn of a letter signed by "Frank Meyers," addressed to "friends of the Nazi," urging all who are "sick of Black arrogance and Jewish lies" to become "one of the elite fighters for the Nordic White Man against the Jewish-Bolshevist terrorists and race-mixers." The letter—circulated nationally—advises persons "interested in meeting other local Nazis, or if you would like to join a discussion and educational group" to contact Meyers at his Milwaukee P.O. box number.[13]

The story also reports that veteran Chicago publisher Balm L. Leavell, editor of *New Crusader,* has exposed

a plot to exterminate Negroes by the local "chapter of the American Nazi Party." . . .

Leavell revealed the Chicago Nazi group had "set 1972 as the year for the extermination or deportation of the city's Negroes" and the organization's fund-raising campaign, adding that "robbery and even murder will be countenanced by party leaders if the crime is productive of money for the operation."

*"Reports continued to come in from various quarters [in Indonesia in 1926] concerning illegal terrorist organizations . . . which aimed at drawing criminals into the [Communist]*

*party to commit thefts, etc., in order to enlarge party funds
with part of the loot, while mention was also frequently made
of attempts to collect money to buy firearms (explosives) in
order to put reactionary officials . . . out of the way."* [14]

The article noted the failure of "an initial effort to amass
cash for the Nazi war chest" when the 25-year-old " 'propaganda
minister' for the Chicago Nazi chapter" was seized and charged
with taking part in a $26,000 robbery.

Yet, the Muslims and American Nazis seem to have something in common, for, we learn from Professor Lincoln, the
Muslims call the Jews "the brains of the white race." They
"manipulate the rest of the whites—to say nothing of the
so-called Negroes." "One Jew is smarter than a roomful of
'white men.' " The Jews "have a stranglehold on public opinion through their control of mass communications." They
"hire gentiles to 'front' for them so as not to antagonize the
public; but on crucial issues . . . they control the thinking of
the people." [15]

In America [says Malcolm X] the Jews sap the very lifeblood of
the so-called Negroes to maintain the state of Israel. . . . This
every Black Man resents. . . . The Jew . . . keeps the so-called
Negroes agitated about such nonsense as sitting beside a white
man on a bus, thus keeping them too busy to think about building supermarkets and department stores. Meanwhile, the white
man is so busy trying to segregate the Negroes in the back of the
bus that *he* has no time for business. The Jew then steps in and
provides the food, clothes and services for both contestants. . . .[16]

In fact in February 1962, two short years before we learn
of "a plot to exterminate Negroes" by the Chicago chapter
of the Nazi party, George Lincoln Rockwell, the number
one American Nazi, was a guest speaker, by invitation from
Elijah Muhammad, at the annual convention of the Black
Muslims, in the International Amphitheatre—in Chicago.

. . . and we went inside, where we were welcomed by Elijah
Muhammad's very impressive "storm troops" (which he calls the
"Fruit of Islam").
Then I told them . . . I believe and the American Nazi
Party believes, that the black man has had a rotten deal in

America. . . . We feel that we owe our own black men the millions of "foreign aid" now being poured out by our nation to Communist countries.[17]

You will recall that our analysis of several issues of *Muhammad Speaks* showed us that the Black Muslims think very favorably of many of these Communist countries.

"Elijah Muhammad is a leader who is trying what I am trying to do. In the past, if the black people had wanted to slaughter the white people they would have some cause." [18]

And apparently it works both ways:

> . . . *I say my hat is off to any white man who wants to be white! Because I don't want to be white.* . . .
> . . . Mr. Rockwell . . . has spoke well. He has lived up to his name. He is not asking you and me to follow him. He endorsed the stand for self that you and I are taking. Why should not you applaud? . . .[19]

How do you figure it?

Here's a man whom any American of any color would deplore—and who is supposed to be against Communism—and Mr. Muhammad—who isn't supposed to be against Communism—invites him as an honored guest to his convention.

Could it be they have something more in common than racism?

Then there's the case of Carl Braden, who as you will recall, is a former convict from the state of Kentucky. Guess what got Mr. Braden into trouble.

Well, he accidentally got involved in a bit of house-bombing, of course. What else? Mr. Braden and his wife Anne bought a new house in a white neighborhood of Louisville, and conveyed it to some Negro friends named Wade. Before you could say "agent provocateur," things began to happen. A cross was burned, but no one saw who did it. A couple of rocks were tossed, but no one saw who did it. A few shots went through the door, but no one saw who did it.

A committee of humanitarians turned up to protest, including a gentleman by the name of Vernon Baun. Mr. Baun had served on the Communist side of the civil war in Spain and, as chance would have it, he was a demolition expert.

So when the house went up no one got hurt.[20]

Now, let us be impeccably precise. I am not making any accusations. I am not charging that Mr. Braden personally had anything to do with blowing up the four little girls in Birmingham.

And I am *not* saying that it is absolutely impossible that some *genuine* Southern white man—probably after being provoked by the States Righters and Mr. Stoner, of course—*really did* blow them up. There are a few criminals in the state of Mississippi and a few criminals in all of the other states and a few criminal Frenchmen, Germans, Dutchmen and Greeks and a few criminals among white men, Negroes, Indians and Chinese.

So it's perfectly possible, and we can all quickly agree on the policy that any of them known to have blown up little girls—of any color—should be caught according to the rules of law, tried according to the rules of evidence, convicted in an American court—and speedily hung from the nearest tree.

So it's not impossible that Mr. Braden didn't do it—who knows—after all, he's a very busy man.

And it's also possible that Lee Harvey Oswald—or one of his colleagues—didn't murder NAACP leader Medgar Evers in June 1963, and then obligingly leave the rifle at the scene so that its owner, Byron de la Beckwith, a "right-wing extremist," could soon be picked up.

Lee, of course, was a busy guy too.

*I submit all these facts and ideas solely so that you will better be able to evaluate the next in the endless series of strange bombings in the South; and what it may mean the next time you hear some "right-wing extremist" defend capitalism—and at the same time denounce the Jews.*

### Notes

1. From the Stalin archives of the National War College in Washington, D.C., as quoted in *Coronet*, vol. 29, no. 3 (January 1951), p. 25.

2. *Muhammad Speaks*, vol. 3, no. 2 (October 11, 1963), p. 2.

3. V. I. Lenin, *"Left-Wing" Communism*, published by "The Toiler," (no imprint and no date), p. 36.

    4. New York *Times* (September 29, 1961), p. 10.
    5. New York *News* (July 22, 1964), pp. 3, 13.
    6. William A. Nolan, *Communism Versus the Negro* (Chicago, Henry Regnery Company, 1951), p. 185. Nolan's references here are to *Life* (September 13, 1948), p. 33; and to Marjorie MacKenzie, column, Pittsburgh *Courier* (September 18, 1948), p. 19.
    7. New York *Times* (December 2, 1964), p. 9.
    8. *U.S. News & World Report,* vol. 56 (June 15, 1964), pp. 60-61.
    9. Claude Lightfoot, in *Negro Liberation, A Goal for All Americans* (New York, New Currents Publishers, July 1964), p. 36.
    10. Cleveland *Plain Dealer* (February 5, 1964), p. 8.
    11. Hardgrove S. Norris, *Focus* (St. Augustine, Fla., July 7, 1964), p. 2.
    12. New York *World-Telegram* (January 18, 1965), p. 1.
    13. *Muhammad Speaks,* vol. 3, no. 12 (February 28, 1964), p. 20.
    14. Harry J. Benda and Ruth T. McVey, editors, *The Communist Uprisings of 1926-1927 in Indonesia: Key Documents* (Ithaca, N.Y., Cornell University, 1960), p. 11.
    15. C. Eric Lincoln, *The Black Muslims in America* (Boston, Beacon Press, 1961), p. 166.
    16. *Ibid.,* pp. 166-167.
    17. *Stormtrooper,* no. 1 (February 1962), pp. 7, 9.
    18. Chicago *Sun-Times* (February 26, 1962), p. 1; photographically reproduced in *Stormtrooper,* no. 1 (February 1962), p. 11.
    19. *Muhammad Speaks* (February 1962); photographically reproduced in *Stormtrooper,* no. 1 (February 1962), p. 9.
    20. See the New York *Times* (October 2, 1954), p. 6, and New York *Times* (December 14, 1954), p. 26 for indictment and conviction. Louisville authorities apparently felt that "the bombings may have been planned to make it appear that Mr. Wade was being persecuted by white persons incensed by his moving into the neighborhood."

## CHAPTER XVIII

It's Very Simple

. . . The old Communist principle still holds: "Communism must be built with non-Communist hands." We do know that Communist influence does exist in the Negro movement and it is this influence which is vitally important. It can be the means through which large masses are caused to lose perspective on the issues involved and, without realizing it, succumb to the party's propaganda lures.[1]
J. Edgar Hoover

The publication of this book will probably be met with a silence so profound that it will closely resemble the Rev. Dr. King in the course of giving a straight answer. And this unhappy state will end only if enough Americans somehow hear about it and decide that the book is worth their time and money to buy and read.

A point will then approach at which it will begin to seem strange—to honest Americans—that little or nothing has been said about it in the daily newspapers and in book reviews. So you will begin to hear that there is a typographical error on page 154 and that this invalidates the whole book; that the book has about it the odor of "fascism"; that the Rev. Dr. King, a winner of the Nobel Peace Prize, is "sick and tired," and that is that; that a "distinguished psychiatrist" has read the book and states that I am definitely in need of "psychiatric treatment."

In fact, if the situation gets desperate, the most terrifying of all charges may be unleashed: that there is nothing in the book but some "wild charges."

The wild charge will of course be made that the evidence in this book is unsound. It's the wrong kind of evidence, is what you will hear. It isn't substantive evidence, it's circumstantial—and you can't prove a thing with circumstantial evidence.

So let's say a word about circumstantial evidence.

The "humanitarians," unfortunately, have not gone to the trouble to define it. But, as we have seen, they seem to imply that the only acceptable evidence would be the serial number on somebody's party card. The only thing wrong with this, ladies and gentlemen, is that we are dealing here with a conspiracy, and the Communist *party,* though very important, is, as evidenced in the countries the conspiracy has captured, *only one small part of it.* So the point is that to accuse the overwhelming majority of members of the conspiracy of also belonging to the Communist party really would be a wild charge—simply because they really *don't* belong to the party.

Now, how would you identify a member of a conspiracy?

Suppose you break down the locked door of a windowless room and find inside a man with a knife. While you are watching, he plunges the knife into another man's back. That's substantive evidence.

You break down the locked door of a windowless room and find inside a man on the floor. The man on the floor is dead. In his back there's a big hole. Kneeling over him is another man, who happens to be holding a bloody knife. That's circumstantial evidence.

Your attorney will tell you that if you can show an American judge and jury, in an American court of law, enough of the right kind of circumstantial evidence, they can find a man guilty, and sentence him. So your attorney will tell you that the question isn't whether or not you're using circumstantial evidence—it's *what kind* of circumstantial evidence you've got. Americans will agree that if you have the right kind, it is at least grounds for indictment—especially if the man with the knife has a smile on his face.

Likewise, there's nothing *necessarily* unfair about "guilt by association."

There is also an old saying that "a man is known by the company he keeps."

But the question arises: Couldn't it be possible that the

facts mean something else? Couldn't it be possible, in spite of all we have learned, that the civil rights movement is really what it is said to be?

Yes, it is "possible." But we are not asking what is possible. We are asking—by means of the iron epistemology I hope we both share—what is likely, what is *probable*. We are asking what explanation most reasonably satisfies these political facts in this historical context.

Now, why is secrecy so important to this conspiracy?

> Premier Castro explained in his speech today that he had hidden his belief in Communism from the Cuban people and from his American friends for years "because otherwise we might have alienated the bourgeoisie and other forces which we knew we would eventually have to fight." . . .
> Referring to his policy of keeping secret his belief in Marxism during the early days of the revolution, he said:
> "If it were known then that the men who led the guerrilla fighting had radical ideas, well, all those who are making war against us now would have started it right then." [2]

So the point to the secrecy is that the conspiracy has to have it—simply because it *is* a conspiracy.

The conspiracy has to practice secrecy to hide the fact that the conspiracy isn't a "workers'" movement, or a "people's" movement, or a "mass" movement at all.

It's nothing but a small band of thugs—many of them wearing silk hats and striped trousers—who are fully aware that in an open battle they would be irrevocably destroyed.

What we saw in the summer of 1964 was only maneuvers; what is planned for this and succeeding summers is of course the actual war:

> . . . Those who have studied events in China and Vietnam [says William Worthy] believe that, as state power is used to repress upheavals and rioting in the ghettos, Negroes in the Armed Forces will defect to protect their homes, taking with them their own guns and stolen weapons as well. . . .

. . . I am also convinced that Negro ghettos and casbahs will close ranks to protect members of the underground after their sorties and "missions" in the white community. As in South Africa, where sabotage is increasing, arrests and imprisonment will merely stimulate a search for more effective and safer techniques. Many of the youth warn more or less openly that spies and informers, black or white, will be "dealt with" in the same way that all past revolutionary movements have handled police agents who get caught.[3]

And as we have learned, it would be a war—if you allow it to be fought—not just against white men, but against *all Americans,* white—*and black:*

Mrs. Arthur Cordier, a Belgian liberated from Communist Congolese rebels, described in the New York *Times* for November 12, 1964, pages 1 and 3, how rebels forced her to watch as they hacked her husband and two sons to death. The *Times* also describes the executions of *black African civilians* deemed "enemies of the revolution."

"At least 800 such 'enemies' were massacred here, many of them burned alive at the foot of the Lumumba monument in the center of town."

That is what Communism is all about.

If you were so unlucky as to be a Jew in Nazi Germany, you still had one chance: it was possible to escape.

And you would escape of course—to the United States.

But you *are* in the United States. You can't escape because there's nowhere else to go.

So what can you do?

You will remember that whenever you turn over a damp rock with the toe of your boot, a host of things comes crawling out as if you had caught them at something dirty.

So how would you handle a conspiracy? Well, what you would do, of course, is expose it. Just turn the rock over.

". . . Every such exposure of the tactics of Communism," says an FBI report exposing the Communist preparation and leadership of the May 1960 riots in San Francisco, "can be used to destroy its ideological appeal and used to strengthen this nation against the psychological pressures Communists constantly apply against every aspect of our society to weaken us." [4]

The point is that it can be done. In fact, it's easy. All it takes is the toe of your boot—and your will to use it.

So let's do it.

Let's do it now.

*Let's turn the rock over.*

On the basis of all the granitic evidence we have seen, I charge that America's "race problem" and the "civil rights movement" supposed to end it, have both been planned by the Communists, as we have seen, built up by the Communists, as we have seen, and, most important, *conducted* by the Communists, as we have seen.

I charge—on the basis of what we have seen—that despite all of the idealistic and good people who have been deceived and pulled into the operation or into support of it, the "civil rights movement" is for the most part a Communist operation under the cloak of which the Communists hope to capture this country.

I charge that there is a real problem between the races in this country today, and that it has been caused almost in its entirety by the Communists to help them to capture the country.

I charge that the growing hopelessness and despair among Negro Americans today *is* real—and that it is largely the work of the Communists—as we have seen.

I charge that the Communists have done everything in their power to create this despair by convincing Negro and white Americans that black men can be nothing but incompetent, helpless and unmanly—that, in short, they are "niggers"— and that the only way they can avoid starvation is for Massa Big Daddy government to feed them.

I charge therefore that the Communists—under the cloak of civil rights—are trying to get American citizens who happen to be black to exchange the benevolent slavery of the

Old Plantation for the malevolent slavery of the New Plantation.

I charge that the growing hostility between black and white Americans *is* real and that it is for the most part the work of the Communists—as we have seen.

I accuse the Rev. Dr. Martin Luther King, Jr. of knowing all this, and yet of deliberately doing everything he can to bring all of it about to such an extent that whether he is or not in actuality a member of the Communist conspiracy can be of interest only to his psychiatrist.

I accuse the Rev. Dr. King of being in effect one of the country's most influential workers for Communism and *against* the Negroes.

I accuse President Kennedy and President Johnson of knowing this but nevertheless not only closing their eyes to it, but lending a hand.

I therefore accuse them both of having betrayed their oath of office.

As we have seen, this—all of this—is obvious.

If newspaper editors had been doing their jobs, a book explaining it would be redundant.

All it takes to see it is a willingness to open one's eyes.

In fact: *It's very simple.*

You now have the facts. It is probable that the decision you make about what you have read in this book will help to determine the course not only of your own, your children's, and their children's lives, but will determine whether the culmination of the long and painful struggle for civilization—our country—is to be replaced for a thousand years with an age so dark that the Dark Ages will seem like the Italian Renaissance.

You can decide to act.

Or you can decide to do nothing.

But you must make a decision.

Because—whether you like it or not:

*The buck stops with you.*

## NOTES

1. *U.S. News & World Report,* vol. 56, no. 18 (May 4, 1964), p. 33.

2. New York *Times* (December 3, 1961), p. 4.

3. William Worthy, "The Red Chinese American Negro," *Esquire,* vol. 62, no. 4 (October 1964), pp. 175, 179.

4. *U.S. News & World Report,* vol. 49, no. 4 (July 25, 1960), p. 71.

# Index